O L

Hou

ant.

Treasury of Great Hymns
and their stories

Guye Johnson

BOB JONES UNIVERSITY PRESS
Greenville, South Carolina 29614

Treasury of Great Hymns and Their Stories
by Guye Johnson
© 1986 Bob Jones University Press
Greenville, South Carolina 29614

Printed in the United States of America.

ISBN: 0-89084-249-3

Cover art and design: Beth Whigham

This book is dedicated
To Mrs. Bob Jones, Sr., whose accounts
of the music in her husband's evangelistic
meetings have been a blessing;
To Mrs. Bob Jones, Jr., who has used her singing voice
for the Lord and has been active in music club work;
To my mother, Mrs. A. J. Ellenburg, who reared two
daughters on the great hymns of the church.

Contents

vii   Thematic List of Hymns

xv   Foreword

xix   Suggestions for Using This Book

Treasury of Great Hymns and Their Stories

1   Worship

25   Praise

62   Thanksgiving

73   Birth of Christ

93   Saving Work of Christ

134   Wisdom and Truth

143   Confession and Forgiveness

153   Comfort

182   Guidance and Trust

233   Commitment and Service

257   Warfare

280   Church and Kingdom

306   Nation

Appendixes

317   Comparative Chart of Hymns

333   Chronological List of Hymns

337   Bibliography

Indexes

341   Scripture Index

345   Tune Index

349   General Index

357   Alphabetical List of Hymns

Thematic List of Hymns

Worship

1 All People That on Earth Do Dwell
  William Kethe
4 Fairest Lord Jesus
  anonymous
8 Great God of Wonders!
  Samuel Davies
10 Holy, Holy, Holy! Lord God Almighty
  Reginald Heber
13 My Jesus, I Love Thee
  William Ralph Featherston
16 O Worship the King
  Robert Grant
19 The Spacious Firmament on High
  Joseph Addison
21 This Is My Father's World
  Maltbie Davenport Babcock

Praise

25 All Hail the Power of Jesus' Name
  Edward Perronet
29 Come, Thou Almighty King
  anonymous
32 Come, Thou Fount of Every Blessing
  Robert Robinson

35   Crown Him with Many Crowns
Matthew Bridges and Godfrey Thring

41   O for a Thousand Tongues to Sing
Charles Wesley

45   Praise, My Soul, the King of Heaven
Henry Francis Lyte

48   Praise Ye Jehovah
Bob Jones

50   Praise Ye the Lord, the Almighty
Joachim Neander

52   Rejoice, the Lord Is King
Charles Wesley

55   Rejoice, Ye Pure in Heart
Edward Hayes Plumptre

58   Ye Servants of God, Your Master Proclaim
Charles Wesley

Thanksgiving

62   Come, Ye Thankful People, Come
Henry Alford

64   Doxology
Thomas Ken

70   Now Thank We All Our God
Martin Rinkart

Birth of Christ

73   Angels, from the Realms of Glory
James Montgomery

75   Away in a Manger
anonymous

78   Hark! the Herald Angels Sing
Charles Wesley

81   Joy to the World! the Lord Is Come
Isaac Watts

83   O Come, All Ye Faithful
John Francis Wade

87   O Little Town of Bethlehem
Phillips Brooks

90   Silent Night, Holy Night
       Joseph Mohr

Saving Work of Christ

 93   Alas! and Did My Saviour Bleed
       Isaac Watts
 96   Amazing Grace
       John Newton
101   And Can It Be That I Should Gain
       Charles Wesley
104   Christ the Lord Is Risen Today
       Charles Wesley
107   Hail, Thou Once-Despised Jesus!
       John Bakewell
111   Jesus Paid It All
       Elvina M. Hall
113   Jesus, Thy Blood and Righteousness
       Nicolaus Ludwig von Zinzendorf
116   O Sacred Head, Now Wounded
       Bernard of Clairvaux
120   Tell Me the Old, Old Story
       Arabella Katherine Hankey
124   The Ninety and Nine
       Elizabeth Cecilia Clephane
126   There Is a Fountain Filled with Blood
       William Cowper
129   When I Survey the Wondrous Cross
       Isaac Watts

Wisdom and Truth

134   Bob Jones University Hymn
       Bob Jones
137   Break Thou the Bread of Life
       Mary Artemisia Lathbury
140   O Word of God Incarnate
       William Walsham How

Confession and Forgiveness

143 Just As I Am, Without One Plea
     Charlotte Elliott
146 O Jesus, Thou Art Standing
     William Walsham How
148 Pass Me Not, O Gentle Saviour
     Fanny J. Crosby
150 Softly and Tenderly
     Will L. Thompson

Comfort

153 Abide with Me: Fast Falls the Eventide
     Henry Francis Lyte
156 Be Still, My Soul
     Katharina von Schlegel
158 Hiding in Thee
     William O. Cushing
160 I Heard the Voice of Jesus Say
     Horatius Bonar
163 I Must Tell Jesus
     Elisha Albright Hoffman
165 I Need Thee Every Hour
     Annie Sherwood Hawks
167 It Is Well with My Soul
     Horatio G. Spafford
171 Peace, Perfect Peace
     Edward Henry Bickersteth
174 The Sands of Time Are Sinking
     Anne Ross Cundell Cousin
179 What a Friend We Have in Jesus
     Joseph M. Scriven

Guidance and Trust

182 All the Way My Saviour Leads Me
     Fanny J. Crosby
184 Blessed Assurance, Jesus Is Mine
     Fanny J. Crosby

186   Count Your Blessings
      Johnson Oatman, Jr.

189   Great Is Thy Faithfulness, O God My Father
      Thomas O. Chisholm

192   Guide Me, O Thou Great Jehovah
      William Williams

196   He Leadeth Me, O Blessed Thought
      Joseph Henry Gilmore

199   How Firm a Foundation
      anonymous

202   I Think When I Read That Sweet Story of Old
      Jemima Thompson Luke

204   Jesus, Lover of My Soul
      Charles Wesley

208   My Faith Looks Up to Thee
      Ray Palmer

211   My Hope Is Built on Nothing Less
      Edward Mote

214   O God, Our Help in Ages Past
      Isaac Watts

217   O Love That Wilt Not Let Me Go
      George Matheson

220   O Perfect Love, All Human Thought Transcending
      Dorothy Frances Gurney

223   Rock of Ages, Cleft for Me
      Augustus Montague Toplady

226   The King of Love My Shepherd Is
      Henry Williams Baker

229   There Is a Name I Love to Hear
      Frederick Whitfield

Commitment and Service

233   Jesus, and Shall It Ever Be
      Joseph Grigg

236   Jesus Calls Us
      Cecil Frances Alexander

239   More Love to Thee, O Christ
      Elizabeth Payson Prentiss

242   O Jesus, I Have Promised
      John E. Bode

245   Spirit of God, Descend upon My Heart
      George Croly

248   Take My Life, and Let It Be
      Frances Ridley Havergal

252   Take the Name of Jesus with You
      Lydia Baxter

254   Trust and Obey
      John H. Sammis

Warfare

257   Am I a Soldier of the Cross
      Isaac Watts

259   A Mighty Fortress Is Our God
      Martin Luther

263   Lead On, O King Eternal
      Ernest Warburton Shurtleff

266   Onward, Christian Soldiers
      Sabine Baring-Gould

271   Soldiers of Christ, Arise
      Charles Wesley

272   Stand Up, Stand Up for Jesus
      George Duffield, Jr.

275   The Son of God Goes Forth to War
      Reginald Heber

Church and Kingdom

280   Blest Be the Tie That Binds
      John Fawcett

283   Faith of Our Fathers!
      Frederick W. Faber

287   For All the Saints
      William Walsham How

290   Glorious Things of Thee Are Spoken
      John Newton

294   I Love Thy Kingdom, Lord
      Timothy Dwight

298   Jesus Shall Reign Where'er the Sun
Isaac Watts
300   The Church's One Foundation
Samuel John Stone

Nation

306   Battle Hymn of the Republic
Julia Ward Howe
309   God of Our Fathers, Whose Almighty Hand
Daniel C. Roberts
311   My Country, 'Tis of Thee
Samuel F. Smith

Foreword

The background of nearly every hymn with the power to touch Christian hearts contains a story, and so it is with this book. Mrs. Estelle Siddons Stollenwerck, the grandmother of Dr. Bob Jones, made it a point to have her young grandson memorize the great hymns of the faith. Having been nurtured on the classics of hymnody, Dr. Jones was particularly struck by the decline in the quality of church music as he grew older. It seemed that there was a "watering down" process whereby doctrinal hymns, especially those emphasizing the blood of the Lord Jesus Christ, dropped out of use and could no longer be found in the hymnbooks. Dr. Jones and his father, the founder of Bob Jones University, decided that *The Fellowship News*, a periodical published by the University, should contain a hymn story in every issue. Dr. Grace W. Haight, who helped Dr. Jones, Sr., edit the weekly, taught hymnology at the University and used her extensive files on hymns and hymn stories to produce this regular feature. It is from these files that many of the stories in this book have been edited.

Treasury of Great Hymns and Their Stories is not meant to be a technical study of hymns but to inspire Christians to understand the hymns they sing. Too often believers sing in a perfunctory manner, giving no thought to the vital messages found in the hymns. The apostle Paul exhorted Christians to sing with the spirit and also with the understanding (I Corinthians 14:15). The Psalmist tells us,

> *Make a joyful noise unto God, all ye lands: Sing forth the honour of his name: make his praise glorious. (Psalm 66:1-2)*
>
> *I will sing unto the Lord as long as I live: I will sing praise to my God while I have my being. (Psalm 104:33)*
>
> *Praise ye the Lord: for it is good to sing praises unto our God; for it is pleasant; and praise is comely. (Psalm 147:1)*

Singing praise to God is an important part of our worship, and we must do it with sincerity and understanding.

While this book has a devotional purpose, accuracy has not been neglected. Those who have been involved in any kind of research in hymnology realize how often the sources conflict with one another. Hymn stories are often not recorded until long after the fact, and contradictory versions of how hymns originated are not at all uncommon. In addition embellishment of the stories often occurs to increase their effect as devotional aids and sermon illustrations. In the preparation of this book, every effort has been made to determine the facts in each case.

The reader should note that the writers of the hymns we sing come from widely different theological backgrounds. Anglicans, Methodists, Baptists, Presbyterians, and others have all been included, for each group has made its contribution to the heritage of worship in the church. In some cases men of questionable theology have written excellent hymns; there may be some who did not in fact know the Lord Jesus Christ as personal Saviour, though it is not for us to judge. Occasionally what we mean when we sing their hymns is not at all what the composers meant. For some readers this will lessen their appreciation of the words; for others it will not. In any case, we should not sing what we do not believe. However, most of the one hundred examples included in this collection should be acceptable to all orthodox believers.

This book is sent forth with the suggestion that parents and leaders, in their training of young people, promote the messages and stories of great hymns. Encourage the young people to research the life and times of each author and to glean therefrom inspiration and instruction for serving their Lord with greater fervency. So many contemporary church songs are unfit for the worship of our holy God because they have unworthy music of worldly origin and unedifying or unsound words. To exchange the majestic hymns of doctrine and praise of the past for the trite, repetitious songs of the present that emphasize the singers' wants and needs is to trade jewels for ashes.

In closing I would like to acknowledge Joan Pinkston, who drew up the original list of hymns to be included; Mary Lang, who checked the manuscript; Dr. A. Duane White, hymnologist, who provided his expertise to ensure historical accuracy; and David Woehr, the editor. It is the prayer of each one who contributed to this book that every reader will be blessed. Although most of us are unable to write a hymn, we can sing, individually and collectively, and bring honor to the Lord, bless hearts, and lead souls to Christ.

Guye Johnson

Suggestions for Using This Book

The stories behind the great hymns are a fascinating but sadly neglected area of devotional enrichment. This book is designed to be as helpful as possible for the layman in delving into the rich store of hymnology. Since each story is complete in itself, the reader may open to any hymn in this book and enjoy it. However, there are many ways of systematic study that will bring even greater profit.

The hymnstories have been arranged according to theme, an excellent way to begin mining the treasure of hymnody. Be sure to read the hymns themselves and refer to them when they are mentioned in the text. Seeing each stanza printed separately, rather than line by line with the other stanzas as in most hymnbooks, helps one to catch the flow of thought. We are all guilty of singing without paying attention to the words, and this is a good remedy.

The appendix has been provided to open other avenues of study. The chart shows the basic facts about each hymn at a glance and will help you in various types of comparative study. If the reader desires to study the hymn as it has developed in church history, he may read the book according to the order of the chronological listing. It will be interesting to many readers to examine the index of hymntunes to discover the various texts that have been sung to the same tune. A church choir might add some variety to its repertoire by singing an old hymn to a new tune. Be your own judge as to which melody best expresses the message of a text as to emphasis, mood, and tempo. The Scripture index helps illustrate how various hymn writers have incorporated the words and thoughts of the Bible into their poetry. There is also a general index so that this book can be used as a reference tool.

Those in positions of leadership in the church and in schools can use this book to good advantage also. A Sunday school class might look at the story behind a great hymn before the regular Bible lesson or during its opening exercises. A teacher of history, music, or Bible in a Christian school will probably find a hymn that fits well into his subject matter, providing an interesting aside from the regular material as well as awakening the students' interest in good Christian music. A songleader can provoke the congregation to concentrate on the words they are singing by mentioning some of the background of at least one song in the evening church service. Those teachers who have some knowledge of church history might want to have a series of lessons on the development of hymns, using this book as a starting point. Certainly every preacher will find in this book rich material to illustrate his sermons.

Treasury
of Great Hymns
and Their Stories

Worship

All People That on Earth Do Dwell
1561

All people that on earth do dwell,
Sing to the Lord with cheerful voice;
Him serve with fear, His praise forth tell;
Come ye before Him and rejoice.

Know that the Lord is God indeed;
Without our aid He did us make;
We are His folk, He doth us feed,
And for His sheep He doth us take.

O enter then His gates with praise,
Approach with joy His courts unto;
Praise, laud, and bless His Name always,
For it is seemly so to do.

For why? the Lord our God is good,
His mercy is forever sure;
His truth at all times firmly stood,
And shall from age to age endure.

To Father, Son, and Holy Ghost,
The God whom heaven and earth adore,
From men and from the angel-host
Be praise and glory evermore.
—William Kethe

In earlier days *The Psalter* (a hymnbook of para-phrased Psalms) was a precious possession. It influenced Christian thought and speech. Perhaps the oldest paraphrase to enjoy continued use is "All People That on Earth Do Dwell," based on Psalm 100. It has been suggested that this psalm contains "a promise of Christianity, as winter at its close contains a promise of spring." Called "the church's official hymn of thanksgiving," the hymn also has a flavor of Job 38-40 and Psalm 134.

Though there is some question as to authorship, this psalm is generally ascribed to William Kethe. The earliest record about him tells us that he was among those who fled England during the reign of "Bloody Mary" and that he was probably Scottish. Mary Tudor, who reigned from 1553 to 1558, tried to restore Romanism in England. Many Protestants crossed the English Channel to Holland, Germany, and Switzerland, and those who stayed faced bitter persecution. Mary had nearly three hundred burned at the stake, among them the famous Latimer, Ridley, Cranmer, and Hooper.

William Kethe fled first to Germany. There the exiles, at the sound of a bell each day, would close their shops, stop all conversation and work, and gather at the nearest church. Taking from their pockets a small book of Psalms with notes, they would sing heartily before and after the sermon; many testified to the comfort of this custom. Later, Kethe began to take letters of encouragement to exiles in such places as Basel and Strassburg.

In 1556 Kethe went to Geneva, Switzerland. There he assisted in translating the Scripture into English to produce the Geneva Bible (also called "The Breeches Bible"), the version that came to America on the *Mayflower*.

When Queen Mary died in 1558, "Good Queen Bess" ascended the throne, bringing to an end the atrocities that had plagued the people who rejected the idolatry of Romanism and refused to recognize the pope as lord of the consciences of Christians.

Kethe returned to England in 1561 to become vicar at Childe Okeford in Dorsetshire. Although Okeford had only one church, that church boasted of two rectors. In 1563 Kethe was granted a leave of absence from the church to serve as chaplain in the Queen's forces under command of the Earl of Warwick at Le Havre. Upon his return to Okeford, Kethe resumed his pastoral duties, serving well until his death in 1594 (some hymnologists say 1608).

Twenty-five of Kethe's paraphrases were published in the 1561 edition of *The Anglo-Genevan Psalter.* "All People That on Earth Do Dwell" was one of them, and it was also added to *The English Psalter* in 1565. Dr. C. S. Robinson attributes the hymn's continued use, even among royalty, to "its rugged strength of expression, combined with small touches of wonderful majesty and grace . . . and the matchless devotion and awful reverence for the majesty and holiness of God."

Minor alterations have occurred from time to time. In stanza 1, line 3, "with fear" became "with mirth." In stanza 2, line 1, "The Lord, ye know, is" became "Know that the Lord is." In stanza 2, line 3, "folck" in the original printing became "flock." It is possible that "folck" was a publisher's error that later was corrected, but it is more likely simply an old spelling for "folk," as it is printed in most modern hymnals.

In the 1561 and 1564 reprints of "All People That on Earth Do Dwell" from *The Anglo-Genevan Psalter* Kethe's name began to appear as author. This leaves little doubt that Kethe is the rightful author. Also, the meter seems to favor Kethe.

Shakespeare refers to this hymn in *The Merry Wives of Windsor* (Act II, Scene I). Mrs. Ford says of a would-be suitor, "They [the disposition and truth of his words] do no more adhere and keep place together than the Hundredth Psalm to the tune of 'Green Sleeves.'" Longfellow refers to the hymn in *The Courtship of Miles Standish.* He calls it "that grand old Puritan anthem." The first congregational hymn sung at the coronation of Queen Elizabeth II (June 2, 1953) was this same beloved hymn.

A hymn's popularity, at least in part, stems from its melody. OLD HUNDREDTH was adapted or composed by Louis Bourgeois in 1551, ten years before the writing of "All People That on Earth Do Dwell." The melody is also used in *The Genevan Psalter* and in Thomas Ken's "Doxology" ("Praise God from Whom All Blessings Flow"). In 1541 Bourgeois followed Calvin to Geneva and helped compile *The Genevan Psalter*. Instead of doing guard duty, as did many others, he was assigned to the teaching, writing, and arranging of music. Because some of his hymn alterations were made without Calvin's authorization, the magistrates put Bourgeois into prison. However, Calvin was soon able to obtain his release.

OLD HUNDREDTH first appeared in *The Huguenot Psalter* in 1552. In its original form the rhythm was so sprightly that "Good Queen Bess" classified it with the tunes that she labeled "Geneva jiggs." We know that Bourgeois returned to Paris in 1557 and published a collection of psalms in 1561, but after that we have no further information about his life. H. Augustine Smith suggests that OLD HUNDREDTH, because of its association with the French version of Psalm 134, might also be called OLD HUNDRED AND THIRTY-FOURTH.

Fairest Lord Jesus
XVII century

Fairest Lord Jesus!
Ruler of all nature,
O Thou of God and man the Son!
Thee will I cherish,
Thee will I honor,
Thou, my soul's Glory, Joy, and Crown.

Fair are the meadows,
Fairer still the woodlands,
Robed in the blooming garb of spring:
Jesus is fairer,
Jesus is purer,
Who makes the woeful heart to sing.

Fair is the sunshine,
Fairer still the moonlight,
And all the twinkling starry host:
Jesus shines brighter,
Jesus shines purer,
Than all the angels heaven can boast.

> *Beautiful Saviour!*
> *Lord of the nations!*
> *Son of God and Son of Man!*
> *Glory and honor,*
> *Praise, adoration,*
> *Now and forevermore be Thine!*

—*Münster Gesangbuch*, 1677 (stanzas 1 and 3)
—*Schlesische Volkslieder*, 1842 (stanza 2)

Overall, this hymn is a skillful blend of the author's love of nature and his vision of the superiority of the Altogether Lovely One who rules nature. The simplicity of the words and tune gives the hymn special appeal with children who love the stories of Jesus and also enjoy nature. The hymn suggests that the author met some hard times, which tempted him to sadness. Yet thoughts of the Lord Jesus Christ and the wonderful change the Lord had wrought in his life caused the author's "woeful heart to sing." Whether he regarded the heavens, the earth, or the heavenly hosts, the hymn writer saw the Lord Jesus Christ as far beyond compare.

The "misty past" of "Fairest Lord Jesus" involves many unsubstantiated stories. Some hymnologists have insisted that the Crusaders sang these words as they journeyed to the Holy Land in the twelfth century. C. A. Barry (1830-1915) accepted this story, citing as his proof Franz Liszt's oratorio, *The Legend of St. Elizabeth* (1862), which incorporates what Liszt called a "Crusader's Melody." Barry points out that Liszt, in his preface to *St. Elizabeth*, expressed appreciation to "Herrn Kantor Gottschalg for calling my attention to the 'Pilgrims' Song' which I have used in *St. Elizabeth*." Other hymnologists, more recent and more reliable, discredit this supposed origin, saying that "'Fairest Lord Jesus' is most emphatically not a 'Crusaders' Hymn of the twelfth century,' as is sometimes claimed" and that the earliest evidence of the hymn is 1677. Armin Haeussler (*Story of Our Hymns*) argues that the hymn dates to 1662 and that it emerged from "Jesuit circles, having six verses under the Latin heading, *'Suspirium ad Jesum.'* "

Some authorities view this hymn as a "product of the peasant mind." Julian's *Dictionary of Hymnology* states that the words were "taken down from oral recitations in the district of Glaz," a town in Silesia that became the haven of a band of Hussites who were fleeing from the purge against the Protestants after the Battle of White Mountain (1620). These refugees, tired of the ecclesiastical pomp from which they had bolted, lived close to nature and worshiped God simply. The original anonymous German text of this favorite hymn was published for the first time in 1677 in the *Münster Gesangbuch*, with the tune SCHÖNSTER HERR JESU (a lovely melody in the minor mode, unfortunately not very well known today). By 1839, when von Fallersleben recorded it in the Silesian district of Glaz, the text had been altered considerably. Our usual first and third stanzas are English translations of the 1677 text from the *Münster Gesangbuch*, while the usual second stanza is an English translation from the 1842 version of von Fallersleben in his *Schlesische Volkslieder*. A fourth stanza, beginning "Beautiful Saviour," appears in some hymnals. It is from a translation by J. A. Seiss, first published in *The Sunday School Book* (Philadelphia, 1873).

In general it is accepted that the popularity of the hymn in America dates to 1850. Although the name of Richard Storrs Willis (1819-1900) has appeared as translator of our English version, Willis disclaimed the honor, saying, "I do not even remember how the hymn came into my hands."

That Richard Storrs Willis introduced the hymn to America, however, is undebatable. Although he appeared not to know who made the English translation, Willis printed the three familiar stanzas as we know them today, under the mistaken caption, "Crusader's Hymn," in his *Church Chorals and Choir Studies* (New York, 1850). In a footnote Willis recounted the traditional tale, no doubt unfounded, that the hymn was "wont to be sung by the German knights on their way to Jerusalem." Born in

Boston on February 10, 1819, Willis was educated at Yale and later taught German there. Moving to Detroit, he entered the field of journalism and became a noted writer on musical subjects. He also edited such important works as the American edition of a biography of Felix Mendelssohn and *The Musical World.* Willis' father, Nathaniel Parker Willis, was the founder of *Youth's Companion;* a brother, Nathan Parker Willis, was a poet and an editor of note; and a sister, Mrs. James Parton, was the popular writer, "Fanny Fern." Willis died in Detroit on May 7, 1900.

The tune CRUSADER'S HYMN, to which "Fairest Lord Jesus" is most often sung, is also of uncertain origin. Julian says that the earliest form of the tune appeared as ASCALON in the 1842 collection of Silesian folk songs by A. H. Hoffman von Fallersleben and E. F. Richter, referred to earlier. Another name for the tune is ST. ELIZABETH (so named for its use by Liszt in his oratorio, *The Legend of St. Elizabeth*). In 1916 the *Musical Times* of London traced the tune's source to a melody published by J. G. Schicht in 1819, citing similarity of the first two measures. One authority suggests that the tune that Liszt incorporated into *St. Elizabeth* was the folk tune, that ASCALON (a variant of the tune) was in Richter's edition, and that Willis' tune is probably the original melody.

A probable reason for the idea that "Fairest Lord Jesus," both the text and the accustomed tune, is a "Crusaders' Hymn" stems from a story about Liszt and the writing of *The Legend of Saint Elizabeth.* (Elizabeth was a thirteenth-century saint from Hungary, Liszt's native country.) He wrote to a former organ pupil of his in Germany, Alexander Wilhelm Gottschalg (1827-1908), and asked for a tune that he could incorporate into the oratorio. Reportedly Gottschalg sent to Liszt the tune in question, saying that it was an old "pilgrim song." Liszt's stirring use of it repeatedly in his magnificent oratorio likely led to the tune's being called CRUSADERS' HYMN.

Whoever the mysterious author and composer may be, it is obvious that they had deep love for the Lord, that they wanted to honor the Lord with radiance of life, and that they preferred simple language and unembellished tunes.

Other translations bear the titles "Sweetest Lord Jesu, Lord," by E. Massie (1867), and "Beautiful Saviour! King of Creation," by J. A. Seiss (1873).

Great God of Wonders!
   XVIII century

Great God of wonders! All Thy ways
   Are matchless, godlike, and divine;
But the fair glories of Thy grace
   More godlike and unrivalled shine.

Refrain:

Who is a pardoning God like Thee?
Or who has grace so rich and free?

Crimes of such horror to forgive,
   Such guilty daring worms to spare,
This is Thy grand prerogative
   And none shall in Thy honor share.

Angels and men, resign your claim
   To pity, mercy, love and grace:
These glories crown Jehovah's name
   With an incomparable blaze.

In wonder lost, with trembling joy,
   We take the pardon of our God—
Pardon for crimes of deepest dye,
   A pardon bought with Jesus' blood.

O may this strange, this matchless grace,
   This godlike miracle of love,
Fill the whole earth with grateful praise,
   And all th' angelic choirs above.

—Samuel Davies

The author of "Great God of Wonders" was Samuel Davies, hailed as "one of the most outstanding pioneers in American hymnody," "one of the most brilliant men to adorn the American pulpit during colonial days," and "as a pulpit orator, the most distinguished American of his times."

Born at New Castle, Delaware, on November 3, 1723, Samuel Davies received his early education from the Reverend Samuel Blair, Chester County, Pennsylvania. Financial assistance for his education was provided by the Reverend William Robinson of New Brunswick. In 1747, young Davies moved to Hanover County, Virginia, to serve as missionary and evangelist. There he became the center of a revival that became part of the Great Awakening.

In 1753, Davies accompanied the Reverend Gilbert Tennent to England to solicit funds for the College of New Jersey, the Presbyterian school that later became Princeton University. Davies' sermons were well received not only by the masses, but also by King George II, who invited the young preacher to speak at the Chapel Royal. During Davies' sermon at the Chapel, it is said, King George "constantly whispered words of praise to those who sat near him."

Back in America, Davies succeeded the Reverend Jonathan Edwards as president of the College of New Jersey. He served in this office from 1759 until his death in 1761.

Biographers have described Davies as fervent, devout, zealous, scholarly, and unexcelled in weaving into his sermons current events. For instance, in 1755, the Lisbon earthquake occasioned "warnings and admonitions" from Davies. A pungent sermon on the subject was "The Different States of Sinners and Saints in the Wreck of Nature." (The words of the hymn that accompanied the sermon are included in Edward S. Ninde's *Story of the American Hymn*, 1921.)

After General Braddock's defeat in 1755, Mr. Davies preached to the Colonial Volunteers. Aware that the "courage and coolness of young George Washington (twenty-three years old) had saved the army," Davies said, "I cannot but hope that Providence has preserved that heroic youth, Colonel Washington, in so signal a manner for some important service to his country."

All of Davies' sermons drew large crowds, which often made it necessary to move the services outdoors. Davies was prolific in sermons on divine forgiveness. Having experienced forgiveness for his own sins, he desired that other men should know of the great love that made forgiveness possible through Christ Jesus our Lord. Characteristically, Davies ended his sermons with an original hymn on the subject.

Early in January 1761, Samuel Davies chose as his text, "This year thou shalt die." In February of that same year, the thirty-seven-year-old minister was with the Lord.

Davies' manuscripts were left in care of Dr. Thomas Gibbons, London. In 1769, Dr. Gibbons included sixteen of Davies' hymns in his *Hymns Adapted to Divine Worship*. "Great God of Wonders," the most popular of Davies' hymns, quickly made its way into 100 different hymnals. Erik Routley *(A Panorama of Christian Hymnody)* calls it "a landmark" of "native American hymnody in the colonial days ... quite remarkable and finely-wrought ... monumental and severe, quite unique among American hymns for its theological weight and grandeur." The most common tune used today is SOVEREIGNTY, composed by the English hymnwriter and preacher John Newton (1725–1807).

Holy, Holy, Holy! Lord God Almighty
1826

Holy, Holy, Holy! Lord God Almighty!
Early in the morning our song shall rise to Thee;
Holy, Holy, Holy! Merciful and Mighty!
God in Three Persons, blessed Trinity!

Holy, Holy, Holy! All the saints adore Thee,
Casting down their golden crowns around the glassy sea;
Cherubim and seraphim falling down before Thee,
Which wert, and art, and evermore shalt be.

Holy, Holy, Holy! Though the darkness hide Thee,
Though the eye of sinful man Thy glory may not see,
Only Thou art holy; there is none beside Thee
Perfect in power, in love, and purity.

Holy, Holy, Holy! Lord God Almighty!
All Thy works shall praise Thy name, in earth, and sky, and
*   sea;*
Holy, Holy, Holy! Merciful and Mighty!
God in Three Persons, blessed Trinity!

—Reginald Heber

The lyrics, the tune, and the title of this hymn unite to praise God the Father, God the Son, and God the Holy Spirit. The words are based on Revelation 4:8-11, which reads in part, "And they rest not day and night, saying; Holy, holy, holy, Lord God Almighty, which was, and is, and is to come."

E. E. Ryden *(The Story of Our Hymns)* says of Heber's "Holy, Holy, Holy": "It should be observed that this great hymn is one of pure adoration. There is nothing of the element of confession, petition, or thanksgiving in it, but only worship. Its exalted language is Scriptural throughout, indeed it is the Word of the Most High."

From childhood, the author, Reginald Heber (1783-1826), was an eager student of the Word of God. He became noted for the wealth of Scripture stored in his memory, and his high regard for God's Word is reflected in his hymns.

Oxford scholar Heber was refined, intelligent, and talented. According to many, he was "the most distinguished student of his time." Praise did not affect his simplicity of character, however, for throughout his life he was noted for humility of heart and life. A close friend remarked, "In spite of his high intelligence, he always seeks to accommodate his instruction to the comprehension of all people."

Along with his wife, Amelia Shipley, Heber served in an obscure parish for sixteen years. It was during this period that he wrote most of his hymns. From his youth, Heber felt a strong pull toward the mission field, particularly the land of India. His zeal for missions in India is expressed in his popular hymn, "From Greenland's Icy Mountains." How surprising, then, that he turned down his first two calls to become bishop of Calcutta in the land he claimed to love so much. With the third call, however, he yielded.

Calcutta's climate, coupled with the strenuous work of overseeing his parish, took a heavy toll on Heber's physical strength, and within three years he was with the Lord. Warm and exhausted after confirming forty-two young converts on April 3, 1826, Heber returned to his room to rest until breakfast. When the call to breakfast brought no response from the bishop, a servant went to investigate. Heber was dead of apoplexy. In eulogizing this dedicated man, someone said, "No other man ever made so great a mark on India in so short a time."

NICAEA, the tune written in 1861 expressly for this hymn, was composed by another Englishman, John B. Dykes (1823-1876). An accomplished organist, an Anglican priest, a theological writer of note, he was also a prolific composer of tunes. He wrote about 300 melodies, many of which appear in hymnbooks of all denominations. When Dykes was thirty-eight, the University of Durham gave him the Doctor of Music degree. A notable dispute arose when his bishop, a Low Churchman, opposed the High Church practices Dykes had introduced. Some say the strain of the court battle, which Dykes lost, brought about his last sickness.

NICAEA was named in honor of the council at which the Nicaean Creed was adopted and first promulgated in A.D. 325. This council was remarkable for its doctrinal impact and the host of courageous people who had endured Diocletian's persecution. These people had scarred faces, twisted arms, paralyzed legs, and sightless eyes from suffering for the Faith.

Dykes is considered the finest of the Victorian composers of hymn tunes, as Heber is considered the foremost writer of the literary Victorian hymn.

The stirring words and melody of "Holy, Holy, Holy" have led some authorities to acclaim it "one of the noblest and most majestic odes ever addressed to the Divine Being." Others believe that "it is doubtful if there is a nobler hymn of its kind in all the realm of hymnody."

(For another hymn by Reginald Heber, see p. 276.)

My Jesus, I Love Thee
ca. 1858

My Jesus, I love Thee, I know Thou art mine;
For Thee all the follies of sin I resign;
My gracious Redeemer, my Saviour art Thou;
If ever I loved Thee, my Jesus, 'tis now.

I love Thee because Thou hast first loved me,
And purchased my pardon on Calvary's tree;
I love Thee for wearing the thorns on Thy brow;
If ever I loved Thee, my Jesus, 'tis now.

I'll love Thee in life, I will love Thee in death,
And praise Thee as long as Thou lendest me breath;
And say when the deathdew lies cold on my brow,
If ever I loved Thee, my Jesus, 'tis now.

In mansions of glory and endless delight,
I'll ever adore Thee in heaven so bright;
I'll sing with the glittering crown on my brow,
If ever I loved Thee, my Jesus, 'tis now.

—William Ralph Featherston

Ira D. Sankey related an incident regarding a famous actress and an invalid girl. The actress, while walking down a city street, saw an open door. Peeking inside, she saw an invalid girl lying on a couch, watching passersby. "Perhaps I can cheer that girl," the actress thought, and she went inside. Instead of her offering a word of encouragement, the girl, a devout Christian, led the actress to the Lord. The actress returned home and told her father that she had been converted and could no longer work in the theater group he headed. The father argued that the theater was his livelihood and that she was "top billing" to draw the crowd. Finally, the daughter agreed to fulfill one more obligation with the troupe. The curtain went up, and the actress received her usual applause. Stepping forward, she repeated the words, "My Jesus, I love Thee, I know Thou art mine; For Thee all the follies of sin I resign; My gracious Redeemer, my Saviour art Thou; If ever I loved Thee, my Jesus, 'tis now." A hush went over the audience, and the actress walked quietly off the stage, never to return. By honoring her Lord, she had not only touched the heart of the audience; she had also won her father to the Lord. Both father and daughter then devoted their time and energy in working for the Lord and in winning many converts to Him.

Wherever "My Jesus, I Love Thee" has been sung or read—in churches, in missions, at bedsides of the dying, or at funerals—it has blessed the hearts of those who have sung it and those who have heard it sung. In some books the hymn opens with the words, "My *Saviour*, I love Thee"; occasionally it begins "Lord Jesus, I love Thee."

For many years the author of this hymn was listed as "Anonymous" or "Unknown." Later (perhaps because he composed the tune) A. J. Gordon's name appeared as author. A more thorough search revealed the name of William Ralph Featherston. According to some sources, Featherston wrote the hymn in 1858, in honor of his conversion, and sent a hand-written copy to his aunt in Los Angeles, California. At her suggestion, Featherston had the hymn published, leaving the original, hand-written copy in the family.

The year of the hymn's writing is debatable. Most books say that it was written when Featherston was sixteen. If, as some men say, Featherston was born on July 23, 1846, the author would have been only twelve in 1858. If, on the other hand, he was born in 1842, as other men claim, the author was indeed sixteen. Whichever age is correct, the hymn is even more inspiring, having been written by a young man who felt such deep devotion to the Lord. Mr. Featherston died, still a young man, in Montreal, his birthplace, on May 20, 1873.

It is generally agreed that the first printing of the hymn was in *The London Hymn Book* in 1864. Apparently it first appeared in American hymnbooks beginning in 1868 with D. L. Moody's *North-western Hymn Book*.

Someone has suggested that "hymns bear more fruit when pollenized by a vital tune." GORDON has been vital to "My Jesus, I Love Thee." It was composed by Dr. Adoniram Judson Gordon (1836-1895), a minister who was named for Adoniram Judson, the famous missionary to Burma. Dr. Gordon was born in New Hampton, New Hampshire, on April 19, 1836. He was educated at Brown University and Newton Theological Seminary and was ordained to the Baptist ministry in 1863. His pastorates included churches in Jamaica Plain, Massachusetts, and the Clarendon Street Baptist Church in Boston. During Gordon's twenty-six year ministry at Clarendon Street, the church, spiritually dead and worldly when he came, was transformed into a strong, vibrant, and evangelistic congregation. The Roman Catholic influence in Boston was strong, and Gordon was once arrested for his bold preaching on Boston Commons. In addition to his editing of hymns and tunes, Dr. Gordon was also in charge of *The Watchword*, a monthly religious periodical. In 1878 Brown University honored him with the honorary Doctor of Divinity degree. Dr. Gordon, a close friend of D. L. Moody, died in Boston on February 2, 1895.

O Worship the King
1833

O worship the King, all glorious above,
And gratefully sing His power and His love;
Our Shield and Defender, the Ancient of Days,
Pavilioned in splendor, and girded with praise.

O tell of His might, O sing of His grace,
Whose robe is the light, whose canopy space.
His chariots of wrath the deep thunderclouds form,
And dark is His path on the wings of the storm.

The earth, with its store of wonders untold,
Almighty, Thy power hath founded of old,
Hath 'stablished it fast by a changeless decree,
And round it hath cast, like a mantle, the sea.

Thy bountiful care what tongue can recite?
It breathes in the air, it shines in the light,
It streams from the hills, it descends to the plain,
And sweetly distills in the dew and the rain.

Frail children of dust, and feeble as frail,
In Thee do we trust, nor find Thee to fail;
Thy mercies how tender! how firm to the end!
Our Maker, Defender, Redeemer, and Friend.

O Lord of all might, how boundless Thy love!
While angels delight to hymn Thee above,
The humbler creation, though feeble their lays,
With true adoration shall lisp to Thy praise.

—Robert Grant

Neither in its writing nor in its use is there connected with this hymn the dramatic element found in such hymns as "Amazing Grace" and "It Is Well with My Soul." But in view of its high spiritual tone and the surpassing beauty of its imagery, this hymn is considered one of the finest examples of adoration and praise in the English language. Some hymnologists have labeled it "the model hymn of worship." It was first published in Edward Bickersteth's *Christian Psalmody* in 1833.

Certainly this hymn inspires worship. Based on Psalm 104 (actually a resetting of William Kethe's 1561 paraphrase of Psalm 104), it has caused the hearts of Christians beyond number to soar to lofty heights in spiritual desires and in thanksgiving to "Our Maker, Defender, Redeemer, and Friend!" With the psalmist our hearts would exclaim, "O Lord my God, thou art very great; thou art clothed with honour and majesty. . . . I will sing unto the Lord as long as I live: I will sing praise to my God while I have my being. . . . Bless thou the Lord, O my soul" (Psalm 104:1, 33, 35).

Many of our hymns were penned by clergymen. This hymn was written by a layman in whose personal life and heritage politics and business were intermingled with deep piety. In Harvey's *Best-Loved Hymn Stories* an interesting anecdote is told about this composer's grandfather. Mr. Harvey states: "On April 16, 1746, at Culloden Moor, the last hope of 'the Young Pretender, Bonnie Prince Charlie,' was shattered when the English Army under the Duke of Cumberland cut to pieces the members of his loyal Highlands Clan." Among the fallen was Alexander Grant. And on the very day that Alexander Grant was killed, his wife bore him a son. She called his name Charles in honor of the young prince for whom her husband had given his life.

Charles Grant was an intelligent man. In young manhood he went to India where he became prominent in business circles. At least two sons were born into his family in India. To the elder son was given the name Charles, for his father (later this son was known as Baron Glenelg); and to the younger son (our hymn writer) was given the Scottish name Robert.

Born in Bengal in 1779, Robert returned with the rest of his family to Scotland in 1790.

In Scotland, the father, Charles Grant, became a member of Parliament for the county of Inverness. But his chief interest continued in the direction of India. Sir Charles, as he was known, became a close friend of the Evangelical clergyman William Wilberforce, and he contributed generously to the missionary causes that Wilberforce espoused. It is said that Sir Charles made "straight paths for his feet," and that he inspired others to do the same.

With the heritage of a grandfather who gave his life for his country and of a father who had an outstanding testimony in religious circles as well as in political and business affairs of the places he loved, it is small wonder that Robert Grant reached great heights in these areas. Even though he did not live to a ripe old age (he died at the age of fifty-nine), he made every year count heavily for his country and for his Lord.

At the age of twenty-one Robert Grant was graduated from Magdalen College, Cambridge. Six years later he was called to the bar. For years he practiced law and served as a member of Parliament. In Parliament he introduced a bill to grant various rights to Jews. It was in favor of this bill that Thomas Babington Macaulay, the noted historian and essayist, made his first speech.

In 1834, Robert (by this time a director in the East India Company) was appointed governor of Bombay and knighted. As governor he displayed outstanding administrative ability and also showed impressive literary talent. The fascinating but perplexing country of India, the land he loved so well, became the subject of at least two treatises, and he authored several books on the work of the East India Company.

The high regard in which Sir Robert was held by the people of Bombay is evidenced in the fact that a medical college (built with subscriptions that Robert Grant solicited from rich and poor alike) was named for him as a lasting memorial.

Sir Robert died in Dalpoorie, India, on July 9, 1838. A year later his brother, Baron Glenelg, published twelve of Sir Robert's beautiful hymns in a small volume entitled

Sacred Poems. These were reprinted in 1844 and again in 1866.

Though sometimes the tune HANOVER by William Croft (1708) is used, "O Worship the King" is usually sung to LYONS, attributed to Johann Michael Haydn in William Gardiner's *Sacred Melodies* (1815).

The Spacious Firmament on High
1712

The spacious firmament on high,
With all the blue, ethereal sky,
And spangled heavens, a shining frame,
Their great Original proclaim.
Th'unwearied sun, from day to day,
Does his Creator's power display;
And publishes to every land
The work of an almighty hand.

Soon as the evening shades prevail,
The moon takes up the wondrous tale;
And nightly, to the listening earth
Repeats the story of her birth;
While all the stars that round her burn,
And all the planets in their turn,
Confirm the tidings as they roll,
And spread the truth from pole to pole.

What though in solemn silence, all
Move round the dark terrestrial ball?
What though no real voice nor sound
Amid their radiant orbs be found?
In reason's ear they all rejoice,
And utter forth a glorious voice,
Forever singing as they shine,
"The hand that made us is divine."

—Joseph Addison

Joseph Addison, son of Lancelot Addison, dean of Lichfield, was one of England's most outstanding writers. He was born at Milston in Wiltshire, England, on May 1, 1672. He entered Oxford to study for the ministry, but at the insistence of friends he decided to study law in preparation for an official career.

In 1705 Addison published a poem—"The Campaign"—which dealt with the Battle of Blenheim. This poem launched the young lawyer into politics, and he held several important official posts, including Chief Secretary to Ireland and, under George I, Secretary of State.

In 1716, after a lengthy courtship, Addison was married to the Countess Charlotte of Warwick. So much unhappiness resulted from the union, however, that Addison soon felt compelled to leave home.

Addison, like many great writers and hymnists, suffered poor health all his life. Asthma and dropsy brought him to an early death at forty-seven. On his deathbed he sent for his wayward stepson, the Earl of Warwick, saying, "I want this young man to see in what peace a Christian can die." Death came on June 17, 1719, and Addison was interred in Westminster Abbey. A daughter survived, but she was too young to understand her loss.

Thomas Macaulay described Addison as "compassionate, full of mirth, reverent, an unsullied statesman, an accomplished scholar, and unrivalled as an observer of life and manners, and all shades of human character." John Wesley added, "God raised up Mr. Addison and his associates to lash the prevailing vices . . . and profane customs . . . and to show the excellence of Christianity and Christian institutions."

"The Spacious Firmament on High," considered by many to be Addison's best hymn, is based on Psalm 19. It graced the end of an essay entitled, "An Essay on the Proper Means of Strengthening and Confirming Faith in the Mind of Man." The hymn was prefaced by the words, "The Supreme Being has made the best arguments for His own existence, in the formation of the heavens and the earth, and these are the arguments which a man of sense cannot forbear attending to, who is out of the noise and hurry of human affairs. . . . The Psalmist has very beautiful strokes of poetry to this purpose in that exalted strain (Psalm 19). As such a bold and sublime manner of thinking furnishes very noble matter for an ode, the reader may see it wrought into the following one." The hymn was published in *The Spectator* of August 23, 1712.

The popular tune of this creation hymn is adapted from "The Heavens Are Telling," a chorus in the famous oratorio of Franz Joseph Haydn (1732-1809), *The Creation* (1798). It is said that Haydn, while he was writing this splendid work, knelt in daily prayer, beseeching the Lord's wisdom and strength.

This Is My Father's World
1901

This is my Father's world,
And to my listening ears
All nature sings, and round me rings
The music of the spheres.
This is my Father's world:
I rest me in the thought
Of rocks and trees, of skies and seas—
His hand the wonders wrought.

This is my Father's world,
The birds their carols raise;
The morning light, the lily white,
Declare their Maker's praise.
This is my Father's world:
He shines in all that's fair;
In the rustling grass I hear Him pass,
He speaks to me everywhere.

This is my Father's world,
  O let me ne'er forget
That though the wrong seems oft so strong,
  God is the Ruler yet.
  This is my Father's world:
  The battle is not done;
Jesus who died shall be satisfied,
  And earth and heaven be one.

—Maltbie Davenport Babcock

Each stanza of "This Is My Father's World" begins with the title words. This thought seemed to permeate the author's poems, his prose, and his preaching. In nature he heard "the music of the spheres." Rocks, trees, skies, and seas reminded him of rest. The carols of the birds expressed praise to the Lord. In the grass he seemed to hear the footsteps of the Lord and seemed to hear His voice speaking to him. He wondered, "Why should I so troubled be at wrong, which often seems so strong?" Then he reasoned, "God is the ruler over all. I live in a world that belongs to my Heavenly Father. There is no need for my heart to be sad. The Lord is King. Oh, let the earth be glad and the heavens ring with the truth that God reigns."

Maltbie Davenport Babcock has been described as "one who possessed the sweet singing soul of David, the fiery zeal of the apostle Paul, the eloquence of Apollos, the capacity for friendship of Jonathan, and the heavenly spirit of St. John." Born in Syracuse, New York, on August 3, 1858, he was educated at Syracuse University and Auburn Theological Seminary where he excelled in musicianship, leadership, dramatics, athletics, and religious activity. Being a champion in baseball and swimming, he became popular on campuses throughout the East. He pastored Presbyterian churches at Lockport (New York), Baltimore, and New York City.

At Lockport Dr. Babcock arose early each morning and went to a nearby hill to revel in the beauty of his Heavenly

Father's world. He said, "This world is the best for one who is called according to God's purpose. . . . How long we are to suffer or to serve is for God to say. Let us not look too much out of the schoolroom windows, or too impatiently at the clock. Until God's time comes for us, this world is best for us, and we must make the most of it and do our best for it." Early morning and evening hikes took young Babcock to a distant forest to "behold the fowl of the air," as Scripture instructs. He would listen to the singing of the birds and think, "They are communing with their Maker." Soon he was expressing in verse his observations of nature.

In Baltimore, at the age of thirty, Dr. Babcock quickly became "the city's most popular preacher, counsellor, and friend." His magnetic personality and powerful preaching drew such large numbers of students and faculty of Johns Hopkins University that the university set aside a special room for his use.

In New York Dr. Babcock succeeded Henry Van Dyke at the Brick Presbyterian Church. There it was said that a "manlier man never stood in a Christian pulpit" and that "he inspired other men to resolve that 'with God's help, I'll be a man!' " Dr. Babcock decried "cowardly contentment"—the "letting things go in weak complaisance or shallow optimism, when those things could be bettered, if we cared to better them." He would exclaim,

> Say not, "The days are evil, Who's to blame?"
> And fold the hands and acquiesce—Oh, shame!
> Stand up, speak out, and bravely, in God's Name.

Dr. Babcock trusted the Lord implicitly. He often said, "Anxiety has no place in the life of God's children. . . . The life lived by the faith of the Son of God will find the fulfillment of His Word—'My peace I give unto you.' Fretting weakens a Christian." This godly minister spent an hour before breakfast each day in prayer and meditation.

In 1901, when he was forty-three, Babcock and his wife traveled to Egypt and Palestine. On the way home he was stricken with a mysterious fever and was taken to Naples, Italy. There he died a few days later, May 18, 1901. Six months later the words of this hymn appeared in *Thoughts for Every Day Living*, a book compiled by Mrs. Babcock and Miss Mary R. Sanford. The hymn formed a part of a poem of sixteen stanzas that was entitled "My Father's World."

Dr. Babcock composed many melodies, but the setting of this particular hymn is the tune TERRA PATRIS, written in 1915 by Dr. Babcock's good friend, Franklin L. Sheppard (1852-1930). A businessman in Baltimore, Sheppard was an active layman in the Presbyterian Church and a close friend of Babcock. He originally called the tune "an English melody," thinking that he had simply recalled it from childhood, but it was in fact his own original composition.

Praise

All Hail the Power of Jesus' Name
   1779 (stanzas 1-8)
   1787 (stanza 9)

All hail the power of Jesus' Name!
   Let angels prostrate fall;
Bring forth the royal diadem,
   And crown Him Lord of all!

Crown Him, ye morning stars of light,
   Who fixed this floating ball;
Now hail the Strength of Israel's might
   And crown Him Lord of all!

Crown Him, ye martyrs of our God,
   Who from His altar call;
Extol the Stem of Jesse's rod,
   And crown Him Lord of all!

Hail Him, the Heir of David's line,
   Whom David Lord did call;
The God incarnate, Man divine!
   And crown Him Lord of all!

(Let high-born seraphs tune the lyre
   And, as they tune it, fall
Before His face who tunes their choir,
   And crown Him Lord of all.)

Ye chosen seed of Israel's race,
   Ye ransomed from the fall,
Hail Him who saves you by His grace,
   And crown Him Lord of all!

Sinners, whose love can ne'er forget
   The wormwood and the gall,
Go spread your trophies at His feet,
   And crown Him Lord of all!

Let every kindred, every tribe,
  On this terrestrial ball,
To Him all majesty ascribe,
  And crown Him Lord of all!

O that with yonder sacred throng
  We at His feet may fall!
We'll join the everlasting song,
  And crown Him Lord of all.
—Edward Perronet (stanzas 1-8)
—John Rippon (stanza 9)

    Edward Perronet, who wrote this imperishable hymn of praise to God the Son, was the descendant of at least two generations of Huguenot (French Protestant) refugees. His father, Vincent Perronet, was a vicar in the Church of England who cooperated with Whitefield and the Wesleys.

    Edward Perronet was born in Sundridge, Kent, England, on August 2, 1726. His early education was under a tutor at home. After studying for the Anglican priesthood, Edward aligned himself with the Wesleys. In his staunch support of early Methodism, Edward suffered much persecution. John Wesley noted some of the persecution in his *Journal* of 1749: "From Rochdale we went to Bolton, and soon found that the Rochdale lions were lambs in comparison with those at Bolton. Edward Perronet was thrown down and rolled in mud and mire. Stones were hurled and windows broken."

    John Wesley admired Edward Perronet. John Julian's *Dictionary of Hymnology* quotes a letter, written by John Wesley to Perronet in 1750, which says, "You and Charles *behave* as I wish you to do, but you cannot or will not preach *where* I want you to preach. There are others who will preach *where* I want them to preach, but they will not *behave* as I wish them to behave. If I had more helpers and preachers who in general had the proper understanding of serving God as sons in the Gospel, the work in Ireland and England would have prospered much more than it has."

Edward Perronet's first notable writing, published in 1757, was a caustic poetic satire on the Established Church entitled "The Mitre." Although it was published anonymously, Perronet's part in the writing was soon discovered, and hearty disapproval came from more than one source. Lady Selina Hastings, Countess of Huntingdon, who had supported the Methodist revival by employing its preachers as chaplains, refused to permit Perronet to appear in her chapels. Even John Wesley was upset about the poem, and he set out to suppress its use. (In later years John Wesley had to admit, "For forty years I have been in doubt concerning the question, 'What obedience is due to heathenish priests and infidels?'")

Because of John Wesley's strict demands with regard to the sacraments (he felt that they should be administered only at parish churches and that all congregations should be brought to these churches), Edward Perronet parted company with him. The two men continued to be friends, but John Wesley refused to admit into his collection any of Perronet's hymns.

Edward's closing years were spent at Canterbury. He pastored an independent church and continued his evangelistic efforts until January 2, 1792, when he went to be with the One he had loved and served. The last words of the saintly Perronet were this doxology: "Glory to God in the height of His divinity! Glory to God in the depth of His humanity! Glory to God in His all-sufficiency! And into His hands I commend my spirit." Perronet, described by David R. Breed as "a Christian genius; a man of distinguished pedigree; of great and varied native gifts; learned, witty, consecrated and influential," was buried in the cloisters of the great cathedral at Canterbury.

"All Hail the Power of Jesus' Name" was published anonymously in *The Gospel Magazine* (Augustus M. Toplady's journal) in 1779. In 1785 it appeared in *Occasional Verses, Moral and Sacred* in London. Although the hymn ranked twenty-one in a list by Benson, David R. Breed says that "it ranks just as high as one desires to place it. It is superfine every way. It is partic-

ularly fine in its unusual Scriptural allusions. . . . It con-
templates the lordship of Jesus from the time when 'the
morning stars sang together' to the 'everlasting song' of
the New Jerusalem, though the last verse [stanza]—'O,
that with yonder sacred throng'—was added by Rev. John
Rippon in 1787." (Rippon also omitted a stanza or two,
such as number 5 above, and made numerous alterations.)

The first tune to which this song was sung (MILES
LANE) was composed in 1779 by William Shrubsole, a
young organist. So fond was Perronet of Shrubsole that
in his will Perronet left to the young man all his property,
stating that it was "in consideration of that pure and
disinterested affection he has ever shown me from our
first acquaintance even when a proverb or a reproach,
cast off by all my relations, disinherited unjustly, and left
to sink or swim as afflictions and God's providence should
appoint."

In the United States, "All Hail the Power of Jesus'
Name" is usually sung to the tune CORONATION. This
tune was composed in 1793 by a Massachusetts carpenter, Oliver Holden (1765-1844), who later became
proprietor of a Boston music store, an author, a publisher,
a lay preacher, and a representative in the United States
Congress. Another popular tune is DIADEM (1838) by
James Ellor (1819-1899). Ellor, a hatmaker who led the
music at a Wesleyan chapel near Manchester, England,
wrote the tune when he was only nineteen. But no matter
how inspiring the tunes, the lofty thoughts of the hymn
itself would set on fire the soul of any true Christian.

"All Hail the Power of Jesus' Name" is a magnificent
hymn without which Edward Perronet would be virtually
unknown in our day. Each time the song is sung, it
testifies, "He being dead, yet speaketh."

Come, Thou Almighty King
ca. 1757

Come, Thou Almighty King,
Help us Thy name to sing,
*   Help us to praise:*
Father all-glorious,
O'er all victorious,
Come, and reign over us,
*   Ancient of days.*

Come, Thou Incarnate Word,
Gird on Thy mighty sword,
*   Our prayer attend:*
Come, and Thy people bless,
And give Thy word success:
Spirit of holiness,
*   On us descend.*

Come, Holy Comforter,
Thy sacred witness bear
*   In this glad hour:*
Thou who almighty art,
Now rule in every heart,
And ne'er from us depart,
*   Spirit of power.*

To the great One in Three
Eternal praises be,
*   Hence, evermore:*
His sovereign majesty
May we in glory see,
And to eternity
*   Love and adore!*

—Anonymous

Our first record of "Come, Thou Almighty King" dates from 1757. Some hymnologists ascribe the hymn to Charles Wesley. They base their arguments on its appearance in a tract along with a hymn that John Wesley attributed to his brother Charles. To most authorities, however, the author is "Unknown." They reason that "the meter is foreign to Charles Wesley, and neither John nor Charles Wesley allude to the hymn in any of their writings."

Although little is known about the writing of this great Trinitarian hymn, William J. Hart (*Unfamiliar Stories of Familiar Hymns*) gives an interesting illustration of its use. Former President Calvin Coolidge died suddenly on June 7, 1933. He was buried on Saturday. When church convened the next day, Mrs. Coolidge and her son were in their usual pew. Mrs. Coolidge seemed to take comfort in singing the opening hymn—"Come, Thou Almighty King . . . Holy Comforter." No doubt this story could be repeated in the lives of countless Christians.

Many hymns, including "Come, Thou Almighty King," follow an invitation pattern. Whereas some invitations are suited for use at the end of a service, others are designed to open a service. Some hymn invitations are addressed to individuals. In this category are "Come, Ye Sinners, Poor and Needy," "Come Ye Disconsolate," and "Come, Ye Thankful People, Come." Other invitations are addressed to Deity, invoking His aid in praising Him. Examples are "Come, Thou Fount of Every Blessing," "Come, Thou Quickening Spirit," and "Come, Saviour Jesus." "Come, Thou Almighty King" addresses the full Godhead, calling Him "Almighty King," "Incarnate Word," "Holy Comforter," and "Great One in Three."

To omit a stanza of this hymn would be to ignore a part of the Godhead. In stanza 1 the petitioner invites the Almighty, the glorious, the all-victorious King, to come and reign over him and give him aid in offering proper praise to the "Ancient of Days." Stanza 2 petitions the "Incarnate Word," "Spirit of Holiness," to come and give His Word success. Stanza 3 requests the "Holy Comforter," the "Spirit of Power," to come and never depart. The final stanza expresses eternal praise and love to the "Great One in Three" whom the author expects to see in glory.

Augustine Smith (*Lyric Religion*) suggests a joyful

attitude in the singing of this hymn. He cautions against too fast a tempo, however, saying that "to sing it too fast robs the hymn of its dignity."

"Come, Thou Almighty King" made its debut in the 1757 tract described above, which also included Charles Wesley's hymn, "Jesus, Let Thy Pitying Eye." The tract was bound in the British Museum's copies of the 1757, 1759, and 1760 editions of George Whitefield's *Collection of Hymns for Social Worship.* In 1763 it was featured in a collection by Martin Madan (which has led some to think Madan wrote it). To some degree, "Come, Thou Almighty King" imitates "God Save the King" (ca. 1743). Similarity is noted in both meter and style. Observe this stanza from "God Save the King":

O Lord our God, arise;
Scatter his [the king's] enemies,
  And make them fall.
Frustrate their knavish tricks,
Confound their politics;
On him our hearts we fix:
  God save the king.

Now compare this omitted stanza from "Come, Thou Almighty King":

Jesus, our Lord, arise,
Scatter our enemies,
  And make them fall!
Let Thine almighty aid
Our sure defense be made,
Our souls on Thee be stayed;
  Lord, hear our call.

Because of its unusual meter, so similar to that of "God Save the King," some think that this hymn was written to be sung to the same tune (which we know as AMERICA). In any case, the hymn was sung for some time to this tune. An interesting story from the days of the American Revolution relates that upon being surprised in church on Long Island one Sunday morning by a detachment of British soldiers, a group of worshipers,

when ordered to rise and sing "God Save the King," rose
and sang heartily, indeed, the expected tune, but with
the words of "Come, Thou Almighty King."

In our day "Come, Thou Almighty King" is usually sung
to the tune ITALIAN HYMN (also called TRINITY, FAIR-
FORD, FLORENCE, HERMON, GIARDINI, and MOSCOW),
which was one of four tunes contributed by Felice de
Giardini to *The Collection of Psalm and Hymn Tunes
Sung at the Chapel of the Lock Hospital* (London, 1769),
published by Martin Madan. Giardini was born in Turin,
Italy, on April 12, 1716. In his youth he served as a choirboy at the Cathedral of Milan. After a diligent study of
music, he became proficient in several areas: voice, com-
position, harpsichord, strings, and conducting. At thirty-
four Giardini toured Europe, giving concerts as he went.
At the end of his successful tour, he settled in London,
England, where he lived from 1752 to 1784. A venture
into comic opera cost him his money and his reputation.
In 1796 he went to Moscow, where he died on June 8,
1796, less than three months after his first concert there.
The tune is called ITALIAN HYMN perhaps because
Giardini himself was known in England as "the Italian."
The name MOSCOW for the same tune is in reference
to the city where the composer died, and TRINITY obvi-
ously refers to the content of the text of the hymn.

Come, Thou Fount of Every Blessing
1758

*Come, Thou Fount of every blessing,
  Tune my heart to sing Thy grace;
Streams of mercy, never ceasing,
  Call for songs of loudest praise.
Teach me some melodious sonnet,
  Sung by flaming tongues above;
Praise the mount—I'm fixed upon it—
  Mount of Thy redeeming love.*

Here I raise mine Ebenezer;
  Hither by Thy help I'm come;
And I hope, by Thy good pleasure,
  Safely to arrive at home.
Jesus sought me when a stranger,
  Wandering from the fold of God;
He, to rescue me from danger,
  Interposed His precious blood.

O to grace how great a debtor
  Daily I'm constrained to be!
Let Thy goodness, like a fetter,
  Bind my wandering heart to Thee:
Prone to wander, Lord, I feel it,
  Prone to leave the God I love;
Here's my heart, O take and seal it,
  Seal it for Thy courts above.

—Robert Robinson

This autobiographical hymn has been described as "a mixture of thanksgiving, petition, and revelation of the gospel," and "a spring of praise bubbling up from many verses of Scripture." Its recurring theme is "prone to wander." It was written in 1758 for Whitsunday and published the following year. Its fourth stanza, omitted by Martin Madan in 1760, seems never to have been printed again.

In stanza 1 the author confesses that his heart tends to get out of tune, causing him to neglect the Source of all blessing. *Fount* implies a rich and constant Source, and *mount* suggests a boundless love. *Ebenezer*, stanza 2, bespeaks divine help (cf. I Samuel 7:12). Looking backward the writer says, "It is by Thy help that I am here." Looking forward he exclaims, "By Thy good pleasure I shall arrive safely at home." He ends the stanza with the thought that the Lord has rescued him from danger by interposing His precious blood. Stanza 3 acknowledges a daily debt to grace. Twice it refers to our tendency to stray from God. Then the author beseeches the Lord to bind his wandering heart as fetters might bind a prisoner's feet.

Robert Robinson was born at Swaffham in Norfolk, England, on September 27, 1735. At eight he was attending a Latin school. At ten he lost his father. The widowed mother, a deeply spiritual woman, prayed that Robert might become a minister. Because of financial difficulties, however, she had to apprentice him to a barber at fourteen, thus interrupting his formal education.

In 1752 Robinson and some friends got a fortune-teller drunk and made her tell their fortunes. When she predicted that Robinson would live to see grandchildren, he said, "Then I must start mending my ways." First he went to hear George Whitefield. His intention was to "ridicule the poor deluded Methodists"; he came away "envying their happiness." Two years and seven months later Robinson not only yielded his heart to the Lord, but he entered the ministry as well.

Robinson was "a man of fine intellect, but unstable as water." Certainly instability affected his church membership. He became successively a Calvinistic Methodist, an Independent, and a Baptist. In his latter years, because of an association with the Unitarian theologian and scientist, Joseph Priestley, Robinson was labeled a Unitarian. His writings and preaching seem to indicate otherwise. One of his outstanding works was "A Plea for the Divinity of Jesus Christ," and his preaching strongly emphasized that "the death of Jesus Christ obtained the remission of sins." He died in 1790.

Robinson once commented that "a common good book, like a good man, is not without its defects." He should know. Although he was considered the "spiritual father of the noted Robert Hall and spiritual grandfather of Charles Spurgeon whom Hall inspired," Robinson was full of defects. An example occurred in his latter years on a stagecoach. A lady passenger, grieved by his levity, sought to convert him. She quoted this hymn, then added, "These words might help you as they have helped me." Robinson sobbed, "Madam, I am the poor, unhappy man who composed that hymn many years ago. I would give a thousand worlds, if I had them, to enjoy the feelings I had then."

The usual tune for "Come, Thou Fount of Every Blessing" was originally called GOOD SHEPHERD or HALLELUJAH. Later it became NETTLETON in honor of Asahel Nettleton (1783-1844), evangelist and hymn collector. The anonymous tune was introduced in 1813 in an important collection of John Wyeth (1770-1858), who was not, however, a composer. Wyeth was a printer, publisher, and musician. Another popular tune, WARRENTON, comes from *The Sacred Harp* (1844).

Crown Him with Many Crowns
1851 and 1874

Crown Him with many crowns,
The Lamb upon His throne;
Hark! how the heavenly anthem drowns
All music but its own!
Awake, my soul, and sing
Of Him who died for thee,
And hail Him as thy matchless King
Through all eternity.

Crown Him the Lord of love!
Behold His hands and side,
Rich wounds, yet visible above,
In beauty glorified:
All hail, Redeemer, hail!
For Thou hast died for me:
Thy praise shall never, never fail
Throughout eternity.

Crown Him the Lord of life,
Who triumphed o'er the grave,
And rose victorious in the strife
  For those He came to save;
  His glories now we sing
  Who died, and rose on high,
Who, died eternal life to bring,
  And lives that death may die.

Crown Him the Lord of heaven!
  One with the Father known,
One with the Spirit through Him given
  From yonder glorious throne!
  To Thee be endless praise,
  For Thou for us hast died;
Be Thou, O Lord, through endless days
  Adored and magnified.

—Matthew Bridges and Godfrey Thring

It was the year 1905. The London Bible Society was holding a Centenary Thanksgiving with the Marquis of North Hampton presiding. First the marquis read messages from numerous Protestant rulers of Christendom; then he said, in substance, "We have read the congratulations of earthly rulers. Now let us honor the Great Ruler, the King of kings, by singing, 'Crown Him with Many Crowns.'"

This popular hymn is based on Revelation 19:12 ("and on his head were many crowns"), and the name of the tune is the Greek word for "crowns" (*diademata*) in that verse. The first printing of the hymn was in *Hymns of the Heart* (1851) by Matthew Bridges (1800-1894). It contained six stanzas. Later, Godfrey Thring (1823-1903) altered the hymn (1874), and most often today only four stanzas appear in our hymnals. The four-stanza arrangement usually follows this order: stanza 1 by Bridges, with the remaining stanzas being by either Bridges or Thring or combinations of stanzas by both authors.

One early arrangement of the hymn had the following order: Stanza 1 (Bridges) discusses Christ's Kingship in general, the crown being placed upon the head of "the Lamb upon His throne" following Revelation 22:1. The "heavenly anthem" comes from the worshipping angels and elders of Revelation 5:11-14. In stanza 2, "Crown Him the Virgin's Son . . ." (Bridges), He is portrayed as the Incarnate Son who fulfilled ancient prophecies. (This stanza is omitted in most hymnals.) Stanza 3, "Crown Him the Son of God . . ." (Thring), depicts His unique personality of two natures—the Pre-existent God, yet also man. As the Babe of Bethlehem, He appeared as a creature of time and space, becoming subject to the limitations of human frailty. Stanza 4 (Bridges) depicts Him as "Lord of Love," as expressed in the atonement; and stanza 5 (Bridges) calls Him the "Lord of Peace," bespeaking the perfect peace that comes through Him. In stanza 6 (Bridges) He is the "Lord of Years," an aspect of the third crown, yet with the addition of creative power. Before time began He was Creator-God; when time ends, He will still be God. Godfrey Thring felt that there should be seven crowns, and He added the "Lord of Life."

Because hymnals do not include them, it is interesting, inspirational, and instructive, to read the six stanzas of Bridges' original hymn (from *Hymns of the Heart,* 1851):

Crown Him with many crowns,
　The Lamb upon His throne;
Hark! how the heavenly anthem drowns
　All music but its own:
　Awake, my soul, and sing
　Of Him who died for thee,
And hail Him as thy matchless King
　Through all eternity.

Crown Him the Virgin's Son!
　The God Incarnate born,—
Whose arm those crimson trophies won
　Which now His brow adorn!
　Fruit of the mystic Rose
　As of that Rose the Stem:
The Root, whence mercy ever flows,—
　The Babe of Bethlehem!

Crown Him the Lord of peace!
Whose power a sceptre sways,
From pole to pole,—that wars may cease,
*   Absorbed in prayer and praise:*
*   His reign shall know no end,*
*   And round His pierced feet*
Fair flowers of paradise extend
*   Their fragrance ever sweet.*

Crown Him the Lord of love!
*   Behold His hands and side,—*
Rich wounds, yet visible above,
*   In beauty glorified;*
*   No angel in the sky*
*   Can fully bear that sight,*
But downward bends his burning eye
*   At mysteries so bright!*

Crown Him the Lord of years!
*   The Potentate of time,—*
Creator of the rolling spheres,
*   Ineffably sublime!*
*   Glassed in a sea of light,*
*   Where everlasting waves*
Reflect His throne,—the Infinite!
*   Who lives,—and loves,—and saves.*

Crown Him the Lord of heaven!
*   One with the Father known,—*
And the blest Spirit, through Him given
*   From yonder triune throne!*
*   All hail! Redeemer,—Hail!*
*   For Thou hast died for me;*
Thy praise shall never, never fail
*   Throughout eternity!*

It is likewise helpful to read Thring's hymn, and then to see how the works of the two authors have been combined to form the lines we sing today. Thring wrote, in *Hymns and Sacred Lyrics*, 1874:

Crown Him with crowns of gold,
All nations great and small,
Crown Him, ye martyred saints of old,
The Lamb once slain for all;
The Lamb once slain for them
Who bring their praises now,
As jewels for the diadem
That girds His sacred brow.

Crown Him the Son of God
Before the worlds began,
And ye, who tread where He hath trod,
Crown Him the Son of man;
Who every grief hath known
That wrings the human breast,
And takes and bears them for His own,
That all in Him may rest.

Crown Him the Lord of light,
Who o'er a darkened world
In robes of glory infinite
His fiery flag unfurled,
And bore it raised on high,
In heaven—in earth—beneath,
To all the sign of victory
O'er Satan, sin, and death.

Crown Him the Lord of life,
Who triumphed o'er the grave,
And rose victorious in the strife
For those He came to save;
His glories now we sing
Who died, and rose on high,
Who died, eternal life to bring,
And lives that death may die.

Crown Him of lords the Lord,
Who over all doth reign,
Who once on earth, the incarnate Word,
For ransomed sinners slain,
Now lives in realms of light,
Where saints with angels sing
Their songs before Him day and night,
Their God, Redeemer, King.

Crown Him the Lord of heaven,
  Enthroned in worlds above;
Crown Him the King, to whom is given
  The wondrous name of Love.
Crown Him with many crowns,
  As thrones before Him fall,
Crown Him, ye kings, with many crowns,
  For He is King of all.

Matthew Bridges was born on July 14, 1800, the youngest son of John Bridges of Wallington House, Surrey. He was educated in the Church of England and for many years served as an Anglican rector. He compiled hymns for the Church and also published several books on history and poetry. In 1828 he published a book against the Roman Catholic Church entitled *The Roman Empire Under Constantine the Great.* Yet in 1848, under the influence of those High Church Anglicans such as John Henry Newman who converted to Roman Catholicism, he embraced Romanism. Bridges spent his last years in Quebec, where he died on October 6, 1894.

Godfrey Thring was born in Alford, Somerset, England, on March 25, 1823. After graduation from Oxford in 1845, he spent his life as a clergyman in the Church of England until his retirement in 1893. As a hymnodist he published several volumes of hymns and other poetry. He died in Shanley Green, Surrey, on September 13, 1903.

The tune DIADEMATA was written especially for this hymn by Dr. George Job Elvey (1816-1893) for the *Appendix* to the 1868 edition of *Hymns Ancient and Modern.* Elvey was born on March 27 or 29, 1816, in Canterbury, England. Musical and spiritual, he began his career as choir boy in Canterbury Cathedral. He studied at the Royal Academy, London, and was organist at St. George's Chapel, Windsor, from 1835 until 1882. In 1840 Oxford granted him a doctorate in music, only two years after he had received the Bachelor of Music degree. Elvey was asked to arrange music for many state occasions. The *Festival March,* which he wrote for the wedding of Princess Louise, resulted in his being knighted in 1871. Though the quantity of his tunes is small, the quality is superb. Elvey died at Windlesham, Surrey, on December 9, 1893, and was buried outside St. George's Chapel, the place of his long ministry.

O for a Thousand Tongues to Sing
  1739

O for a thousand tongues to sing
  My great Redeemer's praise,
The glories of my God and King,
  The triumphs of His grace.

My gracious Master and my God,
  Assist me to proclaim,
To spread through all the earth abroad
  The honors of Thy name.

Jesus! the Name that charms our fears,
  That bids our sorrows cease,
'Tis music in the sinner's ears,
  'Tis life and health and peace.

He breaks the power of canceled sin,
  He sets the prisoner free;
His blood can make the foulest clean;
  His blood availed for me.

He speaks, and listening to His voice,
  New life the dead receive;
The mournful, broken hearts rejoice;
  The humble poor, believe.

Hear Him, ye deaf; His praise, ye dumb,
  Your loosened tongues employ;
Ye blind, behold your Saviour come;
  And leap, ye lame, for joy.

—Charles Wesley

In 1737 John and Charles Wesley were fervent church workers who considered themselves to be in a good spiritual state. In 1738, however, at a place on Aldersgate Street in London, the Wesley brothers came under the influence of some dedicated Moravians who had a peace, a joy, and an assurance that they did not have. John and Charles Wesley recalled having seen some other happy Moravians on the ship which had brought them back to England from America. The Lord dealt with the Wesleys, and soon they had the assurance that they had been genuinely converted. Biographers refer to this change as "the Aldersgate experience."

Customarily, Charles wrote a new hymn every year on his birthday (December 18). It is not surprising, therefore, to know that he penned a hymn on the first anniversary of his new birth. He was thinking on the Lord's goodness in saving him, and he felt such deep gratitude that he had to express his feelings in verse. Again, he was influenced by thoughts of a Moravian leader, Peter Böhler. The Wesleys had never known a man who so constantly praised the Lord as did Peter Böhler. When they questioned Mr. Böhler, they were told, "Had I a thousand tongues, I would praise Him with them all." So in gratitude for his own conversion and in remembrance of Böhler's happy testimony, Charles Wesley wrote this hymn of petition and praise. Another suggestion for the hymn's inspiration is Wesley's enchantment with the German hymn, "O! dass ich tausend Zungen hätte" ("O that I had a thousand tongues") by Johann Mentzer (1658-1734), a German pastor who wrote about thirty hymns.

"O for a Thousand Tongues to Sing" was featured in the Wesleys' *Hymns and Sacred Poems* of 1740. In that collection the hymn was entitled "For the Anniversary Day of One's Conversion." The original title, however, was "Glory to God, and Praise, and Love."

Though at first having eighteen stanzas, the hymn as we use it is comprised of stanzas 7 through 12 of the original hymn, an arrangement that was initiated by Richard Conyers in *A Collection of Psalms and Hymns from Various Authors.* In 1780 the *Wesleyan Hymn Book* also opened the hymn with stanza 7. It changed line 2, however, to "My *dear* Redeemer's praise" instead of "My *great* Redeemer's praise."

Hymnal editors consider the first six stanzas of Wesley's hymn to be for the most part too personal, too intimately related to his conversion experience to be suitable for corporate worship. They are, however, of great interest:

Glory to God, and praise, and love,
*   Be ever, ever given;*
By saints below, and saints above,
*   The church in earth and heaven.*

On this glad day the glorious Sun
*   Of righteousness arose,*
On my benighted soul He shone,
*   And filled it with repose.*

Sudden expired the legal strife,
*   'Twas then I ceased to grieve,*
My second, real, living life,
*   I then began to live.*

Then with my heart I first believed,
*   Believed with faith divine,*
Power with the Holy Ghost received,
*   To call the Saviour mine.*

I felt my Lord's atoning blood,
*   Close to my soul applied;*
Me, me He loved—the Son of God
*   For me, for me He died!*

I found, and owned His promise true,
*   Ascertained of my part,*
My pardon passed in heaven I knew,
*   When written on my heart.*

Many of Wesley's 6500 hymns were written while he was traveling on horseback to serve churches in various communities. Reportedly, he would be riding down the road, thinking on the Lord's goodness and praiseworthiness. Halting the horse in front of a house, he would politely ask for a pen and some paper on which to "write another hymn."

Even on his deathbed Charles Wesley was still writing hymns. He died on March 29, 1788, having served in the ministry fifty years. Shortly before his death he requested pen and paper; then he wrote a poem of praise to the Lord and also a poem to his beloved wife. He handed his pen to his wife, started singing Watts' "I'll Praise My Maker While I've Breath," and soon was in the arms of the Saviour he loved and praised.

Many of Wesley's hymns were published by his brother John, who asked that the hymns "not be tinkered with." The request was ignored, however, and many Wesley hymns—for a time even "Jesus, Lover of My Soul"—went through several alterations. They were indeed "tinkered with."

The German tune AZMON gets its name from the Book of Numbers 34:4-5, a passage that describes the boundaries of Canaan. The name means "strong defense or fortress."

AZMON is attributed to Carl Gotthelf Gläser (1784-1829). Gläser was born in Weissenfels, Germany. He was taught music first by his father, and later by teachers at Saint Thomas' School in Leipzig (renowned because of its greatest teacher, Johann Sebastian Bach). Although Gläser's initial registration at Saint Thomas' was heavy with law courses, successive terms saw him studying music. Gläser taught violin, piano, and voice; he directed choirs and composed music; and he opened a music store, a venture that kept him busy until his death in Barmen on April 16, 1829.

AZMON was introduced in America by Lowell Mason (*Modern Psalmist,* 1839), but it was set to Watts' hymn, "Come, Let Us Lift Our Joyful Eyes." In Mason's *Sabbath Hymn and Tune Book* (1859) and in Charles S. Robinson's *Songs for the Sanctuary* (1879) the tune was labeled DENFIELD. Thomas Hastings (*Selah,* 1856) changed the rhythm and called the tune GASTON. Still another tune is RICHMOND, an eighteenth-century melody that was composed by Thomas Haweis (1734-1820) for use with "O Thou from Whom All Goodness Flows" (*Carmina Christo,* 1792). The present form is attributed to the work of Samuel Webbe, Jr. (1770-1843).

LYNGHAM, possibly the most stirring and exciting tune to which "O for a Thousand Tongues to Sing" is sung, was composed by Thomas Jarman (1776-1861).

(For other hymns by Charles Wesley, see pp. 52, 58, 78, 101, 104, 204, 271.)

Praise, My Soul, the King of Heaven
1834

Praise, my soul, the King of Heaven,
　To His feet thy tribute bring;
Ransomed, healed, restored, forgiven,
　Who like me His praise should sing?
　Alleluia! Alleluia!
Praise the everlasting King.

Praise Him for His grace and favor
　To our fathers in distress;
Praise Him still the same as ever,
　Slow to chide, and swift to bless.
　Alleluia! Alleluia!
Glorious in His faithfulness.

Fatherlike, He tends and spares us;
　Well our feeble frame He knows;
In His hand He gently bears us,
　Rescues us from all our foes.
　Alleluia! Alleluia!
Widely yet His mercy flows!

Frail as summer's flower we flourish,
  Blows the wind and it is gone;
But while mortals rise and perish
  God endures unchanging on.
    Alleluia! Alleluia!
Praise the high Eternal One.

Angels, help us to adore Him;
  Ye behold Him face to face;
Sun and moon, bow down before Him;
  Dwellers all in time and space,
    Alleluia! Alleluia!
Praise with us the God of grace!

—Henry Francis Lyte

"**P**raise, My Soul, the King of Heaven" has enjoyed wide usage, extending from simple street meetings to formal church services and the wedding of Queen Elizabeth II at Westminster Abbey in 1947. The wedding took place on November 20, exactly one hundred years after the death of the hymn's author, Henry Francis Lyte (1793-1847). Elizabeth requested the hymn to be used as the processional hymn at her wedding. Written in 1834, the hymn was published the same year in Lyte's *Spirit of the Psalms*, a collection of new paraphrases of the Psalms.

This hymn is based on the Psalmist's admonition to "praise the Lord, O my soul. Let everything that hath breath praise the Lord. Talk ye of all his wondrous works among the children of men." In five stanzas the poet expresses the thoughts of the entire 103rd Psalm. Compare line 4 of stanza 1 with Psalm 103:2-4: The word *ransomed* condenses the phrase, "Who forgiveth all thine iniquities." *Healed* bespeaks "Who healeth all thy diseases." *Restored* corresponds with the thought, "Who redeemeth thy life from destruction"; and *forgiven* suggests the words, "who crowneth thee with lovingkindness and tender mercies."

Erik Routley (*Hymns and the Faith*) describes "Praise,

My Soul, the King of Heaven" as having in it "everything a hymn should have." He compliments its simple language, saying that it "conceals an unusual degree of skill and concentration." He praises its clarity, which, he says, "leaves room for the imagination," and its several arresting lines that still leave the whole "homely enough to edify the simplest minds and comfort the most distracted persons." The fifth line of each stanza was, in the original, "Praise Him! Praise Him!" It was later changed to "Alleluia! Alleluia!"

Albert Edward Bailey (*The Gospel in Hymns*) contrasts Lyte's state of mind in the writing of "Jesus, I My Cross Have Taken" and "Praise, My Soul, the King of Heaven." In "Jesus, I My Cross Have Taken" Lyte refers to hearts deceiving him, foes hating him, friends shunning him, and men troubling and distressing him. It seems as though he is baring his soul to the Lord about the troubles of ill health and unspiritual people among whom he must minister. In "Praise, My Soul, the King of Heaven" he happily expresses thankfulness that God, in His mercy, has enabled him to rise above the problems of a great task. In effect, he presents the ideal Christian life. Troubles will come, he says, but we must keep our hearts and minds centered on the Lord Jesus Christ.

LAUDA ANIMA (Benedic Anima Mea) was composed for this text in 1869 by Sir John Goss, Mus.D. (1800-1880). The son of organist Joseph Goss, Sir John composed tunes, anthems, and orchestral works and edited and collaborated on various secular and religious works. The supreme desire of Goss' life seemed to be to honor God by means of his music and compositions. It is said that he considered every anthem a sermon in music and that he always prayed for the blessing of God as he began a new work. Critics praise the reverence and dignity of his tunes.

A more recent tune, also written specifically for this hymn, and also called LAUDA ANIMA (Andrews), was composed in 1931 by Mark Andrews (1875-1939) and published in that year as an anthem (G. Schirmer). The tune REGENT SQUARE, to which "Angels from the Realms of Glory" is sung, is also occasionally used with this text.

(For another hymn by Henry Francis Lyte, see p. 153.)

Praise Ye Jehovah
1976

*Praise ye Jehovah, Who from the beginning
    What He established in mercy maintains.
Founding, providing, protecting, abiding,
    Praise to the Saviour Who constant remains.*

*Praise ye Jehovah, for heroes before us,
    Battle-scarred victors at rest from the fray.
Praying, contending, proclaiming, defending,
    Faith of our fathers we will not betray.*

*Praise ye Jehovah, Who like as a father
    Comforts our sorrows and quiets our fears.
Chast'ning, restraining, forgiving, sustaining,
    From the beginning to fullness of years.*

*Praise ye Jehovah, from furnace of testing,
    Fierce though the fire, the Saviour walks there.
Loving, beholding, preserving, enfolding,
    From the beginning till He shall appear.*

*Praise ye Jehovah, for glories awaiting,
    Prizes He giveth and crowns to be won.
Claiming, progressing, obtaining, possessing,
    All He has promised through Jesus the Son.*
—Bob Jones

Anniversary celebrations of nations and institutions are important occasions for reflecting on the past and gaining a vision for the future, and they have often given rise to hymns. In September 1976, when Bob Jones University was approaching its fiftieth-anniversary celebration, Dr. Dwight Gustafson, dean of the School of Fine Arts, discussed the plans with Bob Jones, the chancellor, and told him, "If you'll write some words, I'll write the music." In early October Dr. Jones was in attendance for the anniversary week at the church of Dr. Ian Paisley in Northern Ireland, and the occasion prompted his thinking. The words were soon on paper, the music was composed in a few weeks, and the hymn was published in time for the special Thanksgiving services in November.

The overall design of the hymn shows "a definite progression in God's unchanging care." Prominent throughout is the theme "from the beginning." Stanza 1 suggests faithfulness on the part of One who "in mercy maintains what He has established." Stanza 2 opens with praise "for heroes before us"; it closes with a pledge not to betray the "faith of our fathers." In stanza 3 believers are reminded of unfailing fatherly chastening and discipline; then they are comforted with the thought of divine forgiveness. Stanza 4 brings before us divine care in the midst of earthly trials and difficulties and the hope of our Lord's return. The final stanza, giving assurance of eternal provision for those who are faithful, reminds us of the majestic words of the apostle Paul in II Timothy 4:7-8: "I have fought a good fight, I have finished my course, I have kept the faith: Henceforth there is laid up for me a crown of righteousness, which the Lord, the righteous judge, shall give me at that day: and not to me only, but unto all them also that love his appearing."

Born in 1930, Dwight Gustafson has taught at Bob Jones University since 1954. He completed his B.A. and M.A. there and went on to earn a D.Mus. degree in composition from Florida State University. Besides teaching, serving as dean of the School of Fine Arts, and directing the university symphony orchestra and other musical groups, he has been active in regional music associations and in evangelistic and Bible conference meetings in local churches. His compositions have included not only shorter choral and instrumental works that have been published and widely performed but two one-act operas, an oratorio, and the musical scores for several religious and educational films.

(For another hymn by Bob Jones, see p. 134.)

Praise Ye the Lord, the Almighty
  1680

Praise ye the Lord, the Almighty, the King of creation!
O my soul, praise Him, for He is thy health and salvation!
    All ye who hear,
    Now to His temple draw near;
Join me in glad adoration!

Praise ye the Lord, who o'er all things so wondrously
  reigneth,
Shelters thee under His wings, yea, so gently sustaineth!
    Hast thou not seen
    How thy desires e'er have been
Granted in what He ordaineth?

Praise ye the Lord, who with marvelous wisdom hath made
  thee!
Decked thee with health, and with loving hand guided and
  stayed thee;
    How oft in grief
    Hath not He brought thee relief,
Spreading His wings for to shade thee!

Praise ye the Lord! O let all that is in me adore Him!
All that hath life and breath, come now with praises before
  Him!
    Let the Amen
    Sound from His people again:
Gladly for aye we adore Him.

—Joachim Neander

"Praise Ye the Lord, the Almighty" is a paraphrase of Psalm 103:1-6 and Psalm 150. (Most hymnals use "Praise *to* the Lord," which is closer to the German title, "Lobe den Herren.") It was written in Düsseldorf when the author was thirty years old, during the last year of his life. Biographers have agreed that measured by the standard of words and tune together, it is "the finest hymn of praise ever written." The five-stanza hymn was published in 1680. The usual translation is based on that of Catherine Winkworth (1863) and combines the thoughts from Neander's third and fourth stanzas into a single third stanza.

Joachim Neander (or Neumann, which is the German equivalent of the Greek "Neander" or "new man") was regarded as the greatest German Reformed hymn writer. Born at Bremen, Germany, in 1650, he was the son, the grandson, the great-grandson, and the great-great-grandson of clergymen by the same name.

In his youth, Neander was somewhat wayward. However, at the age of twenty he and some friends went to a church to ridicule the service and "have a little fun," but his heart responded to the gospel message. He accepted the Lord Jesus Christ as his Saviour and surrendered his life to serve Him.

In 1674 Neander, after having tutored five wealthy youngsters at Frankfurt-on-the-Main, accepted a position as headmaster at Düsseldorf's Reformed grammar school. After the example of the Pietist leader Spener, Neander instituted prayer and preaching in addition to the official services, leading others to do the same. The Council of Düsseldorf met, expressed displeasure with Neander's attitude, and voted to suspend him.

Some biographers claim that during his suspension, Neander lived in a cave on the banks of the Rhine and that later the cave became known as Neander's Cave. Other biographers say that this story is without foundation. Wherever he was during his suspension, Neander spent his time in prayer and praise.

After two weeks, the school lifted Neander's suspension

and reinstated him, but in a lesser capacity. First, however, Neander had to sign a declaration that included the words, "Without mental reservation I will abide by the rules of the church and school." The humiliation of his conflict with the school in which he had served seemed to depress Neander, and within a short time he developed consumption and died. Neander is credited with sixty hymns and many hymn tunes.

The English translation of "Praise Ye the Lord, the Almighty" was a product of the genius of Catherine Winkworth (1827-1878). Miss Winkworth, a London native, pioneered higher education for women and became a noted translator of German hymns and books of verse. One of her better-known translations is "Now Thank We All Our God."

The tune for "Praise Ye the Lord, the Almighty" was selected by Neander, and his selection continues to be used. LOBE DEN HERREN ("Praise to the Lord") is from the second edition of *Ander Theil des Erneuerten Gesangbuch,* published in Stralsund in 1665. Its present form and harmonization is that of William Sterndale Bennett and Otto Goldschmidt, musical editors of the *Choral Book for England* of 1863. Much of its popular acceptance was due to its appearance in the 1904 edition of *Hymns Ancient and Modern.* The joyful aspect of hymn and tune warrants a word of caution against too fast a tempo. With changes of rhythm and melody, the tune has been adapted to many other hymns.

Rejoice, the Lord Is King
   1744

Rejoice, the Lord is King!
   Your Lord and King adore!
Rejoice [Mortals], give thanks, and sing,
   And triumph evermore:

Refrain:

Lift up your heart, lift up your voice!
Rejoice, again I say, rejoice!

Jesus, the Saviour, reigns,
The God of truth and love;
When He had purged our stains,
He took His seat above:

His Kingdom cannot fail,
He rules o'er earth and heaven;
The keys of death and hell
Are to our Jesus given:

He sits at God's right hand
Till all His foes submit,
And bow to His command,
And fall beneath His feet:

He all His foes shall quell,
Shall all our sins destroy;
And every bosom swell
With pure seraphic joy:

Rejoice in glorious hope!
Our Lord the Judge shall come,
And take His servants up
To their eternal home:

The original sixth stanza had as its last two lines, instead of the usual refrain, these words:

We soon shall hear the Archangel's voice,
The trump of God shall sound, rejoice.
—Charles Wesley

"**R**ejoice, the Lord Is King" is based on Philippians 4:4, "Rejoice in the Lord alway; and again I say, Rejoice." Christians everywhere have been touched by Paul's words, for they realize that he endured much suffering in his ministry for the Lord. No doubt Paul had also been impressed by the joy of the Christians whom he had helped persecute, as in the stoning to death of Stephen, and he longed to see all Christians radiate such joy.

"Rejoice, the Lord Is King" was written by Charles Wesley. In 1744 John Wesley printed the six-stanza work in *Moral and Sacred Poems.* Two years later the hymn appeared in Charles Wesley's *Hymns for Our Lord's Resurrection.* Today most hymnals include four stanzas, omitting the original fourth and fifth stanzas. The hymn's popularity is said to be on a par with "Hark! the Herald Angels Sing" and "Jesus, Lover of My Soul."

The Lord's resurrection permeates the hymn. The Saviour reigns, having purged our stains and having taken His seat above (stanza 2). Death could not hold Him: He came out of the grave, ascended into heaven, and is seated at the Father's right hand (stanza 4), interceding for us. Someday our Lord will return to this earth to reign in righteousness, and His kingdom cannot fail (stanza 3). His foes shall fall at His feet (stanza 4) and submit to Him. He shall destroy our sins (stanza 5), and at the trumpet's sound (stanza 6), He shall come down and take His servants up. These thoughts called forth spontaneous praise from Charles Wesley (1707-1788), and in this hymn he tries to inspire other Christians to praise the Lord.

The usual tune, DARWALL or DARWALL'S 148TH, is described as sounding a note of triumph and praise. It was composed by John Darwall (1731-1789) in 1770 to accompany Psalm 148. Born at Haughton, Staffordshire, England, at fourteen he entered Brasenose College, Oxford. Although from a musical standpoint Darwall was ranked as an amateur, he composed two volumes of piano sonatas and a tune for each of the 150 psalms (in three volumes).

"Rejoice, the Lord Is King" also stimulated Handel to write the tune GOPSAL, named for Gopsal Hall, home of Charles Jennens, compiler of the libretto for Handel's *Messiah.* According to Robert Guy McCutchan (*Our Hymnody*), Charles Wesley and Handel met at the home of a Mr. Rich whose wife had been converted under Wesley's ministry. Mrs. Rich requested Handel to write tunes for "Rejoice, the Lord Is King," "Sinners, Obey the Gospel Word," and "O Love Divine, How Sweet Thou Art." Handel graciously complied by writing GOPSAL, CANNONS, and FITZWILLIAM. Two centuries later in England, GOPSAL was still used with "Rejoice, the Lord Is King."

(For other hymns by Charles Wesley, see pp. 41, 58, 78, 101, 104, 204, 271.)

Rejoice, Ye Pure in Heart
1865

Rejoice, ye pure in heart!
Rejoice, give thanks, and sing!
Your festal banner wave on high,
The cross of Christ your King.

Refrain:

Rejoice, rejoice,
Rejoice, give thanks and sing!

Bright youth and snow-crowned age,
Strong men and maidens fair,
Raise high your free, exulting song;
God's wondrous praise declare.

Yes onward, onward still,
With hymn, and chant, and song,
Through gate, and porch, and columned aisle,
The hallowed pathways throng.

With ordered feet pass on;
Bid thoughts of evil cease,
Ye may not bring the strife of tongues
Within the Home of Peace.

With all the angel choirs,
With all the saints on earth,
Pour out the strains of joy and bliss,
True rapture, noblest mirth!

Your clear hosannas raise,
And alleluias loud;
While answering echoes upward float,
Like wreaths of incense cloud.

With voice as full and strong
As ocean's surging praise,
Send forth the hymns on fathers loved,
The psalms of ancient days.

Yes, on through life's long path,
Still chanting as ye go,
From youth to age, by night and day,
In gladness and in woe.

Still lift your standard high,
Still march in firm array;
As warriors through the darkness toil,
Till dawns the golden day.

At last the march shall end;
The wearied ones shall rest;
The pilgrims find their Father's house,
Jerusalem the blest.

Then on, ye pure in heart!
Rejoice, give thanks, and sing!
Your glorious banner wave on high,
The cross of Christ your King.

—Edward Hayes Plumptre

Like many other hymns, "Rejoice, Ye Pure in Heart"
was written for a special occasion—a choir festival at
Peterborough Cathedral, England, May 1865, in honor
of St. Stephen's Day (December 26). The hymn is based
on three verses of Scripture. The first verse is Psalm 20:5:

"We will rejoice in thy salvation, and in the name of our God we will set up our banners." The second is Psalm 147:1: "Praise ye the Lord: for it is good to sing praises unto our God; for it is pleasant; and praise is comely." The third is Philippians 4:4: "Rejoice in the Lord alway: and again I say, Rejoice."

The eleven stanzas of this hymn depict the Church, of large size and with flying banners, following behind the banner of the cross and singing a marching song. The hymn calls all ages ("bright youth and snow-crowned age, strong men and maidens fair") to join with "angel choirs" and "all the saints on earth" in the joyful song of "the cross of Christ your King." The suggestion is that in whatever circumstances we may find ourselves ("in gladness and in woe") we are to lift the "standard high" and "march in firm array . . . till dawns the golden day" when "at last the march shall end." "As warriors through the darkness toil," so are we to join angel choirs in praising the Lord in song.

Edward Hayes Plumptre (1821-1891) was a leader in the Church of England. Educated first by private tutor and later at King's College, London, and University College, Oxford, he preached, taught in colleges, lectured, and wrote poems, biographies, and theological works. He also worked on the Old Testament of the Revised Version, which was published in 1885. John Julian said of Mr. Plumptre, "His hymns are elegant in style, and fervent in spirit. . . . The rhythm of his verse has a special attraction for musicians, its poetry for the cultured, and its stately simplicity for the devout and earnest-minded." Glasgow University conferred on him the honorary Doctor of Divinity degree in 1875. He served as dean of Wells for the last ten years of his life. MARION, named for the author's mother, has become the most popular tune for this hymn. It was composed in 1883 by Arthur Henry Messiter (1834-1916).

Messiter was born in Frome, Somersetshire, England, in April 1834. In 1885 he traveled to America, and for thirty years he served Trinity Episcopal Church, New York, as organist and choir leader. His choir set a high standard for American churches, being known for the wide variety and quality of its repertoire patterned after the finest English cathedral choirs. He compiled a book of hymns especially for Trinity Church which included a history of Trinity's choir. He was awarded an honorary Doctor of Music degree by St. Stephen's College in Annandale, New York. Messiter died in New York on July 2, 1916.

An exciting new tune, VINEYARD HAVEN, was written for this hymn in 1974 by Richard Dirksen.

Ye Servants of God, Your Master Proclaim
1744

Ye servants of God, your Master proclaim,
And publish abroad His wonderful name;
The name all victorious of Jesus extol;
His Kingdom is glorious and rules over all.

God ruleth on high, almighty to save;
And still He is nigh, His presence we have;
The great congregation His triumph shall sing,
Ascribing salvation to Jesus, our King.

"Salvation to God, who sits on the throne!"
Let all cry aloud and honor the Son;
The praises of Jesus the angels proclaim,
Fall down on their faces, and worship the Lamb.

Then let us adore and give Him His right,
All glory and power, all wisdom and might;
All honor and blessing, with angels above,
And thanks never ceasing, and infinite love.

The omitted stanzas 2 and 3 that follow are inferior but are indicative of the troublesome times during which Wesley wrote the hymn.

The waves of the sea have lift up their voice,
Sore troubled that we in Jesus rejoice;
The floods they are roaring, but Jesus is here,
While we are adoring He is always near.

When devils engage, the billows arise,
And horribly rage, and threaten the skies;
Their fury shall never our steadfastness shock,
The weakest believer is built on a rock.

—Charles Wesley

In 1744, the birth year of this hymn, Methodists in England were undergoing severe persecution. France and England were at war, and Methodists were falsely accused of being Papists in disguise, working undercover to help dethrone George II and restore the house of Stuart in collusion with Bonnie Prince Charles, the "Young Pretender." In consequence, Methodist meetings were mobbed, Methodist ministers were drafted, and pulpit and pew alike were under a barrage of such things as bricks, cabbages, eggs, and pails of muddy water. These indignities came from ministers and from some of the so-called "gentlemen of the town." Even the Wesley brothers were brought before the magistrates. Like Paul, however, the Wesleys kept their hearts and minds centered on the Lord Jesus Christ and did much writing to honor His Name and to stimulate courage and faith in their followers.

During the time of this persecution, the Wesleys wrote several hymn pamphlets entitled *Hymns for Times of Trouble and Persecution.* One booklet of thirty-three hymns published in 1744 included this hymn—"Ye Servants of God, Your Master Proclaim." Based on Psalm 93:1-4 and Revelation 7:9-12, the hymn was designed to encourage Christians to keep their focus on the One "whose kingdom is glorious" and who "rules over all." In effect the Wesleys said, "Such persecution as we are enduring but leads to higher service for the Lord. No matter where His servants may be, with them is One who is 'almighty to save.' God is on the throne; therefore let us 'cry aloud, and honor His Son and our Saviour.'"

"Ye Servants of God, Your Master Proclaim" has been sung to at least two tunes. The first tune, HANOVER, was composed by William Croft (1678-1727) in 1708. Published anonymously that year in the sixth edition of *Supplement to the New Version of Psalms* by Dr. Brady and Mr. Tate, the tune was simply labeled "A New Tune for the 149th Psalm of the New Version and 104th Psalm of the Old." However, it was set to Psalm 67, "Our God, bless us all with mercy and love." At first the tune was poorly received; in a word, critics labeled it "bad." Eventually, however, the tune gained recognition as "a graceful, high-class, and singable tune."

The first version of HANOVER varied somewhat from the tune as we know it today. For a time it was attributed to Handel, which is probably why it was named HANOVER. Handel was court composer to the Elector of Hanover before moving to England; and this same Elector of Hanover eventually ascended the English throne as King George I. Other tune titles include BROMSWICK (perhaps to honor the reigning House of Brunswick), TALLY'S (used by John Wesley because he supposed Thomas Tallis had written the tune), ST. GEORGE'S (for George III), and OLD 104TH.

William Croft was born in 1678, in what is now Ettington, Warwickshire, England, six miles from Stratford. In his early life Croft served as chorister under John Blow at the Chapel Royal. Later he became organist at Westminster Abbey. In 1713 he received from Oxford the Mus.D. degree. Although Dr. Croft's early music was geared toward the theater, even then he included a few church anthems and hymns. This gifted composer is credited with "changing the Genevan-style tune to the English-Psalm tunes." Discouragement plagued Croft at times, yet he kept pressing forward in favor of better church music. Erik Routley called Croft the "greatest English composer of hymn tunes between Lawes and Parry."

The second tune LYONS was used in Boston in 1822

by Lowell Mason in *Handel and Haydn Society Collection of Church Music.* It had been introduced to America, however, by Mason's teacher, Oliver Shaw, in *Sacred Melodies* (Providence, 1818). The most familiar use of the tune is its association with "O Worship the King." LYONS appeared first, however, in a form for mixed voices and orchestra in Volume II of William Gardiner's *Sacred Melodies from Haydn, Mozart, and Beethoven* (London, 1815), for use with "O Praise Ye the Lord, Prepare a New Song." Hymnologists offer this word of caution: "The tune should never be sung with catch-breath loveliness, but in the free, hearty, traditional style of an old plain song."

LYONS is attributed to Johann Michael Haydn (1737-1806), younger brother of the great Franz Joseph Haydn. Born in Rohrau, Austria, on September 14, 1737, Michael was gifted and served well in many churches, particularly in Salzburg. As a child he was, like his older brother, a chorister at St. Stephen's Cathedral in Vienna. He became a noted choirmaster, vocalist, violinist, pianist, and organist, though he was never on a par with his brother Joseph. (Joseph, however, considered his brother's hundreds of sacred compositions far superior to his own.) Michael died in Salzburg on August 10, 1806.

(For other hymns by Charles Wesley, see pp. 41, 52, 78, 101, 104, 204, 271.)

Thanksgiving

Come, Ye Thankful People, Come
1844

Come, ye thankful people, come,
Raise the song of harvest home:
All is safely gathered in,
Ere the winter storms begin;
God, our Maker, doth provide
For our wants to be supplied:
Come to God's own temple, come,
Raise the song of harvest-home.

All the world is God's own field,
Fruit unto His praise to yield;
Wheat and tares together sown,
Unto joy or sorrow grown;
First the blade, and then the ear,
Then the full corn shall appear:
Lord of harvest, grant that we
Wholesome grain and pure may be.

For the Lord our God shall come,
And shall take His harvest home;
From His field shall in that day
All offenses purge away;
Give His angels charge at last
In the fire the tares to cast;
But the fruitful ears to store
In His garner evermore.

Even so, Lord, quickly come
To Thy final harvest-home;
Gather Thou Thy people in,
Free from sorrow, free from sin;
There, forever purified,
In Thy presence to abide:
Come, with all Thine angels, come,
Raise the glorious harvest-home.

—Henry Alford

This hymn was first published in 1844 under the title, "After Harvest." It is a paraphrase of Mark 4:26-29 and Matthew 13:36-43, and may also be based on Psalm 126:6—"He that goeth forth and weepeth, bearing precious seed, shall doubtless come again with rejoicing, bringing his sheaves with him"—and envisions the day of our Lord's return to "gather His people in, free from sorrow, free from sin." The author made a few changes in his hymn and in 1867 republished it in his book, *The Year of Praise.*

Henry Alford, D.D., was the son of the Reverend Henry Alford, Rector of Aston Sanford, and was born in London, England, on October 7, 1810. Quite early in life he dedicated himself to the Lord's service. At age fifteen he made a vow to the Lord and wrote it on the flyleaf of his Bible. He said, "I do this day, in the presence of God and my own soul, renew my covenant with God and solemnly determine henceforth to become His and to do His work as far as in me lies." Alford never swerved from his vow.

Biographers have described this hymnist as "a pious young student, an eloquent preacher, a sound biblical critic, a man of great learning and taste, one of the most gifted men of his day, and an affectionate man, full of good humour." They have noted the many hymns from his pen, saying that "although they are evangelical, as a whole they have not been heart-warming enough to be popular with churches."

Alford was educated at Trinity College, Cambridge, from which in 1832 he was graduated with honors. Ordained in 1833, he served many churches before accepting the position of dean of Canterbury in 1857. He became affectionately known as Dean Alford and served at Canterbury until his death on January 12, 1871.

About four years prior to his death, Alford wrote "Ten Thousand Times Ten Thousand," another hymn which "represented the maturity of his hope and faith" and which was sung at his funeral at Canterbury Cathedral. "Ten Thousand Times Ten Thousand" has appeared in many hymnals, though not because of its merit as a hymn.

Rather the selection was based on the hymn's "courage of the Church Militant, soon to become the Church Triumphant." That the author was living in view of heaven at the time he wrote this hymn is apparent in such words as "sparkling raiment bright," "armies of ransomed saints," "rush of hallelujahs," "raptured greetings," "knitting severed friendships," and "the reign . . . of the Lamb for sinners slain." Alford was always a superior preacher whose gaze was set toward the eternal city. On his tomb, at his own request, were Latin words which mean, "The inn of a traveler on his way to Jerusalem."

Henry Alford's literary skills were manifest in every department of literature. He wrote fifty books, the most outstanding of which was his four-volume *Exposition of the New Testament.* This work occupied the author's time for more than twenty years. Alford also composed many tunes. When he wrote the treble and bass for "Forward Be Our Watchword," he said to a friend, "I have written hat and boots; you add the coat and trousers."

ST. GEORGE'S WINDSOR, the popular tune of "Come, Ye Thankful People, Come," was composed in 1858 by Sir George Job Elvey. Elvey was born in Canterbury, England, in 1816. He received a Doctor of Music degree from Oxford in 1840, was organist of St. George Royal Chapel, Windsor, from 1835-1883, and was knighted in 1871. He died in 1893.

Doxology
1695

Praise God, from whom all blessings flow;
Praise Him all creatures here below;
Praise Him above, ye heavenly host;
Praise Father, Son, and Holy Ghost!
—Thomas Ken

Haeussler, in *The Story of Our Hymns*, describes hymn singing as "an organic part of public worship, and . . . therefore couched in the language of prayer, praise, faith, and self-commitment. . . ." For more than 200 years the four lines of praise quoted above have poured from the hearts and lips of innumerable Christians.

We are told in the book *Who Wrote Our Hymns* by Christopher Knapp that "the Doxology . . . has been the death song of martyrs and the paean of victorious armies. When peace was sealed at Appomattox, the Doxology rolled like the voice of mighty thunder from State to State and from ocean to ocean."

Another writer has said, "It is the most famous and widely used of all doxologies in the English tongue, sung almost every Sunday in all churches, and on other occasions to give expression to great joy or triumph." Whenever gratitude for blessing wells in the hearts of people, it seems to find spontaneous expression in this praise to the Trinity.

The word *doxology* comes from two Greek words— one meaning "opinion, praise, glory," and the other meaning "to speak." Although Ken wrote his Doxology as the closing stanza of each of three hymns ("Evening," "Morning," and "Midnight") that he wrote for the devotions of Winchester College students, it has been given a far wider use.

The tune to which the Doxology is almost universally sung is OLD HUNDREDTH. The composer, or perhaps arranger, was Louis Bourgeois (1510-1561), a Frenchman who became a Protestant and moved to Geneva, Switzerland. He made a great contribution to congregational singing in the Reformed churches by composing the tunes for the *Genevan Psalter*. Bourgeois composed this particular tune for the French version of Psalm 134 (1551), but we know it as OLD HUNDREDTH because of its use with Kethe's "All People That on Earth Do Dwell," the paraphrase of Psalm 100 from the *Anglo-Genevan Psalter* of 1561.

During the Civil War, men in a certain prison saw

hosts of their number die and be removed, and saw hosts of other men come in to replace them. One night a group of new prisoners arrived. One of them, a young minister, sat down outside; putting his face into his hands, he sobbed uncontrollably. Suddenly, from an upper window he heard a cheerful voice singing, "Praise God, from whom all blessings flow. . . ." At the beginning of each new line, other voices joined in the singing, until finally the whole prison resounded with these heartening words. The young preacher took courage and began to sing, "Prisons would palaces prove/If Jesus would dwell with me there."

Another interesting story of this hymn regards a cotton famine in Lancashire, England. Unemployment had led to destitution. When a wagonload of cotton finally arrived, the men, in gratitude to the Lord for His goodness, unharnessed the horse, pulled the wagon through the streets, and with tears of joy streaming down their faces fervently sang, "Praise God, from whom all blessings flow. . . ."

Carl Price (*More Hymn Stories*) refers to a time when Charles Wesley was preaching in a tumbled-down house in Leeds. The floor gave way with a crash and threw the entire congregation of a hundred people to a room below. Dust and mortar covered the people, and several were injured. However, no lives were lost. Wesley called out, "The Lord is with us. Let us sing, 'Praise God, from whom all blessings flow.'"

Another authority reports that in April 1936, newspapers in Canada and the United States had large headlines of an abandoned-mine disaster in Nova Scotia. Three men—a physician and a lawyer (who had purchased the rights to this mine) and a guide—were exploring the purchase. At the 141-foot level, a cave-in occurred, cutting off all means of escape. The situation was further complicated by rising waters. Rescue squads managed to force down to the imprisoned men a pipe through which they sent food and a telephone line, and four Salvation Army men furnished food and spiritual encouragement.

At the end of ten days, when the rescuers finally

reached the trapped men, they found that one of them had died. The *Associated Press* said of the rescue, "Humble in the face of death, but thankful that two lives had been saved, the miners who succeeded in the rescue, the officials who directed their work, and the spectators who were drawn to the isolated settlement by the international anxiety attending the entombment, joined in singing, 'Praise God, from whom all blessings flow. . . .'"

These lines of such prolonged use were penned by a man of notable background. Thomas Ken was born in July 1637, at Berkhampstead in Hertfordshire, England. Orphaned early in life, he was reared by a sister, Ann, who was the second wife of Izaak Walton (whose book *The Compleat Angler* has charmed so many fishermen).

Ken's boyhood and conversion experience are passed over by most biographers. It is simply noted that he was conscientious and godly. At fifteen, Ken entered Winchester College. Later, he attended Oxford and in 1666 was elected to a fellowship at Winchester College, where his name may still be seen carved on one of the stone pillars. By the time he was twenty-five, Ken launched a preaching career which soared to great heights but which nonetheless was beset by numerous trials.

During a period of service at Winchester Cathedral, Ken had to refuse a request by his monarch. King Charles II was planning a visit to Winchester to check the progress of a new palace under construction. He was to be accompanied by his mistress, Nell Gwynne, and he asked that she be allowed to stay at Ken's residence. Friends advised Ken to "go along" with the king's request. Otherwise, they said, Ken might lose his head. But Ken stated firmly, "Not for the king's kingdom will I do this horrible thing." And to ensure that it would not happen, Ken called in a builder to repair his residence. The first thing the clever builder did was to take off the roof!

When King Charles heard of Ken's refusal, he marked in his mind, "This man Ken is a man of virtue." In 1679, King Charles appointed Ken as chaplain to Princess Mary—(who later became the wife of William of Orange).

In 1684 when the sees (church offices) of Bath and Wells became vacant, the king surprised everyone by asking, "Where is the good little man who refused a lodging to poor Nell? I want to bestow upon him these sees." Declining the usual coronation banquet, Ken gave the allotted money to charity.

As chaplain to the king, Ken faithfully sought to lead the monarch to the Lord. Often after one of his deplorable revels, the king would say, "Now I must go and hear good Bishop Ken tell me my faults." One day Ken preached on the theme of John the Baptist's warning to Herod Antipas with regard to his sin in taking his brother's wife. Then, looking directly at the king, Ken made this application: "So you, O king, are also guilty of violating God's law by openly flaunting your immorality before the British people." Ken was reminded by a friend that John the Baptist's boldness cost him his head. Ken calmly replied, "And I would gladly lose mine if it would bring the king to his senses."

Eight days after Ken had been made bishop, King Charles suffered a stroke. Immediately he sent for the chaplain. Although some authorities claim that Ken convinced the king to give up his mistress and to beg his queen's forgiveness and that the king "died in the faith," other authorities say that "Ken's pious words appear to have fallen on deaf ears." Whichever statement is true, we are sure that Ken's conscience was clear in that he had faithfully discharged his responsibility to witness to the king.

Josiah Miller (*Our Hymns*) says of Ken, "His inflexibility in maintaining what he believed to be right, and his courage in reproving kings where it was necessary, made him many and powerful enemies." In 1688, Ken was one of seven bishops who refused to publish the "Declaration of Indulgence" by which King James II intended to advance the cause of the Church of Rome in England. After a short imprisonment the men were acquitted of all charges against them, but Ken, of course, lost his office. Not having felt highly elated at his elevation, he felt no deflation when deprived of it, and God provided the material means His faithful servant needed. Lord Weymouth granted him 80 pounds a year, and after her accession Queen Anne, at Bishop Hooper's suggestion, allotted him 200 pounds yearly out of the public treasury.

Ken's piety is reflected in this oft-repeated prayer:

> Teach me to live, that I may dread
> The grave as little as my bed.

During his last year of life, Ken's health was severely impaired, and he carried a shroud with him in his travels. To those who questioned this strange practice, he explained, "I have always made it a practice to be prepared." Someone of more recent times has made this challenging comment with regard to Ken's statement: "We do not know when death may claim us; and the true preparation is to have Christ, the robe of righteousness."

He died in 1711, four months before his seventy-fourth birthday. Ken was buried at a simple service in a lowly tomb, his body being borne to the grave by twelve poor men.

As a fitting eulogy to this fearless preacher, this benefactor of the poor, this outstanding educator, this famous hymn writer who gave us the most famous four lines in hymnody, we quote the following comments by men who have written hymnology books:

> It is something to follow the course of a good man who, amid the strife of parties, is faithful to himself and to his God: who desires not high position, yet accepts it when it falls to his lot, and when conscience forbids him to retain it, can leave it without a wistful look behind.

> James II pronounced him the most eloquent preacher among the Protestants at that time.

> He approached as near as infirmity permits to the ideal perfection of Christian virtue.

The next time you sing this great doxology, think of A. Haeussler's challenge, "Let us put new vitality and spirit into our worship. Let us sing."

Now Thank We All Our God
1636

Now thank we all our God,
  With heart and hands and voices,
Who wondrous things hath done,
  In whom His world rejoices;
Who, from our mother's arms,
  Hath blessed us on our way
With countless gifts of love,
  And still is ours today.

O may this bounteous God,
  Through all our life be near us,
With ever joyful hearts
  And blessed peace to cheer us;
And keep us in His grace,
  And guide us when perplexed,
And free us from all ills
  In this world and the next.

All praise and thanks to God
  The Father now be given,
The Son and Him who reigns
  With them in highest heaven,
The one eternal God,
  Whom earth and heaven adore;
For thus it was, is now,
  And shall be evermore.

—Martin Rinkart

This hymn of gratitude, often known as the *Te Deum* of Germany and England, was not written as a choral hymn, but as a grace to be sung before meals in the author's home. According to some hymnologists, stanzas 1 and 2 paraphrase a passage from the Apocrypha, Ecclesiasticus 50:22-24: "Now therefore bless ye the God of all, which only doeth wondrous things every where, which exalteth our days from the womb, and dealeth with us according to his mercy. He grant us joyfulness of heart, and that peace may be in our days in Israel for ever; That he would confirm his mercy with us, and deliver us at his time!" Stanza three incorporates the ancient doxology, *Gloria Patri*. In every stanza, however, is the thought of Psalm 103:1-2,4: "Bless the Lord, O my soul: and all that is within me, bless his holy name . . . and forget not all his benefits . . . Who redeemeth thy life from destruction."

The hymn is rooted in the horrors of the Thirty Years' War (1618-1648), which began as a spiritual conflict between Protestant and Roman Catholic princes in Germany but degenerated into a political war for the conquest of territory. Martin Rinkart, a pastor in Eilenburg, Saxony, played an important role in the affairs of that town. Since Eilenburg was a walled town, it became a refuge for hordes of fugitives. With these fugitives came a plague that claimed 8000 lives, among them Rinkart's beloved wife. Often Rinkart was the only minister in town, and he had to work long hours in caring for the sick and burying the dead (he buried 4480 people in the year 1637, sometimes as many as 40 to 50 a day). Rinkart, although hardly able to provide food and clothing for his own family, mortgaged future incomes for several years in order to help the impoverished people.

On more than one occasion Rinkart saved Eilenburg from the Swedish army. One incident involved a 30,000-taler tax to aid the Protestant cause. Rinkart, knowing that his townsmen were unable to afford such a heavy tax, went to the Swedish camp to plead for mercy. When the general rejected the plea, Rinkart turned to his people and said, "Come, my children, we can find no mercy with men; let us take refuge with God." And falling to his knees, he offered prayer and led his followers to sing, "When in the hour of utmost need. . . ." So touched was the heart of the Swedish commander that he reduced the tax to 1350 talers.

In the midst of the turmoil, Rinkart was always ready to lift his voice in song. He properly assigned the hardships to Romans 8:28, "And we know that all things work together for good to them that love God, to them who are the called according to his purpose," and gave thanks always "for all things," as God had commanded (Ephesians 5:20).

From his birth, Rinkart had been groomed to endure hardship. Born in Eilenburg on April 23, 1586, he was the son of a poor coppersmith who was unable to pay for his son's education. Rinkart, through much industry, paid his own way through the University of Leipzig.

On December 8, 1649, Martin Rinkart was called from his earthly labors to take up his heavenly abode. Two centuries later, Miss Catherine Winkworth (1827-1878) translated "Nun danket alle Gott" into English. This faithful translator exemplified true Christian womanhood; she was a tender, sympathetic, refined intellectual and a champion of women's education.

The tune to "Now Thank We All Our God" (NUN DANKET) was composed by Johann Crüger (1598-1662), one of the most distinguished German musicians of his day and at various times a private tutor in Berlin; the Cantor of St. Nicholas' Church, Berlin; a Master at the Gymnasium; and an editor and contributor to several important German hymnological works of the seventeenth century.

Birth of Christ

Angels, from the Realms of Glory
1816

Angels, from the realms of glory,
   Wing your flight o'er all the earth;
Ye who sang creation's story,
   Now proclaim Messiah's birth:

Refrain:

Come and worship, Come and worship,
Worship Christ, the new-born King.

Shepherds, in the field abiding,
   Watching o'er your flocks by night,
God with man is now residing,
   Yonder shines the infant Light:

Sages, leave your contemplations,
   Brighter visions beam afar;
Seek the great Desire of nations,
   Ye have seen His natal star:

Saints before the altar bending,
   Watching long in hope and fear,
Suddenly the Lord, descending,
   In His temple shall appear:

Sinners, wrung with true repentance,
   Doomed for guilt to endless pains,
Justice now revokes the sentence,
   Mercy calls you, break your chains:

—James Montgomery

This lovely Christmas hymn appeared in *The Shef-
field Iris* on December 24, 1816, under the title "Nativity,"
and later as "Good Tidings of Great Joy to All People."
Someone has commented that "considering the factors

of comprehensiveness, appropriateness of expression, force and elevation of sentiment, it challenges comparison with any hymn ever written."

The theme "Come and worship Christ, the new-born King" is a skillful blend of Scripture. Stanza 1 calls upon angels not to remain in Bethlehem, but to go to all the world with the good news of "Messiah's birth." "Creation's story" suggests Job 38:7. "God with man residing," stanza 2, brings before us Isaiah 7:14, Matthew 1:23, and John 1:14. Stanza 3 hints of Haggai 2:7 and Matthew 2:2. In stanza 4 the author refers to the second coming of Christ, having in mind, perhaps, I Thessalonians 4:16 and Malachi 3:1. Most hymnals omit stanza 5. An 1855 doxological substitution by the Reverend Isaac Gregory Smith says:

Lord of Heaven, we adore Thee,
  God the Father, God the Son,
God the Spirit, One in glory,
  On the same eternal throne.
Hallelujah! Hallelujah!
Lord of Heaven, Three in One.

James Montgomery was born on November 4, 1771, in Irvine, Ayrshire, Scotland. His parents died as Moravian missionaries in the West Indies when James was only six years old. According to a prearranged plan, the young lad became the ward of the Brethren school in Fulneck, England. Here the children "were taught to regard the Lord as their Friend and Brother."

It was in his tenth year that Montgomery began to write serious poetry. At sixteen he fled Fulneck and accepted employment in a retail shop, first in Mirfield and later in Wath. From place to place he roamed, seeking to sell his poetry. Alas! no one seemed interested! He found employment in a grocery store for awhile; then he became assistant and finally editor of a newspaper and remained its editor for thirty-one years. Twice he was imprisoned for his outspoken stand that put him afoul of the prevailing Tory government. Many of his hymns were born in prison. He was an active supporter of foreign missions, Bible societies, and the abolition of the slave trade.

Montgomery was forty-three years old before he felt fully assured of his salvation. Writing to his brother, he said, "On my birthday, after many delays and misgivings and repentings, I wrote to Fulneck for readmission into the Brethren congregation; and on Sunday last I was publicly invested with my title to that goodly heritage. Rejoice with me for this unspeakable privilege bestowed on so unworthy and ungrateful a prodigal as I have been."

On April 29, 1854, Montgomery led evening prayer, as usual. The next morning he did not answer a knock at his door. The "knocker" opened the door and saw the aged poet lying on the floor unconscious. That afternoon Montgomery drifted into a sleep from which he never awoke. Montgomery's nearly four hundred hymns, which he described as "embodying some experience in my life and which I trust will be helpful to others," are the legacy of this gifted man to a needy world.

REGENT SQUARE is an example of the best in English hymn tunes. Composed in 1867 by the noted organist, Henry Thomas Smart (1813-1879), its name derives from the Regent Square Presbyterian Church, London.

Away in a Manger
ca. 1885 (stanzas 1 and 2)
ca. 1892 (stanza 3)

Away in a manger, no crib for a bed,
The little Lord Jesus laid down His sweet head;
The stars in the bright sky looked down where He lay,
The little Lord Jesus, asleep on the hay.

The cattle are lowing, the Baby awakes,
But little Lord Jesus, no crying He makes;
I love Thee, Lord Jesus! look down from the sky,
And stay by my cradle, till morning is nigh.

Be near me, Lord Jesus, I ask Thee to stay
Close by me for ever, and love me, I pray;
Bless all the dear children in Thy tender care,
And fit us for heaven, to live with Thee there.

—Anonymous

In all the tinsel and glitter that dominates the modern celebration of Christmas, it is easy to lose sight of the great mystery of the Incarnation. How was it possible that the Lord of Glory became a little child? This popular Christmas carol brings to our minds that great enigma in words that a child can understand. The song's simplicity perhaps conveys the wondrous truth better than the difficult abstractions of the theologians, at least for young minds. Though "little," He is "Lord"; though a "Baby," He has "all the dear children in [His] tender care."

Though certainly minor in comparison with the Incarnation, the mystery of who wrote this carol has intrigued and frustrated hymnologists. "Not So Far Away in a Manger, Forty-one Settings of an American Carol" (*Notes* of the Music Library Association, December 1945) is an extremely helpful article by Richard S. Hill that clears up some of the mystery of its authorship. While we still do not know who wrote the words of this favorite children's Christmas carol, we do know that it was *not* Martin Luther. Nor did Luther compose any of the tunes to which the words are sung.

Apparently the Evangelical Lutheran Church in North America is responsible for the earliest publication of this text: in J. C. File's *Little Children's Book* (Philadelphia, 1885). J. E. Clark's tune, ST. KILDA, was published with the words. In 1887, this time in Cincinnati, the second appearance of the text was in *Dainty Songs for Little Lads and Lasses* by James R. Murray. This publication gave this erroneous information: "Luther's Cradle Hymn (composed by Martin Luther for his children and still sung by German mothers to their little ones)." Initials "J. R. M." apparently indicate that Murray composed MUELLER, the familiar tune found in most hymnals and Christmas carol books. Subsequent compilers simply perpetuated Murray's error.

The two publications mentioned above included only the first two stanzas of the hymn. Stanza three, also anonymous, appeared in one of Charles H. Gabriel's collections, *Gabriel's Vineyard Songs* (Louisville, 1892).

In addition to Murray's tune, MUELLER, "Away in a Manger" is often sung to William J. Kirkpatrick's CRADLE SONG (1895), as well as to the tune of the song, "Flow Gently, Sweet Afton." James Ramsey Murray (1841-1905), who apparently composed the most familiar tune for this carol (MUELLER), was born in Andover, Massachusetts, March 17, 1841, of Scottish emigrant parents. After a good music education and service in the Civil War, he spent his life as a music teacher and music publisher. He died in Cincinnati, Ohio, March 10, 1905.

William James Kirkpatrick (1838-1921), composer of CRADLE SONG, was born on February 27, 1838, in Ireland, but immigrated as a youth, with his parents, to Pennsylvania. After editing his first hymn collection at twenty-one (*Devotional Melodies*, 1859), he served in the Union Army as a fife-major and then entered the furniture business. When his first wife died in 1878, he left his secular employment entirely for his music ministry. He was active in conducting music at camp meetings and musical conventions and as a composer of the music for gospel songs. Among his best known songs are " 'Tis So Sweet to Trust in Jesus," "He Hideth My Soul," "When Love Shines In," and "Jesus Saves." CRADLE SONG is certainly one of his major contributions. He helped edit over one hundred collections of Christian songs. He died in Germantown, Pennsylvania, September 29, 1921.

Hark! the Herald Angels Sing
1739

Hark! the herald angels sing,
"Glory to the newborn King;
Peace on earth, and mercy mild,
God and sinners reconciled."
Joyful, all ye nations, rise,
Join the triumph of the skies;
With the angelic host proclaim,
"Christ is born in Bethlehem!"
Hark! the herald angels sing,
"Glory to the newborn King!"

Christ, by highest heaven adored;
Christ, the everlasting Lord!
Late in time behold Him come,
Offspring of the Virgin's womb.
Veiled in flesh the Godhead see;
Hail the incarnate Deity,
Pleased as man with men to dwell [appear],
Jesus our Emmanuel.

Hail the heaven-born Prince of Peace!
Hail the Sun of Righteousness!
Light and life to all He brings,
Risen with healing in His wings.
Mild He lays His glory by,
Born that man no more may die,
Born to raise the sons of earth,
Born to give them second birth.

Come, Desire of nations, come!
Fix in us Thy humble home;
Rise, the woman's conquering Seed,
Bruise in us the serpent's head;
Adam's likeness now efface,
Stamp Thine image in its place:
Second Adam from above,
Reinstate us in Thy love.

—Charles Wesley

The hymns "Hark! the Herald Angels Sing," "Love Divine, All Loves Excelling," and "Jesus, Lover of My Soul" have been described as a "triumvirate of hymns never surpassed by a single author." It is the opinion of some critics that in popularity "Hark! the Herald Angels Sing" heads the list of all hymns. Others class it with Toplady's "Rock of Ages," saying that it is excelled by none, not even Bishop Ken's Morning and Evening Hymns.

Under the title of "Hymn for Christmas," the spirited "Hark! the Herald Angels Sing" first appeared in ten stanzas of four lines each in the collection *Hymns and Sacred Poems* (1739). Gradually the number of stanzas was reduced to eight, to six, and finally to three eight-line stanzas with a refrain of the first two lines. (Most modern hymnals include only the standard three stanzas, though some include four, as printed here.)

Surprisingly, "Hark! the Herald Angels Sing" was the only hymn by Charles Wesley (1707-1788) to appear in the Anglican *Book of Common Prayer.* Conjectures in this regard abound. Some suppose that the Anglicans, although upset with the Wesleys and their Methodism, dared not ignore them altogether. So, in an effort to appease Wesleyan sympathizers, they chose a seasonal hymn that would honor the Wesleys only one month each year. Another conjecture is that the printer lacked one hymn to fill an allotted space, and he chose "Hark! the Herald Angels Sing" because it was the proper length.

In the original "Hymn for Christmas Day," lines 1 and 2 read, "Hark! how all the welkin [vault of heaven] rings, Glory to the King of Kings." In one of many revisions— that of George Whitefield (1753)—the lines were changed to read, "Hark! the herald angels sing, Glory to the newborn King." Theological liberals made this revision: instead of "Late in time, behold Him come, Offspring of the virgin's womb," they said, "Long desired, behold Him come, Finding here His humble home." Perhaps the most violent alteration retained only one word of the original— the word "Hark!"

"Hymn for Christmas Day" was 120 years old before

a permanent tune was found. William Hayman Cummings was studying *Festegesang* (meaning "festival song"), a choral composition by Felix Mendelssohn (1809-1847). *Festegesang* was Mendelssohn's contribution to the Gutenberg festival in Leipzig (1840), which honored the anniversary of the invention of the printing press. The thought came to Cummings that the second chorus of the work, entitled "Lied," would serve well as a tune for Wesley's Christmas song, and he quickly adapted it. The use of his music as a sacred work would have surprised Mendelssohn, for he had said, "Singers and hearers will like this work, but it will never be suitable for sacred words." How wrong he was!

Cummings' adaptation of Mendelssohn's tune has had many titles: JESU REDEMPTOR, BERLIN, BETHLEHEM, NATIVITY, ST. VINCENT, and MENDELSSOHN (the last being the current, and certainly the most appropriate, title). To make the words and tune fit, Cummings had to combine two four-line stanzas, making four eight-line stanzas, and repeat the first two lines as a refrain.

William Hayman Cummings (1831-1915), a native of Sidbury, Devonshire, England, achieved prominence quite early in life as a boy soprano. Cummings became a noted tenor, specializing in oratorio work. At sixteen he sang in the premiere performance of Mendelssohn's *Elijah,* which was conducted by Mendelssohn himself. He was in great demand as a vocalist, a conductor, and an organist. Cummings succeeded Sir Joseph Barnby as principal of London's Guildhall School of Music and served as professor at the Academy of Music. He wrote a cantata, *The Fairy Ring* (1873), as well as church music, part songs, and glees. The University of Dublin honored him with the Mus. D. degree in 1900.

(For other hymns by Charles Wesley, see pp. 41, 52, 58, 101, 104, 204, 271.)

Joy to the World! the Lord Is Come
1719

Joy to the world! the Lord is come;
  Let earth receive her King;
Let every heart prepare Him room,
  And heaven and nature sing.

Joy to the earth! the Saviour reigns;
  Let men their songs employ;
While fields and floods, rocks, hills and plains,
  Repeat the sounding joy.

No more let sins and sorrows grow,
  Nor thorns infest the ground;
He comes to make His blessings flow
  Far as the curse is found.

He rules the world with truth and grace,
  And makes the nations prove
The glories of His righteousness,
  And wonders of His love.

—Isaac Watts

Bachelor Isaac Watts (1674-1748) was sitting under a tree on the estate of the Abney family with whom he resided. From a human standpoint, he had cause to be mournful: his lady love had rejected his marriage proposal, and ill health often brought such severe pain that he was unable to occupy his pulpit. In Watts' favor, however, was his deep love for the One who had called him to preach and to write.

Dr. Watts loved the Psalms, and he had a deep desire to "Christianize the Psalms" by incorporating in them "all of the glow and glory of the New Testament story." On this particular day he was meditating on Psalm 98—especially verses 6-9: "Make a joyful noise unto the Lord. . . ." His heart was stirred, and from his pen began to flow the immortal words that have become known as

"the most jubilant Christmas carol in the English language."

Overall the hymn prophetically describes both the first and second advents of our Lord. Stanza 1 speaks happily of the first advent. It calls on "earth to receive her king," "every heart [to] prepare Him room, and heaven and nature [to] sing." Stanza 2 expresses joy that "the Saviour reigns" and urges men and all of nature to "repeat the sounding joy." Stanza 3 pronounces a future end to "sin, sorrow, and curse." Originally "sin and sorrow" were in the plural; but because the plural supposedly made singing more difficult, someone altered the words by putting them in the singular. Most hymnals have now returned to Watts' "sins and sorrows." Stanza 4 exultingly refers to a day when the Lord Jesus Christ "shall rule the world with truth and grace" and shall "make all nations prove the glories of His righteousness and wonders of His love."

The tune ANTIOCH was composed in 1836 by Lowell Mason (1792-1872), who purportedly incorporated phrases from *Messiah* by Handel (1685-1759). Some suggest that he created the tune by combining "Lift Up Your Heads" and "Comfort Ye, My People" into a medley.

Some authorities regard the tune as "far removed from Handel." Other authorities label it "awkward," "laughable," and "ridiculous," because of its "frightfully awkward repetition of each line." These critics argue that repetition makes the singing of the tune most difficult, but multitudes of carol singers over many Christmas seasons have not seemed to mind too much. Other titles of the tune include JERUSALEM, MEDIA, COMFORT, HOLY TRIUMPH, and MESSIAH.

Statues of Watts and Handel stand in the Poet's Corner of Westminster Abbey, where Handel was buried in 1759. Their true memorials, however, are their immortal contributions to Christian worship. As Samuel Johnson, the famous literary critic, who appreciated Watts even though they disagreed on the matter of church government, wrote, "Happy will be that reader whose mind is disposed by his verses or his prose, to imitate him in all but his nonconformity, to copy his benevolence to man and his reverence to God. Few men have left behind such purity of character or such monuments of laborious piety."

(For other hymns by Isaac Watts, see pp. 93, 129, 214, 257, 298.)

O Come, All Ye Faithful
1743

O come, all ye faithful,
Joyful and triumphant,
O come ye, O come ye to Bethlehem!
Come and behold Him,
Born the King of angels;

Refrain:

O come, let us adore Him,
O come, let us adore Him,
O come, let us adore Him,
Christ the Lord.

Sing, choirs of angels,
Sing in exultation!
O sing, all ye bright hosts of heaven above;
Glory to God, all
Glory in the highest;

Yea, Lord, we greet Thee,
Born this happy morning,
Jesus, to Thee be all glory given;
Word of the Father,
Now in flesh appearing;

Stanzas usually omitted:

God of God,
Light of Light,
Lo! He abhors not the Virgin's womb:
Very God,
Begotten, not created;

See how the shepherds,
Summoned to His cradle,
Leaving their flocks, draw nigh to gaze;
We too will thither
Bend our joyful footsteps;

Child, for us sinners
Poor and in the manger,
We would embrace Thee, with love and awe;
Who would not love Thee,
Loving us so dearly?
—John Francis Wade

Conjecture has surrounded the writing, the translation, and the tune of this familiar hymn. Some have traced the words to St. Bonaventura, a pious Franciscan monk of the thirteenth century. William Brooke, in Julian's *Dictionary of Hymnology,* at least comes closer to the time, if not the place of its origin, when he says, "Most probably it is a hymn of the seventeenth or eighteenth century, and of French or German authorship. . . . Towards the close of the [eighteenth] century it was sung both in England and in France at Benediction during Christmastide. As early as 1797 the hymn was sung at the Chapel of the Portuguese Embassy. . . ." Although the hymn may have first appeared in Roman Catholic services, a few alterations made it popular in Protestant circles as well.

Fortunately, much of the controversy concerning this hymn has been resolved by recent scholarship. Dom John Stéphan presents convincing evidence in his study, *Adeste Fideles: A Study on Its Origin and Development* (1947), that John Francis Wade was the actual author and composer. Seven manuscripts, each containing four Latin stanzas, with music, and each signed by Wade, have been discovered in seven separate locations (one in Ireland and six in England), the most recent having been found in 1946 by Maurice Frost. This one dates from 1743 and is considered by Stéphan to be the original one.

John Francis Wade (ca. 1710-1786), an English layman, was a music teacher who made his living chiefly
by copying and selling music in Douai, France. The best
we can tell, we are indebted to him for both the text and
the music of "O Come, All Ye Faithful."

The three stanzas which appear in most hymnals, as
well as the original second stanza which begins, "God
of God, Light of Light," were the four original Latin
stanzas. Several others appeared later and have occasionally been included in hymnals.

Estimates of the number of translations range from
thirty-eight to fifty, the most popular being that of Canon
Frederick Oakeley (1802-1880). Oakeley's translation began, "Ye faithful, approach ye," and was written in 1841
for use at the Margaret Street Chapel, London, during
his tenure there. The opening line was changed to "O
come, all ye faithful" in 1852 in F. H. Murray's *Hymnal
for Use in the English Church.* Oakeley's translation
embodies the four original stanzas probably written by
John Francis Wade.

Ranking high in the myriads of other translations are
Edward Caswall's 1849 translation, beginning, "O come,
all ye faithful, triumphantly sing," and John Mason Neale's
translation, which opens with the words, "Be present, ye
faithful."

Frederick Oakeley, D.D., whose translation of this
hymn appears in most hymnals, was born on September
5, 1802, in Shrewsbury, England. His father was a distinguished former governor of Madras. At Oxford Oakeley
won special honors in Latin and was invited to become
a fellow at Balliol College. He took orders in the Church
of England and served eighteen years. When he became
involved with the Oxford movement and began to write
controversial papers favoring the Roman Church, Oakeley
was suspended by the Church of England. This prompted
him to join the Roman Catholic Church. From 1852 until
his death on January 29, 1880, he served as canon of
the diocese of Westminster.

The tune of this hymn has many titles. ADESTE

FIDELES derives from the opening words of the Latin text (see below). AIR OF READING was used by Vincent Novello, organist at the Portuguese Embassy. Two men bore the name of John Reading—John Reading, Sr., and John Reading, Jr. Whichever man was organist at Winchester Cathedral from 1675 to 1681 has been considered by some as the composer of this tune. Another source, obviously unaware of Stéphan's scholarship, says that "the air, because of its English style and rhythm, might be called 'Old English Air.'" The *Hallowell Collection* of 1817 lists the tune as OPORTO. According to some authorities, PORTUGUESE HYMN rightfully belongs to the chapel master, Marcas Antonio da Fonesca (or "Il Portogallo"). Other authorities say, "It cannot be this man, for he was not born until 1763, which was eleven years after the hymn was written." Actually, PORTUGUESE HYMN was accidentally and erroneously applied to this composition. During a visit to Portuguese Chapel in 1785, the Duke of Leeds heard the tune and falsely assumed that it had been written especially for the chapel. In his use of the tune, he always referred to it as "Portuguese Hymn." Often this same tune accompanies "How Firm a Foundation."

In all seven of the Latin manuscripts the music appeared in triple meter. It appeared in duple meter for the first time in Samuel Webbe's *Essay on the Church Plain Chant* (London, 1782). Modern hymnals usually print the music in 4/4 time. The tune was first published in the United States in Benjamin Carr's *Musical Journal* (Philadelphia, December 29, 1800). Notwithstanding the fact that the hymn has been translated into English quite often, the original Latin text is frequently sung. The first stanza, from which the tune gets its name, reads:

Adeste, fideles,
Laeti triumphantes;
Venite, venite in Bethlehem;
Natum videte regem angelorum.
Venite, adoremus Dominum.

O Little Town of Bethlehem
1868

O little town of Bethlehem,
   How still we see thee lie!
Above thy deep and dreamless sleep
   The silent stars go by.
Yet in thy dark streets shineth
   The everlasting light;
The hopes and fears of all the years
   Are met in thee tonight.

For Christ is born of Mary,
   And gathered all above,
While mortals sleep, the angels keep
   Their watch of wondering love.
O morning stars, together
   Proclaim the holy birth!
And praises sing to God the King,
   And peace to men on earth!

How silently, how silently,
   The wondrous gift is given!
So God imparts to human hearts
   The blessings of His heaven.
No ear may hear His coming,
   But in this world of sin,
Where meek souls will receive Him still,
   The dear Christ enters in.

Where children pure and happy
   Pray to the blessèd Child,
Where misery cries out to Thee,
   Son of the mother mild;
Where charity stands watching
   And faith holds wide the door,
The dark night wakes, the glory breaks,
   And Christmas comes once more.

O holy Child of Bethlehem!
  Descend to us, we pray;
Cast out our sin, and enter in;
  Be born in us today.
We hear the Christmas angels
  The great glad tidings tell;
O come to us, abide with us,
  Our Lord Emmanuel.

—Phillips Brooks

While Phillips Brooks was rector of the Holy Trinity Episcopal Church in Philadelphia, he was asked to write a special song for the Sunday school Christmas celebration. "What shall I write?" he wondered. "How can I challenge the hearts and minds of our Sunday school with regard to Christ's birth—the place and manner of His birth, the reason for His birth, and the necessity of our new birth?" After much prayer, he felt that the Lord was bringing into focus an experience he had had two or three years earlier in the Holy Land.

On Christmas Eve he had stood for a long time on a hillside and looked out over sleeping Bethlehem. In his imagination Brooks could see a weary couple making their way to the stable of an inn. There was no room for them in the guest section; too many "great ones" had made advance reservations. A few moments later, he seemed to hear angel voices announcing to surprised shepherds, "Behold, I bring you good tidings of great joy, which shall be to all people. For unto you is born this day, in the city of David, a Saviour, which is Christ the Lord." He imagined that he could hear the heavenly host praising God and saying, "Glory to God in the highest, and on earth peace, good will toward men."

"How sad," he thought, "that in the inn there was no room for the One of whom the angels sang—no room for the Son of God who—though He was rich—yet for man's sake became poor, that through His poverty we might be made rich. But conditions have not changed; men still reject this One who willingly took upon Himself

the form of man in order to pay the penalty of the sin
of man." From this reverie, Brooks turned to go to a
midnight service to which he was pledged, and prayed,
"O Holy Child of Bethlehem! Descend to us, we pray; Cast
out our sin, and enter in; Be born in us today."

Brooks put his thoughts into verse, and when he had
finished, he went to Lewis H. Redner, the organist and
Sunday school superintendent, and said, "If you will write
a suitable tune for these words, I will name it for you."
On Christmas Eve the tune still had not come to Redner.
Somewhat discouraged, he went to bed; and, as he slept,
he dreamed he heard angels singing. He awoke, took up
pen and paper, and set down the melody he felt was a
direct gift from heaven.

Phillips Brooks' interest in hymns dated back to his
childhood. He was born in Boston on December 13, 1835.
Family devotions, especially on the Lord's Day, were
important to his parents. At these Sunday sessions, each
child would recite a hymn from memory; by the time he
was ready for college, Phillips Brooks could accurately
quote 200 hymns.

Brooks went on to become an Episcopal minister,
pastoring churches in Philadelphia and Boston. He also
taught at the Philadelphia Divinity School. The crowning
honor bestowed on him was his election as bishop of
Massachusetts in 1891. His death in 1893 was universally
lamented.

Though not very well known today, except as the author
of his Christmas carol or perhaps for his classic *Lectures
on Preaching,* Phillips Brooks was one of the most famous
and respected preachers of the nineteenth century. The
force of his personality and his deep insight into the
common experiences of humanity enthralled the masses,
who constantly crowded out the regular parishioners from
his services, and drew high praise from religious leaders
of every denomination. Unfortunately, his theology was
rather weak, for he had a low view of biblical inspiration.
Though he spoke warmly of Christ and often sounded
evangelical, his dislike of precise doctrinal statements and

his emphasis on the universal fatherhood of God and brotherhood of man put him in the moderate camp of his day. Nevertheless, he was an inspiring and eloquent speaker, and in "O Little Town of Bethlehem" we find some of the many practical and noble truths that he taught the multitudes so long ago.

The tune that Lewis H. Redner (1831-1908) composed for Brooks' hymn is called ST. LOUIS. As Sunday school superintendent of Philadelphia's Holy Trinity Episcopal Church for nineteen years, Redner raised the attendance from 36 children to over 1000. The English melody FOREST GREEN, arranged by Ralph Vaughan Williams in 1906, is also very well suited to "O Little Town of Bethlehem." Combining the two tunes is a simple and very effective arrangement for variety.

Silent Night, Holy Night
1818

Silent night! Holy night!
All is calm, all is bright
Round yon virgin mother and Child!
Holy Infant, so tender and mild,
Sleep in heavenly peace,
Sleep in heavenly peace.

Silent night! Holy night!
Shepherds quake at the sight!
Glories stream from heaven afar,
Heavenly hosts sing Alleluia,
Christ the Saviour is born!
Christ the Saviour is born!

Silent night! Holy night!
Son of God, love's pure light
Radiant beams from Thy holy face,
With the dawn of redeeming grace,
Jesus, Lord, at Thy birth,
Jesus, Lord, at Thy birth.

—Joseph Mohr

Many stories have been woven around the writing of "Silent Night," but one of the most popular ones is this. It was Christmas Eve, 1818, in a village near Salzburg, Austria. Clergyman Joseph Mohr, age twenty-six, received into his study his church organist and friend, Franz Gruber, age thirty-one. Gruber said, "Pastor, the church organ is broken, and it will be impossible to get it repaired in time for the Christmas service tomorrow evening. Our Christmas music is ruined." Mohr sought to console his friend, saying, "Everything will turn out all right. You will see."

When Gruber returned to his home, Mohr decided to make some pastoral visits. One visit was to the home of a woodcutter to welcome a new baby. On his way home from the visit, Mohr climbed to the mountaintop to enjoy the starlit evening. His mind began to wander to the humble surroundings of the woodcutter's family; then he began to think of the lowly birthplace of the Christ child. He thought of the message of the angels centuries before: "For unto you is born this day in the city of David a Saviour, which is Christ the Lord." And soon he was thinking poetically of the circumstances of that holy night, and he hurried home to record his thoughts.

Early the next morning the young minister rushed over to Gruber's home and gave the new words to him as a Christmas gift. "God be praised!" cried Gruber. "We have often expressed sorrow that the perfect Christmas hymn had not been written. Now we have it." "Then write an appropriate tune," Mohr challenged. "I cannot do it," Gruber protested. "The organ will not work." Mohr went into the next room and returned with a guitar. "You can play three chords on this instrument," he said, "and the melody I want is a simple one in two-part harmony. When you have finished, we will perform the song as a duet at tonight's Christmas service."

Gruber began to hum and strum. Soon he exclaimed, "Why the song sings itself!" And within a short while the finished work was in the pastor's hands. "We will call it 'The Tyrolese Song,' " Mohr said, "because it originated in the Tyrolean Alps." The hymn found immediate success with Mohr's congregation.

In early spring, 1819, Karl Mauracher, an organ builder from the Zillertal valley, came to the little mountain church to repair the organ. When the repairs were completed, he asked Gruber to play a number. Mohr persuaded Gruber to play their new Christmas song, and Mauracher was spellbound. "Will you give me a copy?" he asked. "I want to take it back to the village."

Ten years passed. One day Mauracher heard the Strasser children's quartet sing. "They sing like nightingales," he said. "I shall arrange the new Christmas hymn into four parts and ask them to add it to their repertoire." The Strasser children were delighted with the new song, renaming it "The Song from Heaven."

The next year the Strasser family journeyed to the Leipzig Fair to sell their chamois-skin gloves, an item for which they were well known. The children, in an effort to attract trade, performed in front of the Strasser booth. When they sang the new Christmas hymn, the music director for the Saxon court heard it and invited them to sing it on Christmas Eve for the king and queen in the Royal Saxon Court Chapel. Twenty-two years later a choir performed the number before King Frederick William IV of Prussia, who ordered it to be given first place at all future Christmas concerts within the bounds of his domain.

"Silent Night" was written, of course, in German. It was translated by the Reverend John Freeman Young (1820-1885), Episcopal bishop of Florida, and it was published in America in 1863 in J. C. Hollister's *Sunday-School Service and Tune Book.*

Joseph Mohr was born on December 11, 1792, at Salzburg, Austria. He died at Wagrein, Austria, on December 4, 1848. Franz Gruber was born on November 25, 1787, at Hochburg, Austria, and died on June 7, 1863, at Hallein, Austria.

Saving Work of Christ

Alas! and Did My Saviour Bleed
1707

Alas! and did my Saviour bleed,
And did my Sovereign die?
Would He devote that sacred head
For such a worm as I?

Was it for crimes that I had done
He groaned upon the tree?
Amazing pity! grace unknown!
And love beyond degree!

Well might the sun in darkness hide,
And shut His glories in,
When Christ, the Mighty Maker, died
For man, the creature's sin.

Thy body slain, sweet Jesus, Thine—
And bathed in its own blood—
While the firm mark of Wrath Divine
His soul in anguish stood.

Thus might I hide my blushing face
While His dear Cross appears;
Dissolve my heart in thankfulness,
And melt mine eyes to tears.

But drops of grief can ne'er repay
The debt of love I owe;
Here, Lord, I give myself away—
'Tis all that I can do.

—Isaac Watts

Isaac Watts said of his hymn writing, "I have made no pretence to be a poet. But to the Lamb that was slain, and now lives, I have addressed many a song, to be sung by the penitent and believing heart." Converts beyond number have walked the "sawdust trail" or the carpeted aisles of churches to the invitation of "Alas! and Did My Saviour Bleed." Fanny Crosby dated her conversion to the singing of this hymn. It was November 20, 1850. Miss Crosby (1820-1915) had attended numerous revivals and had answered the altar call, hoping to find the peace of salvation. She was well versed in Scripture and could quote much of it from memory; she honored God in every possible way; yet somehow peace and joy alluded her. On this particular night when the altar call was given, the audience began to sing Watts' "Alas! and Did My Saviour Bleed." When they came to the words, "Here, Lord, I give myself away—'Tis all that I can do," Miss Crosby realized that all she needed was to yield herself to the Lord. Later she said, "I surrendered myself to the Saviour, and my very soul flooded with celestial light. I sprang to my feet, shouting 'Hallelujah.' " In 1903 Miss Crosby expressed this experience in verse. She said,

I surrendered myself to the Saviour,
At the Cross I was kneeling,
When the Lord, Himself revealing,
Gave me peace in believing,
When I sought His mercy there.

She titled the new hymn "At the Cross."

When he wrote "Alas! and Did My Saviour Bleed," Watts headed it "Godly Sorrow Arising from the Sufferings of Christ." Alterations have been made by many men. In stanza 1, line 4, "For such a worm as I" has appeared variously as "For such a one as I," and "For sinners such as I." Stanza 3, line 3, "When Christ, the Mighty Maker, died," originally stated, "When *God*, the Mighty Maker, died." Other changes include "When Christ, the Lord of Glory [the Great Creator], died." Watts favored the change that says, "When Christ, the Great Creator, died." Of the six original stanzas, only four are used in most modern hymnals. Stanzas 4 and 5 are usually omitted.

Many biographers have conjectured that "Alas! and

Did My Saviour Bleed" stemmed from Watts' bout with smallpox at fifteen, which left him outwardly unattractive and which eventually cost him the woman he loved. When Watts proposed to Miss Elizabeth Singer, he received the answer, "I admire the jewel [his talent], but I cannot accept the casket [his outward appearance]." This rejection brought to his mind the wonder of God's love that accepted him as he was. Biographers base their conjecture on the question of stanza 1, which asks, "Would He devote that sacred head/ For such a worm as I?" Although they did not marry, Watts and Miss Singer remained friends for more than thirty years.

The popular tune AVON, whether it is called MARTYRDOM, FENWICK, DRUMCLOG, INVERNESS, or ALL SAINTS, appeared at the close of the eighteenth century. Its first printing was in leaflet form for use in music classes. Twenty-five years later the hymn appeared in a book. According to *The Scottish Hymnbook* of 1827, the tune was written by Hugh Wilson, who selected the title of "Fenwick" to honor his birthplace. R. A. Smith (*Sacred Music Sung in St. George's Church*, 1825) published the tune under the title "An Old Scottish Melody." J. Robertson (*The Seraph, a Selection of Psalms and Hymns*, Glasgow, 1827) attributed the tune to Wilson. The composer supposedly wrote the tune shortly before 1800.

After Mr. Wilson's death on August 14, 1824, his heirs obtained legal confirmation that he had owned the copyright. Miss Anne Gilchrist, in *The Choir*, July 1934, points out that because the conflict involved copyright and not authorship, the tune was probably an adaptation that Wilson made from an old Scottish melody. AVON appeared in America in *The New Baptist Praise Book* of 1914. The fact that AVON and MARTYRDOM are usually in different keys and vary slightly in the bass is of no consequence. "Overall," it is said, "the tune is one of the most dignified and most celebrated of all psalm-tunes."

Hugh Wilson was born in 1764 in Fenwick, Ayrshire, Scotland. From his father, a shoemaker, he learned shoemaking. However, he used his leisure hours for things of his own liking, including making sundials, which became popular in Fenwick and nearby places. At the head of his list of interests, however, was music, and he spent much time in teaching music and academic studies. In 1800 he moved to Pollokshaws. There he met Mr. William Dunn, who gave him an important position in his mills. Hugh founded the first Sunday school in Pollokshaws. His most popular tune and the only Wilson tune in current use was AVON or MARTYRDOM. Before his death, Mr. Wilson caused his manuscripts of poems, hymns, and tunes to be destroyed.

(For other hymns by Isaac Watts, see pp. 81, 129, 214, 257, 298.)

Amazing Grace
1779

Amazing grace! how sweet the sound,
That saved a wretch like me!
I once was lost, but now am found,
Was blind, but now I see.

'Twas grace that taught my heart to fear,
And grace my fears relieved;
How precious did that grace appear
The hour I first believed!

Through many dangers, toils and snares,
I have already come;
'Tis grace hath brought me safe thus far,
And grace will lead me home.

The Lord has promised good to me,
His Word my hope secures;
He will my shield and portion be
As long as life endures.

Yes, when this flesh and heart shall fail,
  And mortal life shall cease,
I shall possess, within the veil,
  A life of joy and peace.

The earth shall soon dissolve like snow,
  The sun forbear to shine;
But God, Who called me here below,
  Will be forever mine.
—John Newton

When we've been there ten thousand years,
  Bright shining as the sun,
We've no less days to sing God's praise
  Than when we first begun.
—Anonymous, XIX century

No matter how many people have loved this hymn and have been blessed by its message—and there have been thousands and thousands—no one has ever had a more complete understanding of the words than the author himself had. Whether he wrote the hymn to be used at his wife's funeral, as some have claimed, or whether he wrote it to reflect the great change that had taken place in his own life, it is a marvelous picture of the transforming power and the all-sufficiency of divine grace. Having drunk heavily and long at the cistern of sin, Newton was awed by this grace that had brought him into the sharp contrast of partaking freely of the fountain of living water, the water of eternal life!

Who could measure the depth of this man's sin? His life at sea was so full of reckless abandon to sin as to be beyond estimate. But if we could not measure the depth of his sin, how much less are we able to measure the sovereign grace that removed his sin from him "as far as the east is from the west."

Newton (1725-1807) said of his past, "Had you seen me go by, so pensive and solitary in the dead of night, to wash my one shirt upon the rocks, and afterwards put it on wet that it might dry upon my back while I slept; had you seen me so poor a figure that when a ship's boat came to the island, shame often compelled me to hide myself in the woods from the sight of strangers; especially had you known that my conduct, principles, and heart were still darker than my outward condition—how little would you have imagined that one, who so fully answered to the 'hateful and hating one another' of the apostle, was reserved to be so peculiar an instance of the providential care and exuberant goodness of God."

Usually when someone who has been in the clutches of sin repents of that sin, people begin to ask, "What happened? What caused him to turn to the Lord?"

There were several influences that figured in Newton's conversion. First of all—and this should be a challenge to all godly parents—his conversion is proof of the Scripture that says, "Train up a child in the way he should go: and when he is old, he will not depart from it" (Proverbs 22:6). Even though Newton's mother died when Newton was seven, she had trained her boy well in the Scriptures. At the age of four he could answer questions on the catechism and could recite a number of passages of Scripture and some of Dr. Watts' hymns. Mrs. Newton often said to her young son, "I am praying that someday you will become a minister of the Word of God."

A second influence in Newton's conversion was his sweetheart, Mary Catlett, who later became his wife. John and Mary met under interesting circumstances. Mr. Newton, concerned about the welfare of his wayward son, made arrangements for John to go to Jamaica for several years. But first John was allowed to visit some of his mother's distant relatives. While visiting them, John fell in love with a girl, not yet fourteen, by the name of Mary Catlett. The thought of several years in Jamaica without this girl became intolerable to John; and he, always quick to figure a way out for himself, prolonged his visit until the ship to Jamaica had sailed. This was not the only time John tried this trick. And it was not the only time his disappointed and enraged father threatened to disown him!

During the years of John's horrible traffic in slaves—years of such despondency and discouragement that he thought of drowning himself—the memory of sweet Mary Catlett sustained him. Mary took every means to keep Newton informed of her love, her concern, and her prayers. Often she would ask captains of various ships to try to locate Newton and tell him that she loved him and was praying for him. The two were married on February 1, 1750, and they spent forty years together, lovingly devoted to one another.

Other influences that figured largely in bringing the penitent to the throne of mercy were his deliverance from a malignant fever in Africa, serving with a godly captain of good testimony on one of the ships, and the reading of *The Imitation of Christ* by Thomas à Kempis. (If you have never read this fine devotional work, I would suggest that you get a copy and read it.)

But perhaps the event that brought into sharpest focus Newton's need of a Saviour was an experience in a violent storm at sea. As the storm in its fury lashed heavy waves against Newton's ship, many of the most hardened seamen cowered in some corner, seeking protection. During the height of the storm, someone uttered an oath using the name of God. The sound of that Holy Name, even in an oath, struck home; and Newton's thoughts turned to his godly mother who had so carefully taught him about God and about God's Word. As Newton continued to do his part to try to steady the ship, he prayed, "O God, if Thou wilt get me safely ashore, I will serve Thee forever." Gradually the storm ceased, and the ship and its crew landed safely in the harbor.

Often people who in times of distress make a vow to the Lord forget the vow when the danger is past, but not John Newton! Although some authorities say that he continued in slave trade for a few years after his conversion (he was a new Christian and was not told that this was wrong), Newton finally surrendered himself completely to the Lord. Under the influence of Whitefield, Wesley, and other friends whom he came to know, he answered the call to preach.

Numbered among Newton's converts were Claudius Buchanan, a missionary to the East Indies, and Thomas Scott, a well-known Bible commentator. But one of Newton's closest friends was William Cowper, the poet. Together they published a song book, *Olney Hymns* (1779), to be used by the plain people. Prior to this time, though psalm singing had given way to hymn singing in dissenting churches, the Church of England continued to reject it as "unscriptural, schismatic, and doctrinally dangerous." But *Olney Hymns* gave the people 349 attractive hymns.

Perhaps a fitting close to this brief biography of the man whose hymns contrast the life of sin with the change that is brought about by God's grace is the following anecdote from *Our Hymnody* by Robert Guy McCutchan:

> When in his late years his eyes failed him so that he could not see to read his notes while preaching, he had an old servant accompany him to the pulpit ... to point out the lines of his manuscript. One morning he read the words "Jesus Christ is precious," paused, and then repeated them. Thinking that Newton had become confused, the servant whispered, "Go on; go on, you said that before." Newton turned and said, "John, I said that twice, and I'm going to say it again." And his voice took on a different quality as he repeated more firmly than before, "Jesus Christ *is* precious!"

Most hymnals print only the first three of Newton's original six stanzas. Most add, however, an additional stanza which Newton did not write, but which appeared anonymously in numerous nineteenth-century American collections. Its first use as a final stanza of "Amazing Grace" was in 1910 in E. O. Excell's *Coronation Hymns*. Most people who know that Newton wrote the hymn also think erroneously that he wrote this now well-known final stanza.

The tune AMAZING GRACE, to which the words are nearly always sung, is an early American tune of unknown origin (although some in Scotland say that it was an anonymous Scottish tune before it became an anonymous American tune). Its earliest appearance seems to have been in the oblong tune book *Virginia Harmony* of 1831. Like so many other folk tunes set to hymn texts, it is completely pentatonic (that is, using only five different tones).

(For another hymn by John Newton, see p. 290.)

And Can It Be That I Should Gain
1738

And can it be that I should gain
An interest in the Saviour's blood?
Died He for me, who caused His pain?
For me, who Him to death pursued?
    Amazing love! how can it be
    That Thou, my God, shouldst die for me?

'Tis mystery all! The Immortal dies!
Who can explore His strange design?
In vain the firstborn seraph tries
To sound the depths of love divine.
    'Tis mercy all! let earth adore;
    Let angel minds inquire no more.

He left His Father's throne above,
So free, so infinite His grace;
Emptied Himself of all but love,
And bled for Adam's helpless race;
    'Tis mercy all, immense and free;
    For, O my God, it found out me.

Long my imprisoned spirit lay
Fast bound in sin and nature's night;
Thine eye diffused a quickening ray,
I woke, the dungeon flamed with light;
  My chains fell off, my heart was free;
  I rose, went forth, and followed Thee.

Still the small inward voice I hear,
That whispers all my sins forgiven;
Still the atoning blood is near,
That quenched the wrath of hostile heaven:
  I feel the life His wounds impart;
  I feel my Saviour in my heart.

No condemnation now I dread;
Jesus, and all in Him, is mine!
Alive in Him, my living Head,
And clothed in righteousness divine,
  Bold I approach the eternal throne,
  And claim the crown, through Christ my own.

—Charles Wesley

So overwhelmed by his conversion was Charles Wesley (1707-1788) that he often resorted to a favorite means of praising the Lord—the writing of a special hymn. "And Can It Be That I Should Gain" (originally titled "Free Grace") has been described as a "word picture" of Charles Wesley's conversion, a "profound study of the atonement by a soul that is filled with gratitude, appreciation, and awe over the significance and mystery of the sufferings and death of Christ." The hymn was published in 1738, the year it was written, in John Wesley's *Collection of Psalms and Hymns* and in 1739 in *Hymns and Sacred Poems.*

Stanza 1 of Wesley's six original stanzas expresses amazement at the great love of One who "died for me, who caused His pain." Stanza 2 exclaims, " 'Tis mercy all!" In stanza 3 is the suggestion of Philippians 2:6-8: "But made himself of no reputation, and took upon him the form of a servant, and was made in the likeness of men: and . . . humbled himself, and became obedient unto death, even the death of the cross." The freed soul of stanza 3 cries, "O my God, [His mercy] found out me!" Stanza 4 contrasts being "bound in sin" and awaking to a new life in Christ Jesus. Stanza 5, usually omitted, describes the "small inward voice that whispers, all my sins forgiven." The final stanza is reminiscent of Romans 8:1 ("There is therefore now no condemnation to them which are in Christ Jesus") and Ephesians 3:12 ("In whom we have boldness and access with confidence by the faith of him").

John and Charles Wesley often recorded the results of their hymns in services and in personal witnessing. On August 22, 1729, Charles Wesley made the entry that "And Can It Be" had been a help in leading to the Lord "a drunken servant of Mr. Seward."

This hymn was a favorite of John Wesley, and he quoted it on the day of his death. It was Sunday, and a friend came to visit the Reverend Mr. Wesley. In a labored voice, John Wesley said, "There is no need for more. At Bristol my words were 'I the chief of sinners am, But Jesus died for me.'" The friend asked, "Is this the present language of your heart, and do you now feel about conversion as you did when you were first saved?" Mr. Wesley answered, "Oh, yes." The friend quoted from stanza 3 of "And Can It Be," saying, "Bold I approach the eternal throne, And claim the crown through Christ my own." Then the friend added, "'Tis enough; He, our precious Immanuel, has purchased, has promised all." Wesley replied, "He *is* all. He *is* all. I will go." "To joys above," said the friend, "and Lord, help me to follow you." "Amen," said Mr. Wesley.

Critics generally attribute the tune FILLMORE to Jeremiah Ingalls (1764-1828). Some disagree, however, basing their arguments on the fact that the tune does not appear in Ingalls' *Christian Harmony* of 1805. Robert Guy McCutchan suggests that the tune was named for President Millard Fillmore (1800-1874; thirteenth president of the United States, 1850-1853). McCutchan's suggestion is not untenable, inasmuch as the earliest source for the tune FILLMORE is a publication compiled by William G. Fischer and published in 1869 in Philadelphia under the title *Joyful Songs.* In this collection it is said to be arranged by Fischer as sung by Chaplain C. C. McCabe.

Jeremiah Ingalls, the great-grandson of one of the settlers of Andover, Massachusetts, was born there on March 1, 1764. Ingalls was a tavern keeper and singing master at Andover; then he moved to Vermont to serve as choir leader at a Congregational church in Newbury. Ingalls trained all of his sons in music. They played the violin, the clarinet, the flute, and the bassoon, and he filled in with bass viol. Ingalls died at Hancock, Vermont, on April 6, 1828.

Another tune to which this great hymn of Charles Wesley is sung is SAGINA, composed about 1825 by the Scottish poet, Thomas Campbell (1777-1844).

(For other hymns by Charles Wesley, see pp. 41, 52, 58, 78, 104, 204, 271.)

Christ the Lord Is Risen Today
1739

Christ the Lord is risen today, Alleluia!
Sons of men and angels say, Alleluia!
Raise your joys and triumphs high, Alleluia!
Sing, ye heavens, and earth reply, Alleluia!

Lives again our glorious King, Alleluia!
Where, O death, is now thy sting? Alleluia!
Dying once, He all doth save, Alleluia!
Where thy victory, O grave? Alleluia!

Love's redeeming work is done, Alleluia!
Fought the fight, the battle won, Alleluia!
Death in vain forbids Him rise, Alleluia!
Christ hath opened Paradise, Alleluia!

Soar we now where Christ has led, Alleluia!
Following our exalted Head, Alleluia!
Made like Him, like Him we rise, Alleluia!
Ours the cross, the grave, the skies. Alleluia!
—Charles Wesley

Of all the great Easter hymns, this one is perhaps most outstanding. It is based on I Corinthians 15:55-57: "O death, where is thy sting? O grave, where is thy victory? The sting of death is sin; and the strength of sin is the law. But thanks be to God, which giveth us the victory through our Lord Jesus Christ." Originally this hymn included eleven stanzas of four lines each; but in 1760, when the song appeared in Martin Madan's *Collection of Psalms and Hymns,* only eight stanzas remained, several being omitted and many lines rearranged. Only four stanzas are usually sung today.

Throughout the hymn we find the word *Alleluia.* This term, used frequently in the early Church and derived from Hebrew, means "Praise ye the Lord." On Easter morning the early Christians greeted each other with the words, "Alleluia, the Lord is risen." It is this expression that reminds us of Christ's words, "Because I live, ye shall live also" (John 14:19).

Historically the hymn comes to us as a result of John Wesley's ministry. After being ostracized by the Anglican Church, John Wesley determined to establish religious societies to nurture his converts. In Upper Moorfield, near London, he was able to purchase an abandoned iron foundry. The place where the new organization met was soon known as "the Foundry Meeting House," and it was for the opening service in the foundry in 1739 that Charles Wesley composed "Christ the Lord Is Risen Today."

Charles Wesley, next to the youngest of nineteen Wesley children, was born in Epworth, England, on December 18, 1707. Spiritual, poetic, sensitive of spirit, emotional of nature, highly educated, and a strong supporter of the Lord's cause, Charles was endowed with the qualities that led him to be called "the Asaph of the Methodist Church" (Asaph being one of King David's choir leaders whose name may be found in the titles of Psalms 73-83).

Charles Wesley wrote in the time of great revival. His lyrics emphasize the plan of salvation and voice the personal experiences of the saved. His own conversion experience has been described as follows:

> Charles was beset by a lingering illness of such serious nature that he lay in constant fear of death. On Sunday, May 21, 1738, John Wesley and some friends visited Charles. They sang a song, prayed, and then departed. "After they had gone," Charles later recalled, "I prayed, drifted into a deep sleep and seemed to hear a voice saying, 'In the Name of Jesus of Nazareth, arise, and believe, and thou shalt be healed of all thine infirmities.' I cried, 'I believe, I believe'; and when I awoke, I yielded my heart to the Lord, promising to serve Him faithfully all the days of my life."

Charles Wesley has been called "the most prolific writer of all the hymnists." His motto seemed to be "A hymn a day" and "A new hymn for every sermon." At least 6000 hymns are ascribed to him. Aside from the large number of hymns, Wesley was noted for inculcating strong Christian doctrines into his hymns. To him God was great, powerful, and majestic, but He was also a Saviour, a Companion, a Friend, and "an ever present help."

Charles remained a bachelor until he was forty-two. At age forty he fell in love with Sarah Gwynne, and for two years debated with himself whether he should marry her. Finally Charles decided that it was God's will, and the time was set at eight o'clock in the morning, April 8, 1749. At four o'clock on the morning of the wedding day, Charles called his beloved Sarah, his brother John, and a friend. For three hours they prayed and sang hymns.

The long and fruitful career of Charles Wesley ended on March 29, 1788. His doctor, unable to find any serious physical problem, concluded, "Death is the result of old age and weakness from strenuousness of life."

The stirring tune to which this favorite Easter hymn is usually sung is, appropriately, EASTER HYMN. It is the only surviving tune from an important early eighteenth-century tune book, *Lyra Davidica* (1708). It appeared anonymously in this collection in a somewhat different form from the way we sing it today. The present form of the melody came from John Arnold's *Compleat Psalmodist*, though subsequent editions of this work show gradual alteration in the tune. John Wesley called the tune SALISBURY TUNE in his *Foundry Collection* (London, 1742).

(For other hymns by Charles Wesley, see pp. 41, 52, 58, 78, 101, 204, 271.)

Hail, Thou Once-Despised Jesus!
1757

Hail, Thou once-despised Jesus!
Hail, Thou Galilean King!
Thou didst suffer to release us;
Thou didst free salvation bring.
Hail, Thou agonizing Saviour,
Bearer of our sin and shame!
By Thy merits we find favor;
Life is given through Thy name.

Paschal Lamb, by God appointed,
All our sins on Thee were laid;
By almighty love anointed,
Thou hast full atonement made.
All Thy people are forgiven
Through the virtue of Thy blood;
Opened is the gate of heaven,
Peace is made 'twixt man and God.

Jesus, hail! enthroned in glory,
  There forever to abide;
All the heavenly hosts adore Thee,
  Seated at Thy Father's side.
There for sinners Thou art pleading,
  There Thou dost our place prepare,
Ever for us interceding
  Till in glory we appear.

Worship, honor, power, and blessing
  Thou art worthy to receive;
Loudest praises, without ceasing,
  Meet it is for us to give.
Help, ye bright angelic spirits,
  Bring your sweetest, noblest lays;
Help to sing our Saviour's merits,
  Help to chant Immanuel's praise!
—John Bakewell

"**H**ail, Thou Once-Despised Jesus!" heads a long list of hymns attributed to John Bakewell, one of Wesley's lay preachers. To many hymnologists, the hymn is more than the efforts of one man; it is the combined efforts of several men—Bakewell, Toplady, and possibly Madan. "There is no evidence to show whether Bakewell rewrote his hymn for Madan, or whether Madan himself or in collaboration with Bakewell contributed the added lines" (*Companion to the [1964 Methodist] Hymnal,* 1970, p. 206).

"Hail, Thou Once-Despised Jesus!" was written originally in only two stanzas of eight lines each, and appeared first in 1757. Though we have no supporting evidence, the hymn since its first appearance has been attributed to Bakewell. Described as "worshipful and strongly doctrinal," it breathes the atonement and intercession of the Lord Jesus Christ. From His "suffering and humiliation" the hymn moves to His glorification and His worthiness to receive praise.

Three years later the hymn appeared, revised, in Martin

Madan's *Collection of Psalms and Hymns* (1760). This revision paved the way for other revisions, notably that of Augustus M. Toplady, published in *Psalms and Hymns for Public and Private Worship* (1776). In Toplady's revision the second stanza was omitted and a few additions were made to suit Toplady's Calvinistic views (according to Julian, although the original stanza two is retained in the 1776 edition of Toplady in the Princeton Theological Seminary library).

John Bakewell was born in 1721 in Brailsford, Derbyshire, England. At the age of eighteen he read Thomas Boston's *Fourfold State* and began to think deeply about his spiritual condition. Soon he was soundly converted. In 1744 Bakewell entered an active ministry that eventually led to his becoming one of the Wesleys' most ardent supporters and most efficient workers.

A list of Bakewell's close friends reveals something of his stature: John and Charles Wesley, Martin Madan, Augustus Toplady, and Thomas Oliver. (It is said that Oliver wrote "The God of Abraham Praise" while visiting in Bakewell's home.) For a time Bakewell was involved in educational work, serving as master of Greenwich Royal Park Academy. There he introduced the Methodism that was so dear to his heart. As his ministry increased, Bakewell realized that he must give up the educational work; so he asked his son-in-law, Dr. James Egan, to take over the headship of Royal Park Academy.

Bakewell died near Greenwich on March 18, 1819. Interment was in a London churchyard near the grave of his dear John Wesley. On Bakewell's tombstone the inscription says: "Sacred to the memory of John Bakewell, late of Greenwich, who departed this life March 18, 1819, age ninety-eight. He adorned the doctrine of God, our Saviour, eighty years, and preached His Glorious Gospel about seventy years. 'The memory of the just is blessed.'"

AUTUMN, a popular tune for "Hail, Thou Once-Despised Jesus," is described by Robert Guy McCutchan (*Our Hymnody*) as also the work of several men. He cites these possibilities: Louis von Esch; Ludovich Nicholson;

an arrangement by George F. Root; a Spanish melody; a Scotch melody; probably from the eighteenth century; an arrangement from Psalm 42 in *The Geneva Psalter,* 1551; and François H. Barthélémon.

Hymnologists most often fix upon a work by François Hippolyte Barthélémon (1741-1808), noted violinist and composer, as the source for this tune. Born in Bordeaux, France, July 27, 1741, François was educated in nearby schools. His wife, Mary Young Barthélémon, was the niece of the author of *Hymns of the Great Festivals* (Lampe, 1746). François served a brief term in the army but then followed the advice of a friend to devote his full time to music. Most of Barthélémon's compositions were for the theater and public gardens. His one attempt at hymn-tune writing was MORNING HYMN, which he composed for Thomas Ken's "Awake, My Soul, and with the Sun" (1785). Barthélémon, in his older years, met with misfortune, which left him broken-hearted and paralyzed. He died in London on July 23, 1808.

PLEADING SAVIOUR (*Christian Lyre,* 1830, and *Plymouth Collection,* 1855) is thought to be an adaptation of an American folk tune. The tune is named for the hymn that begins, "Now the Saviour stands a-pleading," by John Leland (1754-1841).

A third tune, increasingly sung to "Hail, Thou Once-Despised Jesus," is IN BABILONE, a traditional Dutch melody. Its first publication was in 1710 in a collection of some 1000 Dutch folk songs and dances. It is often seen in an arrangement by Julius Röntgen (1855-1932) which Ralph Vaughan Williams included in *The English Hymnal* of 1906. Röntgen was a well-known performer, conductor, and scholar who counted such luminaries as Liszt, Brahms, and Grieg as his friends and directed the conservatoire at Amsterdam. T. Tertius Noble (1867-1953) made a very majestic harmonization of this tune in 1918.

Jesus Paid It All
1865

I hear the Saviour say,
  "Thy strength indeed is small,
Child of weakness, watch and pray,
  Find in Me thine all in all."

Refrain:

Jesus paid it all,
  All to Him I owe;
Sin had left a crimson stain,
  He washed it white as snow.

Lord, now indeed I find
  Thy power, and Thine alone,
Can change the leper's spots
  And melt the heart of stone.

For nothing good have I
  Whereby Thy grace to claim;
I'll wash my garments white
  In the blood of Calvary's Lamb.

And when, before the throne,
  I stand in Him complete,
"Jesus died my soul to save,"
  My lips shall still repeat.
—Elvina M. Hall

"**J**esus Paid It All" was sparked by a sentence in a pastor's Sunday morning prayer in Baltimore, Maryland, in 1865. Choir member Elvina M. Hall (1820-1889) was stirred by Pastor Schrick's "thanksgiving for the great salvation which we have in Christ Jesus." As Elvina thought on the sacrificial death of our Lord, she was impressed anew with how much all believers owe Him.

Picking up a hymnal, apparently while the minister was praying, Mrs. Hall began to pen on the flyleaf the words, "I hear the Saviour say. . . ." At the end of the stanzas, her heart exclaimed—"Jesus paid it all!" And very quickly she added the refrain with its "Jesus paid it all," its reference to the effects of sin, and its assurance that Jesus Christ cancels sin through His shed blood on the cross.

When Elvina Hall returned home, she carefully copied her words and took them to her pastor. A few days later, while visiting his church organist, John T. Grape (1835-1915), the pastor asked, "John, have you written any new tunes lately?" "Yes," John replied. And he sat down and played the tune. As Pastor Schrick listened, he thought, "Why not try Elvina Hall's words with this new tune?" The idea pleased the organist, for he had been disappointed with his new tune. Even the members of his choir had concurred that it was of "poor quality." Only one person—Mrs. John Grape—had praised the tune. "It is a good tune," she had said, "and it will find good use. You will see." Her appraisal was correct. The tune, when combined with Mrs. Hall's words, quickly became one of our most popular gospel hymns, especially for revival meetings.

Where could one find more appealing words and a more appealing tune than "Jesus Paid It All"? Thousands have argued, "I am too bad to be accepted of the Lord. God cannot save a sinner like me." Yet they have melted under Mrs. Hall's reminder that God's power "can change the leper's spots" and "melt the heart of stone." Others have argued, "I am afraid that I cannot hold out." Mrs. Hall has answered,

And when, before the throne,
  I stand in Him complete,
"Jesus died my soul to save,"
  My lips shall still repeat.

"Jesus Paid It All" was launched in 1868 in *Sabbath Chords.* Credit for its popularity, however, goes to P. P. Bliss and Ira D. Sankey who published the hymn in *Gospel Songs,* 1874. Thereafter it became familiar in the *Gospel Hymn* series.

Jesus, Thy Blood and Righteousness
ca. 1739

Jesus, Thy blood and righteousness
My beauty are, my glorious dress;
'Midst flaming worlds, in these arrayed,
With joy shall I lift up my head.

Bold shall I stand in Thy great day,
For who aught to my charge shall lay?
Fully absolved through these I am,
From sin and fear, from guilt and shame.

The holy, meek, unspotted Lamb,
Who from the Father's bosom came,
Who died for me, e'en me to atone,
Now for my Lord and God I own.

Lord, I believe Thy precious blood,
Which, at the mercy seat of God,
Forever doth for sinners plead,
For me, e'en for my soul, was shed.

Lord, I believe were sinners more
Than sands upon the ocean shore,
Thou hast for all a ransom paid,
For all a full atonement made.
—Nicolaus Ludwig von Zinzendorf

Like many other great hymns, this one sets forth a cardinal doctrine of the Christian faith—atonement for sin through the sacrificial blood of Jesus Christ. It was translated by John Wesley in 1739 from the German hymn "Christi Blut und Gerechtigkeit." The original hymn by Zinzendorf had thirty-three stanzas. Wesley translated twenty-four stanzas, and other editors abridged it even more. Modern hymnals include four stanzas, omitting stanza 3 above.

Nicolaus Ludwig von Zinzendorf was born on May 26, 1700, in Dresden. His father, prime minister at the Saxon court, died when his son was very young. When Frau Zinzendorf remarried, she left Nicolaus with his grandmother, a godly woman who reared the boy to honor and serve the Lord.

From childhood Nicolaus was well groomed for the Lord's service. At eleven he was sent to Royal School in Halle (Handel's native city). There tutors and fellow classmates ridiculed the lad's Christian piety. The sneers he endured made him even more determined to serve the Lord. The experience also taught him to be mindful of downtrodden Christians.

Zinzendorf's guardian felt that he needed to be worldly-minded. When Zinzendorf reached the age of sixteen, consequently, the guardian sent him to Wittenberg to study law. Though Nicolaus was a conscientious student of law, he spent his free hours in the study of theology.

At Düsseldorf, Nicolaus was impressed with the painting *Ecce Homo*. He gazed at Christ wearing the crown of thorns on his head. He read the inscription, "This have I done for thee; what doest thou for me?" With renewed dedication he adopted as his life's motto the thought, "I have but one passion, and that is He, and only He."

Later the young man and a tutor were sent on a tour of Holland, France, and Switzerland. Though he became world conscious, no amount of worldly allurement could shake his desire to serve his Lord.

Nicolaus was also sent to Paris. Even there he refused to succumb to worldly standards. He sought the company of devout Christians who believed as he did—that life is a sacred trust to be used as God should lead. Nicolaus leaned toward becoming a missionary, but wealthy relatives strenuously opposed the idea and skillfully maneuvered him into a position as Judicial Counselor in Dresden.

At twenty-two Nicolaus married a dedicated Christian girl. The couple became deeply concerned about the Hussites, or Bohemian Brethren, who for 300 years had suffered persecution and had been driven out of Moravia by the Thirty Years' War. They bought an estate in Saxony to be used as a refuge for these Christians who had become known as "the hidden seed, for they had to meet almost in secret." The Moravians, as they were now called, built homes at the foot of Hutberg ("Shelter Mountain") and called the community "Herrnhut" ("the Lord's Shelter"). When news of the religious freedom at Herrnhut spread, the center quickly became a flourishing colony.

At twenty-seven Zinzendorf resigned his Dresden appointment to become a full-time worker for the Brethren church on his estate. He traveled extensively, organizing Moravian societies as he went. In London in 1737 he was pleased to enlist the Wesley brothers. John Wesley visited Herrnhut in 1738. Later, though John Wesley greatly admired Zinzendorf and continued to call him "my friend," doctrinal differences caused an official break between the Wesleys and the Moravians. Wesley is said to have admired their pietism (emphasis on a personal religious experience) but not their "quietism" (withdrawal from the world for mystic contemplation). We are indebted to John Wesley for not only the translations of this hymn of Zinzendorf but also for renderings of several other German hymns.

Zinzendorf made three trips to England. The last visit extended four years (1751-1755). His work on behalf of the Moravians won him the title of "the apostle of the Moravians." At one point banished from Saxony, Zinzendorf came to America for several years. Spending most of his time in Pennsylvania, he established several Moravian settlements, such as Bethlehem, Nazareth, Lancaster, Hebron, and York. A few years after Zinzendorf's return to Herrnhut, he was stricken with a fever that after four days claimed his life on May 9, 1760.

Zinzendorf wrote more than 2000 hymns between 1712 and 1760. His hymns have been severely criticized by critics who have felt that the hymns spoke "too intimately of sacred things and seemed to be written in haste." The hymns were designed for use with Zinzendorf's sermons; when he could not find a suitable hymn, he simply wrote one for the occasion.

The tunes MALVERN and UXBRIDGE (pure Gregorian), to which this hymn is sometimes sung, were arranged by Lowell Mason. The more usual tune, however, is GERMANY (also known as FULDA, WALTON, BEETHOVEN, and MELCHIZEDEC), to which the hymn "Where Cross the Crowded Ways of Life" is also customarily sung. It first appeared in William Gardiner's *Sacred Melodies* (1815), where Gardiner (1770-1853) attributed the tune to Beethoven (1770-1827). Later, however, Gardiner could not identify from which work of Beethoven the tune ostensibly came, but reported vaguely that the melody was from "somewhere in the works of Beethoven, but I cannot point it out" (*Music and Friends*, 1838). Scholars consider it best, therefore, to attribute the tune to Gardiner himself. Gardiner's valuable contribution to hymnody was the adaptation of classics of music literature in hymn tunes. He was also instrumental in introducing the work of his three greatest musical contemporaries, Haydn, Mozart, and Beethoven, to England. Later, Lowell Mason adapted some of Gardiner's tunes, as well as his methods of arranging, for his own collections.

O Sacred Head, Now Wounded
    XII century

O Sacred Head, now wounded,
    With grief and shame weighed down;
Now scornfully surrounded
    With thorns, Thine only crown;
O sacred Head, what glory,
    What bliss till now was Thine!
Yet, though despised and gory,
    I joy to call Thee mine.

What thou, my Lord, hast suffered
  Was all for sinners' gain:
Mine, mine was the transgression,
  But Thine the deadly pain.
Lo, here I fall, my Saviour!
  'Tis I deserve Thy place;
Look on me with Thy favor,
  Vouchsafe to me Thy grace.

What language shall I borrow
  To thank Thee, dearest Friend:
For this Thy dying sorrow,
  thy pity without end?
O, make me Thine for ever;
  And should I fainting be,
Lord, let me never, never
  Outlive my love to Thee.

Be near me when I'm dying,
  Oh! show Thy cross to me;
And for my succor flying,
  Come, Lord, and set me free!
These eyes, new faith receiving,
  From Jesus shall not move;
For he who dies believing,
  Dies safely through Thy love.
—Bernard of Clairvaux

This beautiful hymn is the translation of a hymn attributed to Bernard of Clairvaux. The original poem was from a seven-part work entitled *Rhythmica Oratio* in which Bernard had addressed different parts of our Lord's body—His feet, His knees, His hands, His side, His breast, His heart, and His face. In 1656 Paul Gerhardt made a loose translation of part seven, *"Salve caput cruentatum,"* into German. In 1830 James Waddell Alexander of Princeton translated it into English. Each of the successive stages of translation have, surprisingly, enhanced the hymn's power and popularity.

Mark 15:17-20 is the basis of this hymn. The sacred writer says, "And they clothed him with purple, platted a crown of thorns, and put it about his head, And began to salute him, Hail, King of the Jews! And they smote him on the head with a reed, and spat upon him, and bowing their knees worshipped him. And when they had mocked him, they . . . led him out to crucify him."

Depicted in stanza 1 is our Lord on the Cross enduring the grief, the shame, and the crown of thorns. The pious poet says, "I joy to call Thee mine." In stanza 2 the poet accepts personal responsibility for the Lord's suffering, crying, "Mine, mine was the transgression." Stanza 3 deplores weakness of vocabulary that renders him helpless to thank the Lord properly for His death. "Never let me abuse such dying love," the poet begs. In stanza 4 the poet envisions his own death and asks the Lord's succor, pledging not to move His eyes from the One whose love has prompted His death.

The author, Bernard of Clairvaux (1091-1153), was one of the most influential clerics of his day. While he had no taste for ecclesiastical statesmanship, his judgments carried great weight in the councils of the powerful. He is the greatest light of the Cistercian monastic order, and he played a dominant role in the Second Crusade. Though a child of his age and guilty of many of its errors, he was perhaps the most evangelical of the medieval theologians. Calvin held him in high regard, and Luther said, "Bernard is superior to all the doctors in his sermons, even to Augustine himself, because he preaches Christ most excellently." His mystic writings exhibit a humility, a devotion to Christ, and a reliance upon grace for salvation that was rare before the dawn of the Reformation. His greatest influence on us today is through such hymns as "O Sacred Head, Now Wounded," "Jesus, the Very Thought of Thee," and "Jesus, Thou Joy of Loving Hearts," and they express Bernard's most admirable emphases very well.

The German translator of Bernard's hymn, Paul Gerhardt, "ranks, next to Luther, as the most gifted and popular hymn writer of the Lutheran Church." Very little is known of his life. He was born on March 12, 1607, the son of the mayor of Gräfenhainichen, a small town in Saxony, and graduated from the university of nearby Wittenberg. About 1643 he became a tutor in the home of Berlin's Chancellor-Advocate, Andreas Barthold, who believed in strict discipline and in faithfully training children in the way that they should go.

Eventually Gerhardt accepted a pastorate and in 1655 married Barthold's daughter, Anna. Their troubles were many: the Thirty Years' War had wreaked terrible devastation on the land, so poverty was everywhere; their first child died; after Gerhardt took a Berlin church, he was dismissed for refusing to limit his preaching on controversial topics. He firmly took the position of being willing to offer his neck to the sword and thus seal with his blood the evangelical truth. When Paul was ordered out of Berlin in 1666, he and his wife were so poor that they had to travel on foot. Still his faith in the Lord was constant. One day Anna became so discouraged that she burst into tears. Paul tried to solace her by quoting, "Trust in the Lord; in all thy ways acknowledge him, and he shall direct thy path." Anna remained sorrowful, but Paul took courage. Then he began writing a hymn, "Commit thou all thy griefs and ways into His hands. . . ." Within a few hours, Paul received messengers who bore an invitation from Duke Christian to come to Merseburg and make his city their home. Tearfully, but excitedly, Paul handed to his wife the poem, "Commit Thou All Thy Griefs," which he had written for her. Then he gently chided her with the question, "Did I not bid you confide in Him and all would be well?"

When Gerhardt died, his portrait was hung in the church. The portrait bore this apt inscription: "A theologian sifted in the sieve of Satan."

The English translator was the eminent Presbyterian minister, James Waddell Alexander. He was born on March

13, 1804, at Hopewell, Virginia. Educated at Princeton, Dr. Alexander held pastorates in Virginia, New Jersey, and New York before he returned to Princeton to become a professor there. Though an author of note, his fame today rests chiefly on his hymn translations, especially "O Sacred Head, Now Wounded." Dr. Alexander had the testimony of being "brilliant, scholarly, beloved, and revered; a man of great influence and piety." He died at Red Sweet Springs, Virginia, on July 31, 1859.

The tune, HERZLICH TUT MICH VERLANGEN ("Passion Chorale") by Hans Leo Hassler, was adapted from a German love song. The tune was harmonized by Johann Sebastian Bach, who used it at least five times in his *St. Matthew Passion*. It is said that in the will of Frederick William I, king of Prussia, was a request for a band to play this tune at his funeral.

Hans Leo Hassler (1564-1612) was born at Nuremberg, Bavaria. His father was a renowned organist who imparted his knowledge to his three sons, of whom Hans was the most famous. After studying under his father, Hans went to study in Italy. He returned to Germany and held a number of important positions as a musician. Critics have said of Hassler, "He is one of the most outstanding composers of his day. He is one of the founders of German music."

Tell Me the Old, Old Story
   1866

Tell me the old, old story
   Of unseen things above,
Of Jesus and His glory,
   Of Jesus and His love.
Tell me the story simply,
   As to a little child,
For I am weak and weary,
   And helpless and defiled.

Refrain:

Tell me the old, old story,
Tell me the old, old story,
Tell me the old, old story
Of Jesus and His love.

Tell me the story slowly,
  That I may take it in—
That wonderful redemption,
  God's remedy for sin.
Tell me the story often,
  For I forget so soon;
The "early dew" of morning
  Has passed away at noon.

Tell me the story softly,
  With earnest tones and grave;
Remember I'm the sinner
  Whom Jesus came to save.
Tell me the story always,
  If you would really be,
In any time of trouble,
  A comforter to me.

Tell me the same old story
  When you have cause to fear
That this world's empty glory
  Is costing me too dear.
Yes, and when that world's glory
  Is dawning on my soul,
Tell me the old, old story:
  "Christ Jesus makes thee whole."
—Arabella Katherine Hankey

It is said that once when William Gladstone, one of the world's greatest statesmen, was lecturing on the subject of science, industry, and art, he said, "I do not mention any of these things as the great specific for alleviating the sorrow of human life and encountering the evils which defile the world. If I am asked what is the remedy for these things, I must point to something which, in a well-known hymn, is called the 'old, old story,' told of in an old, old Book, and taught with an old, old teaching, which is the greatest gift ever given to mankind."

"Tell Me the Old, Old Story" has been translated into more languages than perhaps any other children's hymn. Though written for children, this hymn has blessed people of all ages and in all circumstances. When Miss Hankey wrote the words, she arranged them in eight four-line stanzas, with each four lines expressing a complete thought. She also composed a simple little melody for her words. Later when Dr. W. H. Doane wrote a new tune for the song, he changed the structure to four stanzas of eight lines each. The change displeased Miss Hankey, although it is the tune that has made the hymn popular.

Each stanza in the author's original arrangement begins with the same yearning appeal—"Tell me." In stanza 1 she longs to hear the story of heaven and of Jesus' love and glory. In stanzas 2 through 4 she begs to hear the story slowly and in simple language. She explained, "God's remedy for sin is something I want to understand, and I want to hear it often, lest I forget it. As weak as I am, I cannot think too well or too fast. I need to have the story explained to me as to a little child." Stanzas 5 through 8 request the story softly, earnestly, seriously, and always—even at the hour of death.

Katherine (Kate) Hankey, born in 1834, was the daughter of a prosperous banker who belonged to a group called the Clapham Sect. (Its members were leaders of the Evangelical party in the Anglican Church, and its aim was "to apply the ethics of Christ to personal, social, political, national, and international affairs.") Like her father, she showed deep interest in people of less fortunate circumstances than her own, and though she devoted much time to Bible teaching among rich girls, she concentrated her efforts on the so-called "factory girls." Many of her trainees became strong Christian leaders.

In 1866 Katherine Hankey was stricken with a serious illness that required a lengthy convalescence. As she lay on her bed and thought of the people who had seemed to be thrilled to hear her tell the story of redemption, she thought, "I wish people would come in and tell me the old, old story." As an outgrowth of this longing, she wrote a lengthy, two-part poem on the life and work of our Lord. "The Old, Old Story" is from Part I, "The Story Wanted," and a companion song, "I Love to Tell the Story," is from Part II, "The Story Told." Proceeds from Miss Hankey's literary endeavors went to missions. She died in London in 1911.

Of his popular tune, William Doane says,

> In 1867 I was attending the international meeting of the Young Men's Christian Association at Montreal. Among those present was Major-General Russell, then in command of the English forces during the Fenian excitement [an insurrection in Ireland]. He arose in the meeting and read the words of the song from a sheet of foolscap paper, the tears streaming down his bronzed cheeks as he read. I was much impressed, and immediately requested the privilege of making a copy. He gave me the copy from which he had read. I wrote the music for the song while on the stage-coach one hot summer afternoon between the Glen Falls House and the Crawford House in the White Mountains. That evening we sung it in the parlors of the hotel and thought it pretty, though we scarcely anticipated the popularity which was subsequently accorded it. It was afterwards published in sheet form in Cincinnati.

William Howard Doane (1832-1915) was a cotton manufacturer, the head of a large woodworking business, and an inventor of much of the machinery he used in his businesses. From childhood he performed well in music, but his hymn writing did not begin until he was stricken with a serious illness in 1862. He composed more than 2200 tunes and compiled more than forty collections.

The Ninety and Nine
1868

There were ninety and nine that safely lay
   In the shelter of the fold;
But one was out on the hills away,
   Far off from the gates of gold—
Away on the mountains wild and bare,
Away from the tender Shepherd's care.

"Lord, Thou hast here Thy ninety and nine;
   Are they not enough for Thee?"
But the Shepherd made answer: "This of mine
   Has wandered away from Me;
And although the road be rough and steep,
I go to the desert to find My sheep."

But none of the ransomed ever knew
   How deep were the waters crossed;
Nor how dark was the night that the Lord passed through
   Ere He found His sheep that was lost.
Out in the desert He heard its cry—
Sick and helpless, and ready to die.

"Lord, whence are those blood drops all the way
   That mark out the mountain's track?"
"They were shed for one who had gone astray,
   Ere the Shepherd could bring him back."
"Lord, whence are Thy hands so rent and torn?"
"They are pierced tonight by many a thorn."

But all through the mountains, thunder-riven,
   And up from the rocky steep,
There arose a glad cry to the gate of heaven,
   "Rejoice! I have found My sheep!"
And the angels echoed around the throne,
   "Rejoice! for the Lord brings back His own!"
—Elizabeth Cecilia Clephane

Elizabeth Cecilia Douglas Clephane was the third
daughter of Andrew Clephane, sheriff of Fife. She was

born in Edinburgh, Scotland, on June 18, 1830, but spent most of her short life in Melrose, Scotland. This saint of God was small of stature, quiet, shy, bookish, a lover of poetry, and at the head of all her classes at school. Having been orphaned at an early age, she was sensitive to the needs and sorrows of those about her.

Miss Clephane was credited with eight songs which were published anonymously and posthumously in *The Family Treasury,* a periodical for Christian homes. These songs included "Beneath the Cross of Jesus" and were published under the general title of "Breathings on the Border." The arrow of conviction has pierced hearts beyond number as they listened to the singing of "The Ninety and Nine." The words to this hymn were written in 1868 for a friend who begged of Miss Clephane a contribution to *The Children's Hour* magazine.

The year was 1874. Miss Clephane had been dead five years. D. L. Moody and Ira D. Sankey had ended a meeting in Glasgow, Scotland. As they boarded the train for Edinburgh, the place of their next meeting, Mr. Sankey purchased a penny newspaper. In the paper he found Miss Clephane's "The Ninety and Nine." "Mr. Moody," he said, "I have found a poem that might be helpful to you in your sermons." "Read it," Mr. Moody replied. But soon Mr. Sankey realized that Mr. Moody was absorbed in a letter he had received from Chicago and was not paying any attention to the reading of the poem. Mr. Sankey tore the poem from the paper and "filed" it in his pocket for future use.

At a noon meeting soon after, Mr. Moody and Dr. Horatius Bonar spoke on "The Good Shepherd." When Dr. Bonar had finished his brief but eloquent address, Moody asked Sankey, "Have you a solo appropriate for this subject with which to close the service?" Mr. Sankey prayed, "O Lord, help me. I do not have an appropriate solo." A voice suddenly seemed to say, "Sing the hymn you found on the train." Panic and Doubt argued, "You can't sing those words. They have not been set to music, and you have never composed a tune. Certainly you could not 'compose' under this pressure." But the inner voice seemed to urge, "Sing the song you found on the train. I will help you with the tune." Mr. Sankey put the poem on the organ, struck an A-flat chord, and began to sing. Note by note the melody poured forth.

At the end of the first stanza, Panic and Doubt came back. They asked, "So what if you got through the first stanza; what makes you think that you can sustain the tune for the other stanzas? It would be terrible for you to have to change the tune or stop singing." Fortunately, the singer did not forget. And later he was able to fit the words and the music together for publishing.

A short time after Mr. Sankey had introduced "The Ninety and Nine," he received a note of gratitude from the author's sister. "I am happy," she wrote, "that Elizabeth's poem has found a place in the service of the One she loved and tried to serve."

Ira D. Sankey was born in Edinburgh, Pennsylvania, on August 28, 1840. He was "born again" at the age of sixteen. An enlistee during the Civil War, he organized a male chorus and assisted the chaplain. Prior to his teaming up with Mr. Moody in 1871, Mr. Sankey served as a bank clerk, music director, and government employee. He died in Brooklyn on August 13, 1908.

There Is a Fountain Filled with Blood
ca. 1771

There is a fountain filled with blood
  Drawn from Immanuel's veins;
And sinners, plunged beneath that flood,
  Lose all their guilty stains.

The dying thief rejoiced to see
  That fountain in his day;
And there may I, though vile as he,
  Wash all my sins away.

Dear dying Lamb, Thy precious blood
Shall never lose its power,
Till all the ransomed Church of God
Be saved to sin no more.

E'er since by faith I saw the stream
Thy flowing wounds supply,
Redeeming love has been my theme,
And shall be till I die.

Then in a nobler, sweeter song,
I'll sing Thy power to save.
When this poor lisping, stammering tongue
Lies silent in the grave.

Two stanzas, omitted from most hymnals, are as follows:

Lord, I believe Thou hast prepared,
Unworthy though I be,
For me a blood-bought free reward,
A golden harp for me.

'Tis strung and tuned for endless years,
And formed by power divine,
To sound in God the Father's ears
No other name but Thine.

—William Cowper

This hymn is based on Zechariah 13:1: "In that day there shall be a fountain opened to the house of David and to the inhabitants of Jerusalem for sin and for uncleanness." Surprisingly, it was written at St. Alban's Asylum during the author's temporary confinement for having made several attempts to take his life. A relative visited Cowper, seeking to ease his depression by telling him of "Jesus' power to save." Cowper burst into tears, saying, "It is the first time that I have seen a ray of hope." Later the poet opened his Bible at random and read Romans 3:25: "Whom God hath set forth to be a propitiation through faith in his blood, to declare his righteousness for the remission of sins that are past, through the forbearance of God." Cowper exclaimed, "There shone upon me the full beams of the sufficiency of the atonement that Christ had made, my pardon in His blood, the fulness and completeness of my justification; and in a moment I believed and received the gospel." So thrilled was Cowper with his new-found hope that he described it in verse, hoping thereby to help other troubled souls.

Many hymn writers have argued that "a fountain filled with blood" is incorrect, that "a better symbolism would be 'a spring bubbling up.' " James Montgomery (1771-1854) altered stanza 1 to read, "From Calvary's cross a fountain flows/Of water and of blood,/More healing than Bethesda's pool,/Or famed Siloam's flood." But the hymn's popularity has followed the original words of the author.

William Cowper was born in Berkhampstead, England, in November 1731. His father was chaplain to King George II, and his mother was a descendant of the poet John Donne. When Cowper was six, his mother died, leaving him with a life-long grief. At ten Cowper was sent to boarding school. The cruelty of the older boys caused him to write, "Day and night I was upon the rack, lying down in horror and rising up in despair." At eleven Cowper was sent by his father to deliver a treatise on suicide. No doubt this morbid subject added "fuel to the fire" of the lad's already pronounced mental problems.

At eighteen Cowper began to study law. Although he was admitted to the bar, he made no attempt to practice his profession. In nine years of so-called law practice Cowper never felt worthy to serve people; nor could he attract business for himself. A concerned relative arranged for Cowper a clerkship in the House of Lords. Cowper felt so inadequate that he made several attempts to take his life.

Suicidal failures, compounded by two unhappy romances, increased the poet's feelings of self-contempt; and as he walked the streets, he felt that all eyes were fixed on him in scorn. He wrote, "The meshes of that fine network, the brain, are composed of such mere spinner's threads in me that when a long thought finds its way into them it buzzes, and twangs, and bustles about at such a rate as seems to threaten the whole contexture." Nevertheless he always added, "Blessed be the God of salvation. Thus did he break me and bind me up; then did He wound me and make me whole."

Providentially, a Mr. and Mrs. Unwin realized the poet's potential and took him into their home. Upon Mr. Unwin's death, John Newton (author of "Amazing Grace") moved Mrs. Unwin and Cowper to Olney. There Cowper helped Newton compile the *Olney Hymns,* to which Cowper contributed nearly seventy original hymns.

When Cowper died on April 25, 1800, it was said that his expression changed at the last from dejection to happiness. A friend commented, "It was as if he saw his Saviour, and as if he realized the blessed fact, 'I am not shut out of heaven after all.' " In "Cowper's Grave" Elizabeth Barrett Browning wrote, "O poets, from a maniac's tongue was poured the deathless singing."

The familiar pentatonic tune, CLEANSING FOUNTAIN, is believed by some to be from Lowell Mason's COWPER, which may have been written for this hymn. Most hymnologists, however, simply call it an early American melody.

When I Survey the Wondrous Cross
1707

When I survey the wondrous cross
On which the Prince of Glory died,
My richest gain I count but loss,
And pour contempt on all my pride.

Forbid it, Lord, that I should boast,
Save in the death of Christ, my God;
All the vain things that charm me most,
I sacrifice them to His blood.

See, from His head, His hands, His feet,
Sorrow and love flow mingled down!
Did e'er such love and sorrow meet,
Or thorns compose so rich a crown?

His dying crimson, like a robe,
Spreads o'er His body on the tree;
Then am I dead to all the globe,
And all the globe is dead to me.

Were the whole realm of nature mine,
That were a present far too small;
Love so amazing, so divine,
Demands my soul, my life, my all.

—Isaac Watts

Watts wrote this soul-searching hymn for use at Communion services. It was inspired by Galatians 6:14— "But God forbid that I should glory, save in the cross of our Lord Jesus Christ, by whom the world is crucified unto me, and I unto the world." But it breathes of many other Scriptures, including our Lord's warning about gaining the whole world and losing one's soul (Matthew 16:26) and Paul's instructions to examine oneself before partaking of the Lord's Supper to avoid eating and drinking unworthily (I Corinthians 11:27).

The word *survey* suggests seriously considering a thing in order to appreciate its value. Watts' use of the word was to inspire people to think seriously on the Lord's death on the cross and its intended effect on our lives. As Watts surveyed the cross, he saw beyond the shame of such death the wonders of divine love that prompted our Lord's death on the cross as the means of salvation.

The phrase *pour contempt* of stanza 1 and the *boast* of stanza 2 warn against inordinate pride in personal accomplishment. Watts was impressed by the fact that although Paul had cause to boast after the flesh—a wonderful heritage, a marvelous education, and high position—his full boast was in the cross of Christ. This inspired Watts to write, "All the vain things that charm me most, I sacrifice them to His blood."

Stanza 3 brings under consideration all that the crucifixion involves. Especially in the author's mind was the thought of the soldiers' piercing our Lord's side to make certain that He was dead. Watts considered the intermingling of "sorrow and love" that flowed "from His head, His hands, His feet," and he felt compelled to challenge others to consider if such sorrow and love had ever met elsewhere. Hinting at the richness of the crowns of earthly monarchs, he suggested that these crowns could not begin to compare with the crown of thorns that pierced the Saviour's brow.

Stanza 4 expresses the precious truth that, by virtue of Christ's sacrificial death, Christians are dead to the world. This thought is derived from the last part of Galatians 6:14, where Paul says that by Christ "the world is crucified unto me, and I unto the world." Romans 6:1-4 and Colossians 2:20 use the same image.

In stanza 5 we find one of hymnody's greatest challenges: the Christian's full dedication demanded by our Lord's perfect sacrifice. In effect, Watts says, "Even if the whole realm of nature were ours to give, it would still fall far short as a gift to such great love. The amazing love that was manifest at Calvary 'demands our souls, our lives, our all.' "

This hymn has been rated highly by literary men, theologians, and hymnists. One has praised it as "the finest hymn in the English language" and another as "second only to 'Rock of Ages.'" An apt description says, "It is logical, artistic, and solemn. It is full of simplicity and splendor. It is a flower of song—the royal jewel of Watts' hymns."

Originally this hymn bore the title of "Crucifixion to the World, by the Cross of Christ." This title followed the practice of the day to summarize a hymn's theme in its title.

"When I Survey the Wondrous Cross" was popularized by George Whitefield, who omitted the fourth stanza, which Watts had set in brackets to indicate that it was the most likely one to be left out, if need be.

The first published appearance of this hymn was in 1707 in Watts' *Hymns and Spiritual Songs*. The words "the Prince of Glory" of line 2 appeared as "the Young Prince of Glory." In the second edition of the hymnal (1709), Watts changed the line to read, "When God, the Mighty Maker, died." Other changes of line 2 state, "When Christ, the Lord of Glory died"; "When Christ, the Great Redeemer, died"; and "When Christ, the Great Creator, died." In the nineteenth century there were numerous hymn collections that printed the hymn with extensive alterations. Julian quotes an authority on hymnology as commenting about one such "mutilation":

> There is just enough of Watts left here to remind one of Horace's saying, that you may know the remains of a poet even when he is torn in pieces.

Some have accused Watts of Socinianism, a rationalistic heresy from the time of the Reformation that is the predecessor of modern Unitarianism. The fact that certain phrases in his hymns were altered in later editions, supposedly to tone down Trinitarian doctrine, induced the Scottish Presbyterians to forbid the use of his hymns. Though some statements in his theological writings are suspect, there is a letter preserved in which he clearly states his belief in the deity of Christ and the Holy Spirit. The whole tenor of his hymns stands in opposition to Unitarian principles.

"When I Survey the Wondrous Cross" figured in the events surrounding Matthew Arnold's death. Arnold, a noted English author and critic, usually referred to God as "the Eternal Somewhat that makes for righteousness and from whom Jesus came." But on the day of his death, he heard Watts' hymn at Ian MacLaren's Church in Liverpool. Later Arnold dined at the home of his brother-in-law who reported, "Throughout the day Matthew kept repeating the opening lines of this hymn. About ten minutes before he died, he repeated these lines again,

saying, 'This hymn is the greatest of all English hymns.'"
Afterwards people conjectured that perhaps Arnold, at
death, might have accepted redemption as it was explained in this hymn.

There have been several tunes for this hymn—I. B.
Woodbury's EUCHARIST (sometimes OLIVET), Henry
Smart's CHORAL, and a tune by G. C. Wells. The popular
HAMBURG derives from the Gregorian chant. This is a
type of church music from the Middle Ages that is
monophonic (i.e., having one melody line and no parts)
and without regular meter. It is named after Gregory the
Great, pope from 590 to 604, though it is probably of
later origin. HAMBURG was arranged by Lowell Mason
(1792-1872) in 1824 from the "first Gregorian tone" or
"Gregorian Chant I." Mason, at that time, was organist
at the First Presbyterian Church in Savannah, Georgia.
He left Georgia, however, and moved to Boston to seek
a publisher for his tunes. HAMBURG was first published
in *The Boston Handel and Haydn Society Collection
of Church Music* (third edition) in 1825.

*(For other hymns by Isaac Watts, see pp. 81, 93, 214, 257,
298.)*

Wisdom & Truth

Bob Jones University Hymn
ca. 1945 (stanzas 1-3, 7, 8)
1961 (stanzas 4-6)

Wisdom of God, we would by Thee be taught;
Control our minds, direct our ev'ry thought.
Knowledge alone life's problems cannot meet;
We learn to live while sitting at Thy feet.

Light of the world, illumine us we pray,
Our souls are dark, without Thy kindling ray;
Torches unlighted, of all radiance bare,
Touch them to flame, and burn in glory there!

Incarnate Truth, help us Thy truth to learn,
Prone to embrace the falsehood we would spurn;
Groping in error's maze for verity,
Thou art the Truth we need to make us free.

Giver of life, we would not live to please
Self or the world, nor seek the paths of ease;
Dying Thou bringest life to sons of men;
So may we dying live Thy life again.

Captain of Might, we yield to Thy command,
Armored by faith, Thy Word our sword in hand;
Fierce though the battle, Thine the victory,
Bravely we'll strive and more than conq'rors be.

Eternal Lord, let heavens pass away,
Earth be removed, no fear our hearts shall sway;
Empires may crumble, dust return to dust;
Secure are they, who in their Saviour trust.

Unfailing love, we are so cold in heart,
To us Thy passion for the lost impart;
Give us Thy vision of the need of men,
All learning will be used in service then.

Great King of kings, this campus all is Thine,
Make by Thy presence of this place a shrine;
Thee may we meet within the classroom walls,
Go forth to serve Thee from these hallowed halls.
—Bob Jones

Bob Jones is the son of the fiery evangelist of the same name who founded Bob Jones University. He was born on October 19, 1911, in Montgomery, Alabama. Led to the Lord about the age of five by his mother, he spent a good part of his early years traveling with his father on the evangelistic circuit and meeting some of the most famous orthodox preachers of his day, such as Billy Sunday, Gipsy Smith, W. E. Biederwolf, and Harry Ironside. He was in the first graduating class of Bob Jones College, which was founded in 1927, and he went on to earn a master's degree from the University of Pittsburgh at the age of twenty-one. He has been awarded honorary degrees from six institutions, including the Doctor of Letters degree from Chungang University in Seoul, Korea.

As a young man, Dr. Jones developed a special interest in art, and he eventually built up what is now recognized by many critics as the finest collection of Baroque paintings in America. Another of his early loves was drama, and he has acted in a variety of roles in plays and Christian films produced at Bob Jones University. He would probably have made an important name for himself on the Shakespearean stage had not God called him to be a preacher of the gospel and to serve as president of Bob Jones University. As a preacher, he has proclaimed the Gospel in innumerable places around the world; as a religious leader, he is recognized as a prominent spokesman for Fundamentalism; as a college president and now chancellor, he has added a touch of culture unique in modern Christian education.

Apart from preaching, teaching, acting, and other activities, Bob Jones has used his pen for the service of His Lord. Besides two novels, several collections of sermons, an anthology of poetry, and other books, he has written a number of hymns. These include "Broken Things," "Forsaken," "Easter's Dawning Light," "Strong in Salvation," and "Anniversary Hymn." His poetry conveys a sense of balance and majesty that a writer attains only by a close study of the classics of English literature. Such qualities have always marked the great hymns of the English language but unfortunately are rarely found in modern Christian music.

According to the author, "University Hymn" has this background:

> I wrote the hymn during the war while I was traveling around the country preaching. I remember very well that I completed one stanza while riding on a train in southern Illinois. At that time the hymn consisted of only five stanzas. Some years later, however, we found that the length of the hymn was too short to permit its use as a processional or recessional at commencement time. The graduating class had grown to such proportions that they, together with the faculty, found it impossible to march in or out of the service with only five stanzas to the hymn. Also, apostasy had widened in religious circles around the world, and I felt a special need to include challenging thoughts on faithfulness, militancy, and confidence. These thoughts are expressed in the stanzas "Giver of life," "Captain of Might," and "Eternal Lord."

The music for "University Hymn," BACCALAUREATE, was composed by Harriette Stollenwerck Parker (1913-1946), the author's cousin. Mrs. Parker served for many years as a member of the music faculty of Bob Jones University. Dr. Jones says of this gifted woman, "Harriette was one of the most godly, sweet-spirited, and cheerful Christians I have ever known. She was also beautiful. I especially remember the lovely pianologues she used to give at Bible Conference and vespers. She would sit at the piano and play a melody while reciting the words of a great hymn." She was killed in an accident when a truck collided with the automobile in which she was riding, but she is still remembered for the noble tune she wrote and her radiant Christian testimony.

(For another hymn by Bob Jones, see p. 48.)

Break Thou the Bread of Life
1877 (stanzas 1 and 2)
pub. 1913 (stanzas 3 and 4)

Break Thou the bread of life,
  Dear Lord, to me,
As Thou didst break the loaves
  Beside the sea;
Beyond the sacred page
  I seek Thee, Lord,
My spirit pants for Thee,
  O living Word.

Bless Thou the truth, dear Lord,
  To me, to me,
As Thou didst bless the bread
  By Galilee;
Then shall all bondage cease,
  All fetters fall;
And I shall find my peace,
  My All in all.

Thou art the bread of life,
  O Lord, to me,
Thy holy Word the truth
  That saveth me;
Give me to eat and live
  With Thee above;
Teach me to love Thy truth,
  For Thou art love.

O send Thy Spirit, Lord,
  Now unto me,
That He may touch mine eyes,
  And make me see:
Show me the truth concealed
  Within Thy Word,
And in Thy Book revealed
  I see the Lord.

—Mary Artemisia Lathbury (stanzas 1 and 2)
—Alexander Groves (stanzas 3 and 4)

This prayer hymn is based on four passages of Scripture: Matthew 14:19, "and took the five loaves, and the two fishes, and looking up to heaven, he blessed, and brake, and gave the loaves to his disciples, and the disciples to the multitude"; John 8:32, "And ye shall know the truth, and the truth shall make you free"; John 6:35, "I am the bread of life: he that cometh to me shall never hunger"; and Matthew 5:6, "Blessed are they which do hunger and thirst after righteousness: for they shall be filled."

Miss Lathbury wrote the first two stanzas of this hymn while sitting beside the blue water of Lake Chautauqua, New York, home of the Chautauqua Literary and Scientific Circle (CLSC). The CLSC, inaugurated in 1874 by Bishop John H. Vincent and Lewis M. Miller, was an outgrowth of a Methodist summer camp meeting that usually lasted for two weeks but which lengthened to two months and broadened to include cultural, literary, and spiritual activities. Miss Lathbury served as Bishop Vincent's private secretary, and when he wanted a study song and a vesper song for the daily sessions, he asked her to write them. As Miss Lathbury sat beside the beautiful lake, praying for guidance with regard to her assignment, she began to think of the feeding of the five thousand at Galilee. "Dear Lord," she prayed, "break Thou the bread of life to me as Thou didst break the loaves beside the sea." And from that prayerful beginning, the words of her "study song" poured forth. Later, as the sun began to set, she felt moved also to write the first two stanzas of the vesper hymn, "Day Is Dying in the West."

The September 13, 1913, issue of the *Wesleyan Methodist Magazine* (London), just five weeks before Miss Lathbury's death, published two additional stanzas of "Break Thou the Bread of Life," written by Alexander Groves (1842-1909). Today some hymnals print only Miss Lathbury's original two stanzas, while others print four stanzas—1 and 2 by Miss Lathbury, 3 and 4 by Groves. Nothing is known about Groves other than that he was born in Newport, Isle of Wight, England, in 1842, and that he died in Henley-on-Thames, Oxfordshire, England, August 30, 1909.

Miss Lathbury was born in Manchester, New York, on August 10, 1841. She was the daughter of a Methodist minister and the sister of two Methodist ministers. Even in her youth she felt a compulsion to dedicate her talents to the Lord. She seemed to hear God saying to her, "Remember, My child, that you have a gift of weaving fancies into verse and a gift with the pencil of producing visions that come to your heart; consecrate these talents to Me as thoroughly and as definitely as you do your inmost spirit."

Upon her graduation from school, Miss Lathbury taught art, sharing a studio with her sister in New York. She was especially well known for her exquisite pictures of children. The "Saint of Chautauqua" contributed stories to various publications, wrote several books, and founded a club, "The Look-Up Legion," that attracted more than 4000 boys and girls to Methodism. The Legion had as its foundation four rules: "Look up, not down; look forward, not back; look out, and not in; and lend a hand In His Name."

An intensely religious woman and as widely acclaimed for her unselfish nature and personal charm as for her art and journalism, Miss Lathbury spent the closing years of her life in East Orange, New Jersey, where she died on October 20, 1913.

Miss Lathbury's Chautauqua hymns were set to music

in 1877 by William Fiske Sherwin (1826-1888), the gifted and dedicated music director of CLSC. Born in Buckland, Massachusetts, on March 14, 1826, Sherwin studied with Dr. Lowell Mason, taught at the New England Conservatory of Music in Boston, composed many gospel songs, and, although a Baptist, directed the large choirs of Chautauqua. Sherwin died in Boston, April 14, 1888, and a memorial window was installed in a small church in Buckland.

"Break Thou the Bread of Life," with the tune BREAD OF LIFE by Sherwin, is often used as a Communion hymn. While this is by no means inappropriate, a close examination of the text, both the two original stanzas and the two added stanzas, reveals that the "Bread of Life" for which we pray in this hymn is the Word of God; we ask the Lord to break it for our understanding, that we might "see the Lord revealed" in "the Book."

O Word of God Incarnate
1867

O Word of God incarnate,
O Wisdom from on high,
O Truth unchanged, unchanging,
O Light of our dark sky,
We praise Thee for the radiance
That from the hallowed page,
A lantern to our footsteps,
Shines on from age to age.

The Church from her dear Master
Received the gift divine,
And still that light she lifteth
O'er all the earth to shine.
It is the golden casket,
Where gems of truth are stored;
It is the heaven-drawn picture
Of Christ, the living Word.

It floateth like a banner
  Before God's host unfurled;
It shineth like a beacon
  Above the darkling world;
It is the chart and compass
  That o'er life's surging sea,
'Mid mists and rocks and quicksands
  Still guides, O Christ, to Thee.

O make Thy Church, dear Saviour,
  A lamp of purest gold,
To bear before the nations
  Thy true light, as of old.
O teach Thy wandering pilgrims
  By this their path to trace,
Till, clouds and darkness ended,
  They see Thee face to face.

—William Walsham How

This hymn is said to have been based on Psalm 119:105 ("Thy word is a lamp unto my feet, and a light unto my path") and Proverbs 6:23 ("For the commandment is a lamp; and the law is light"). However, numerous passages of Scripture are apparent in the stanzas of this hymn, which first appeared in the 1867 supplement to *Psalms and Hymns*, edited by How (1823-1897) and T. B. Morrell.

In substance "O Word of God Incarnate" is a prayer of praise to the Lord Jesus Christ, to whom the author refers under many titles, such as, "Word of God Incarnate," "Wisdom from on High," "Truth unchanged, unchanging," "Light of our dark sky," "Master," and "Saviour." To this great God How offers praise "for the radiance that from the hallowed page, A lantern for our footsteps, Shines on from age to age." Then he calls upon the Church, over whom the Lord is Master, to be faithful witnesses before all nations "Till clouds and darkness ended, They see Thee face to face."

From the pen of Francis Pigou, dean of Bristol, has

come this estimate of Bishop How:

> Walsham How . . . was a man of great personal piety,
> which shone transparently in him. . . . His well-known
> hymns are fragrant with it. . . . he was, like St. Barn-
> abas, "a good man, full of faith and of the Holy Ghost";
> and his ministry was singularly owned and blessed
> of God. It is true that more men are won to God by
> holiness than by cleverness.

MUNICH (also called KÖNIGSBERG), the musical setting for this hymn, is an adaptation from a German melody published in 1693. Felix Mendelssohn made the
adaptation and used it as a chorale in his oratorio, *Elijah*,
which he composed for the National Festival in Birming-
ham, England, in 1847. The writing and the production
of his oratorio "frayed his nerves," and he died within
a year of its production. A mourner said, "There is one
thing that Mendelssohn could not do in music. He could
not play an audience out of the church. The parishioners
enjoyed his music so much that the only way to get them
to leave was to stop the bellows."

(For other hymns by William Walsham How, see pp. 146, 287.)

Confession & Forgiveness

Just As I Am, Without One Plea
1834

Just as I am, without one plea,
But that Thy blood was shed for me,
And that Thou bidd'st me come to Thee,
O Lamb of God, I come! I come!

Just as I am, and waiting not
To rid my soul of one dark blot,
To Thee whose blood can cleanse each spot,
O Lamb of God, I come! I come!

Just as I am, though tossed about
With many a conflict, many a doubt,
Fightings and fears within, without,
O Lamb of God, I come! I come!

Just as I am, poor, wretched, blind;
Sight, riches, healing of the mind,
Yea, all I need, in Thee I find,
O Lamb of God, I come! I come!

Just as I am, Thou wilt receive,
Wilt welcome, pardon, cleanse, relieve;
Because Thy promise I believe,
O Lamb of God, I come! I come!

Just as I am, Thy love unknown
Hath broken every barrier down;
Now to be Thine, yea, Thine alone,
O Lamb of God, I come! I come!

Just as I am—of that free love,
"The breadth, length, depth, and height" to prove,
Here for a season, then above—
O Lamb of God, I come! I come!
—Charlotte Elliott

"This hymn," says Dr. David R. Breed in *The History of Hymns and Hymn-Tunes,* "is the very epitome of the Gospel. It brings into strongest association the 'sacrificial Lamb of God,' His 'shed blood,' His 'promise,' and His 'love'; it meets all the hindrances of the sinner."

That this hymn is written in the first person singular, present tense, is significant: the hymn incorporates phrases and experiences from the author's conversion. In May 1822, Dr. César Malan of Geneva, Switzerland, was being entertained in the home of Charles Elliott. One day while chatting with Charlotte, the invalid daughter of the host, Dr. Malan asked, "Are you a Christian? Have you experienced Christ?" Charlotte was aghast; one did not discuss one's religion, and certainly one did not boast that he was saved. Later, however, her resentment was pierced by "the arrow of conviction from the quiver of the Almighty," and she apologized to Dr. Malan, saying, "I am sorry for my rudeness. Actually I would like to come to Christ, but I do not know how to find Him." Dr. Malan, aware that she had been seeking salvation through works and worthiness, said, "Come just as you are. Cut the cable; it will take too long to unloose it. It is small loss anyway."

It was not until twelve years after her conversion that Charlotte wrote "Just As I Am." Her brother, in an effort to secure funds for the founding of a school for the children of poor clergy, held a bazaar. All the Elliotts but the ailing Charlotte went to assist in the effort. Left alone, the invalid Charlotte became so depressed at the thought of her "uselessness" that she felt she could not bear it. Then she thought, "God's grace is sufficient for all things, and surely my thoughts of uselessness can be conquered by His grace." The thought of God's marvelous grace, which not only saves but also keeps, inspired her to set down in verse "the gospel of pardon, peace, and heaven."

This famous hymn first appeared anonymously in a paper edited by Miss Elliott. A wealthy woman was deeply touched by the words and had them printed in a leaflet and distributed freely. One day after giving her a routine checkup, Charlotte's doctor handed her one of the leaflets, saying, "I believe you will appreciate the sentiment of these words." Imagine her surprise to read her own verse! The first six stanzas were published in the *Invalid's Hymn Book* in 1836; and later that same year in her *Hours of Sorrow Cheered and Comforted* Miss Elliott included the same six stanzas with an additional seventh stanza (printed above) that one rarely sees today.

Miss Elliott was the daughter, granddaughter, and sister of ministers. She was born in Clapham, England, on March 18, 1789, and reared in a cultured and deeply spiritual atmosphere. Miss Elliott died at Brighton, England, September 22, 1871. For most of her eighty-two years, Miss Elliott endured physical agony. She said,

> My Heavenly Father knows, and He alone, what it is, day after day, and hour after hour, to fight against bodily feelings of almost overpowering weakness, and languor and exhaustion, to resolve, as He enables me to do, not to yield to the slothfulness, the depression, the irritability, such a body causes me to long to indulge, but to rise every morning determined on taking this for my motto, "If any man will come after me, let him deny himself, and take up his cross daily, and follow me."

Although wedded to many tunes in its long history, "Just As I Am" is perhaps best known by the tune WOOD-WORTH, composed in 1849 by William B. Bradbury (1816-1868). Among his accomplishments are listed composer, publisher, choral director, manufacturer of musical instruments, and pioneer in bringing musical instruction into the New York City public school. He is credited with "teaching the American people the songs that paved the way for the Moody-Sankey revival movement." Bradbury compiled fifty-nine books of sacred and secular music between 1841 and 1867.

Two other very effective tunes for "Just As I Am, Without One Plea" are SAFFRON WALDEN by Arthur Henry Brown (1830-1926) and ST. CRISPIN by George J. Elvey (1816-1893).

O Jesus, Thou Art Standing
1867

O Jesus, Thou art standing
  Outside the fast-closed door,
In lowly patience waiting
  To pass the threshold o'er:
Shame on us, Christian brothers,
  His Name and sign who bear,
O shame, thrice shame upon us,
  To keep Him standing there!

O Jesus, Thou art knocking;
  And lo! that hand is scarred,
And thorns Thy brow encircle,
  And tears Thy face have marred:
O love that passeth knowledge,
  So patiently to wait!
O sin that hath no equal,
  So fast to bar the gate!

O Jesus, Thou art pleading
  In accents meek and low:
"I died for you, My children,
  And will ye treat Me so?"
O Lord, with shame and sorrow
  We open now the door;
Dear Saviour, enter, enter,
  And leave us nevermore!

—William Walsham How

Most authorities agree that this hymn is How's most famous work. They agree that the hymn first appeared in a supplement to *Psalms and Hymns* (1867) upon which Bishop How and the Reverend Thomas B. Morrell collaborated, but the source of the hymn's inspiration is debated.

According to some hymnologists, the hymn was inspired by William Holman Hunt's painting, *The Light of the World*, which antedates How's hymn by several years.

In the painting Jesus is standing outside a closed door that has no outside latch. Weeds, vines, and fruit around the door indicate that the door has been closed for a long time. A lantern in the hand of Jesus suggests His being the Light of the World who has come to dispel the darkness of sin.

To see in How's hymn the reflection of this painting is easy. Stanza 1 pictures the Saviour standing outside a "fast-closed door," and it pronounces shame on professing Christians for refusing to open the door to the Saviour. Stanza 2 depicts the crucified and risen Saviour as still patiently and lovingly knocking, and the hymnist explains that to bar the gate against such love is a "sin that hath no equal." The final stanza presents the pleading Saviour being invited in by repentant sinners who cry, "Dear Saviour, enter, enter, And leave us nevermore."

Other hymnologists place How's inspiration for the hymn in a poem. How wrote,

> I composed the hymn in 1867, after I had been reading a very beautiful poem entitled "Brothers, and a Sermon." The pathos of the verses impressed me very forcibly at the time. I read them over and over again, and finally, closing the book, I scribbled on an old scrap of paper my first idea of the verses beginning, "O Jesus, Thou art standing." I altered them a good deal subsequently, but I am fortunate in being able to say that after the hymn left my hands it was never revised or altered in any way.

The poem to which How referred is by Jean Ingelow. In it two brothers are listening to a sermon by the village parson. The parson is somewhat downcast, for he realizes that his audience is not listening. Finally he reads Revelation 3:20—"Behold, I stand at the door, and knock: if any man hear my voice, and open the door, I will come in to him, and will sup with him, and he with me"; and taking "fresh marvel" in the words, the parson challenges, "Open the door with shame, if ye have sinned; If ye be sorry, open it with sighs. Albeit the place be bare for

poverty . . . Be not ashamed for that, but open it. . . ." He
urges the "rich and strong" and the "happy young" to
open the door immediately lest "the wounded heart for
evermore withdraw."

The tune ST. HILDA, also known as ST. EDITH, is an
adaptation of the eighteenth-century tune KNECHT composed in 1793. The composer, Justin Heinrich Knecht
(1752-1817), was a gifted German musician and professor
of literature who played many different musical instruments. The adaptation was made by the Reverend Edward
Husband (1843-1908), organist, composer, vicar, and
popular lecturer on church music, who combined the first
two lines of Knecht's tune with two lines of his own in
1871. The tune is named after St. Hilda, the seventh-
century abbess who founded and supervised the famous
nunnery and monastery of Whitby in northeastern
England, known not only for its charity but for being
a center of theological and literary learning.

(For other hymns by William Walsham How, see pp. 140, 287.)

Pass Me Not, O Gentle Saviour
   1868

Pass me not, O gentle Saviour,
   Hear my humble cry;
While on others Thou art calling,
   Do not pass me by.

Refrain:

Saviour, Saviour, hear my humble cry,
While on others Thou art calling,
Do not pass me by.

Let me at Thy throne of mercy
   Find a sweet relief;
Kneeling there in deep contrition,
   Help my unbelief.

Trusting only in Thy merit,
 Would I seek Thy face;
Heal my wounded, broken spirit,
 Save me by Thy grace.

Thou the spring of all my comfort,
 More than life to me;
Whom have I on earth beside Thee?
 Whom in heaven but Thee?
—Fanny J. Crosby

"**P**ass Me Not, O Gentle Saviour," written in 1868, was, according to some authorities, inspired by the prayer "Saviour, do not pass me by," which Miss Crosby (1820-1915) heard a penitent pray at a mission. Within six years this prayer hymn was called the "most popular song in the Moody-Sankey meetings in London." It was the first hymn of Fanny Crosby to receive worldwide attention.

The hymn well expresses the thoughts and attitudes that characterize the sinner who is sincerely seeking divine forgiveness and healing. There is a proper emphasis on humility and contrition, the penitent imploring and pleading rather than demanding pardon or lightly passing over his sin. On the other hand, we see the true character of our Lord as the One who is not only able but willing to give comfort and spiritual relief to those who forsake and repent of their sin and unbelief. Our only basis for coming to God is "Thy throne of mercy," "Thy merit," and "Thy grace."

Because of the great volume of her poetic output, more than 8000 hymns, critics have charged that she "sacrificed quality for quantity." As hymnologist S. W. Duffield said, "It is more to her credit as a writer that she has occasionally found a pearl than that she has brought to the surface so many oyster shells." Nevertheless, we are indebted to her for these "pearls," for they have been an instrument for the conversion of many sinners and the encouragement and edification of many saints.

The tune PASS ME NOT was composed also in 1868,

by William H. Doane, devoted friend of Miss Crosby. Born in Preston, Connecticut, on February 3, 1832, he received training from outstanding American and German masters. He was active as a Sunday school worker and as a successful businessman, editor, and composer. Denison University awarded him an honorary doctorate in 1875. Doane died in South Orange, New Jersey, on December 24, 1915, at the age of eighty-three.

(For other hymns by Fanny Crosby, see pp. 182, 184.)

Softly and Tenderly
1882

Softly and tenderly Jesus is calling,
  Calling for you and for me;
See, on the portals He's waiting and watching,
  Watching for you and for me.

Refrain:

Come home, come home,
Ye who are weary, come home;
Earnestly, tenderly, Jesus is calling,
Calling, O sinner, come home!

Why should we tarry when Jesus is pleading,
  Pleading for you and for me;
Why should we linger and heed not His mercies,
  Mercies for you and for me?

Time is now fleeting, the moments are passing,
  Passing from you and from me?
Shadows are gathering, deathbeds are coming,
  Coming for you and for me.

Oh, for the wonderful love He has promised,
  Promised for you and for me!
Though we have sinned, He has mercy and pardon,
  Pardon for you and for me.

—Will L. Thompson

There is a story that Dwight L. Moody, in the closing days of his life, was visited by his good friend, Will Lamartine Thompson (1847-1909). "Will," Moody is supposed to have said, "I would rather have written 'Softly and Tenderly' than anything I have been able to do in my whole life." Moody was not exalting an invitation hymn above preaching the Word. No one realized more than Moody did that the drawing power of salvation was in the lifting up of the Lord Jesus Christ. At the same time, Moody had seen thousands in his meetings answer the call to "come home, come home . . .," and he knew that countless other evangelists and pastors had had the same experience.

Will Thompson was a gifted writer and composer who was paid well for his works. His critics sometimes called him "that millionaire composer," but Thompson was just a good businessman who simply refused to sell his works at prices below their worth.

Thompson was born in Beaver County, Pennsylvania, and spent most of his life across the state border in East Liverpool, Ohio. Having composed his first song at the age of sixteen, Thompson went on to obtain formal training at Mount Union College (Alliance, Ohio), at the Boston Conservatory of Music, and in Leipzig, Germany. At twenty-eight he began to offer his works for publication. The first man to whom Thompson took his works offered twenty-five dollars for four songs. "After all," the publisher said, "such material can be had in abundance 'free of charge.'" Thompson was insulted. Later, while on a business trip to New York with his father, Thompson sold his works at his own price. Printing presses rolled furiously with Thompson songs and tunes, the most popular song being his "Gathering Shells from the Seashore." He wrote a number of patriotic, romantic, and humorous songs, very well known at the time but now long forgotten.

Thompson opened a music company in Chicago and published secular, sacred, and classical works. He also managed a music store in East Liverpool. In his effort to "sell" a song to an undecided person, he often had to play and sing for hours.

At forty, Thompson began to major on religious writing, apparently because of religious convictions. Thompson also traveled about the countryside in a two-horse wagon that was equipped with a piano. Will wrote and sang such hymns as "There's a Great Day Coming," "Lead Me Gently Home, Father," and his autobiographical "Jesus Is All the World to Me." "Softly and Tenderly" was first published in *Songs of Triumph* in 1882. Evangelists everywhere began using "Softly and Tenderly" to invite sinners to the mourner's bench. D. L. Moody and his song leader, Ira D. Sankey, used the hymn extensively. In hundreds of meetings all across the United States and the British Isles, these men pictured to sinners a Saviour who was "patiently waiting" and "tenderly pleading" for them to come to Him for salvation. "Why should we linger and heed not His mercies?" Sankey would sing; and great hosts would surge forward to surrender to the Lord Jesus Christ.

Thompson married Elizabeth Johnston in 1891, and they had one son. Thompson went home to his Lord on September 20, 1909, just after he and his family had spent a summer abroad. A close friend of Thompson said,

> Will L. Thompson, who always wrote both the words and music, lives in his songs that give wings to the gospel and still bring strength and comfort to many souls. . . . His musical gift was matched by a fine character and a beautiful spirit. . . . Simplicity, sincerity, humility, and righteousness marked his life.

Comfort

Abide with Me: Fast Falls the Eventide
1847

Abide with me: fast falls the eventide;
The darkness deepens; Lord, with me abide!
When other helpers fail, and comforts flee,
Help of the helpless, O abide with me.

Swift to its close ebbs out life's little day;
Earth's joys grow dim, its glories pass away:
Change and decay in all around I see.
O Thou, who changest not, abide with me.

Not a brief glance I beg, a passing word,
But as Thou dwell'st with Thy disciples, Lord,
Familiar, condescending, patient, free,
Come not to sojourn, but abide with me.

Come not in terrors, as the King of kings;
But kind and good, with healing in Thy wings,
Tears for all woes, a heart for every plea;
Come, Friend of sinners, and abide with me.

Thou on my head in early youth didst smile;
And, though rebellious and perverse meanwhile,
Thou hast not left me, oft as I left Thee;
On to the close, O Lord, abide with me!

I need Thy presence every passing hour;
What but Thy grace can foil the tempter's power?
Who, like Thyself, my guide and stay can be?
Through cloud and sunshine, Lord, abide with me.

I fear no foe, with Thee at hand to bless;
Ills have no weight, and tears no bitterness;
Where is Death's sting? where, Grave, thy victory?
I triumph still, if Thou abide with me.

Hold Thou Thy cross before my closing eyes;
Shine through the gloom and point me to the skies;
Heaven's morning breaks, and earth's vain shadows flee;
In life, in death, O Lord, abide with me.

—Henry Francis Lyte

Dr. David R. Breed in *History and Use of Hymns* said of this hymn, "It needs no comment. To read it is to interpret it, and to sing it with any degree of seriousness is to realize its spiritual depth, purity, and beauty."

Some authorities date the hymn to 1820, giving as its inspiration the dying words of W. A. LeHunte, one of Lyte's friends. The LeHunte family claimed documentary evidence in support of the earlier writing. But most authorities set the date as 1847 and argue the following background:

For twenty-three years Lyte had ministered in an English fishing village. Because of a weakened physical condition, he was advised to seek a warmer climate. On September 4, 1847, in a farewell Communion service and a sermon based on the account of Christ and the two disciples on the road to Emmaus, Lyte moved his audience to tears with a challenge to holier living. That evening he strolled to his beloved seashore for a farewell look at the glorious sunset. "How can I leave this place?" he wondered. Then he thought, "But the Lord is sending me away, and He will go with me even as He walked with the disciples on the road to Emmaus. What a thrill they must have felt to hear Him expound the Scriptures concerning Himself. It is no wonder they said to Him, 'Abide with us: for it is toward evening, and the day is far spent'" (Luke 24:29). Lyte, looking toward heaven, prayed, "Not a brief glance I beg, a passing word; but as Thou dwell'st with Thy disciples, Lord—familiar, condescending, patient, free—come not to sojourn, but abide with me . . . who like Thyself my guide and stay can be? Through cloud and sunshine, Oh, abide with me." Arriving back home, the minister went to his room and penned these eight stanzas, five of which are in general use today.

Henry Francis Lyte was born in Ednam, Scotland, on June 1, 1793. Orphaned early in life and extremely poor, he struggled to get an education. At first he planned to be a doctor, but later he decided that the ministry was a "worthwhile profession." It was not until a few more years had passed that he came into deep fellowship with the One he tried to serve. According to Lyte, a dying minister friend sent for him. "What have I to offer a dying man?" he asked himself. Nevertheless, they prayed together and read Scripture; and the dying man's heart was blessed. Later Lyte remarked, "The peaceful attitude of that man at death so impressed me that I fully surrendered my heart and life to the Lord, and my ministry felt the impact."

After serving in several small parishes, Lyte was led to Lower Brixham. Here he ministered for twenty-three years, and having contracted tuberculosis, was advised to go to Italy. To a friend Lyte wrote, "I am meditating flight again to the South; the little faithful robin is every morning at my window, sweetly warning me that autumnal hours are at hand. The swallows are preparing for flight and inviting me to accompany them; and yet, alas! while I talk about flying, I am just able to crawl, and ask myself whether I shall be able to leave England at all."

Lyte traveled as far as Nice, France, and had to stop. Two months later he was with the Lord (November 20, 1847).

"Abide with Me" was set to music (EVENTIDE) by William Henry Monk—editor, composer, teacher, lecturer, and organist. Mrs. Monk said of the tune, "My husband wrote it at a time of great sorrow when together we watched, as always each day, the glories of the setting sun. As the last golden ray faded, my husband took up paper and pencil and in ten minutes had written the tune." Monk was born in London on March 16, 1823, and died there on March 1, 1889.

(For another hymn by Henry Francis Lyte, see p. 45.)

Be Still, My Soul
1752

Be still, my soul: the Lord is on thy side;
Bear patiently the cross of grief or pain;
Leave to thy God to order and provide;
In every change He faithful will remain.
   Be still, my soul: thy best, thy heavenly Friend
   Through thorny ways leads to a joyful end.

Be still, my soul: thy God doth undertake
To guide the future as He has the past.
Thy hope, thy confidence let nothing shake;
All now mysterious shall be bright at last.
   Be still, my soul: the waves and winds still know
   His voice Who ruled them while He dwelt below.

Be still, my soul: the hour is hastening on
When we shall be forever with the Lord,
When disappointment, grief, and fear are gone,
Sorrow forgot, love's purest joys restored.
   Be still, my soul: when change and tears are past,
   All safe and blessed we shall meet at last.

Omitted stanzas:

Be still, my soul: when dearest friends depart,
And all is darkened in the vale of tears,
Then shalt thou better know His love, His heart,
Who comes to soothe thy sorrow and thy fears.
   Be still, my soul: thy Jesus can repay
   From His own fondness all He takes away.

Be still, my soul: begin the song of praise
On earth, be leaving, to thy Lord on high;
Acknowledge Him in all thy works and ways,
So shall He view thee with a well-pleased eye.
   Be still, my soul: the Sun of life divine
   Through passing clouds shall but more brightly shine.

—Katharina von Schlegel

High on the list of outstanding hymn writers of eighteenth-century Germany was Fräulein Katharina von Schlegel. Very little is known about this godly woman except that she was born on October 22, 1697, and that she served the Lutheran church in the capacity of canoness in a women's seminary in Germany. From certain lines of stanza 1—"In every change He faithful will remain" and "Through thorny ways leads to a joyful end"—one might infer that Fräulein von Schlegel or someone close to her had suffered heartaches during which time friends had failed them. Whatever prompted the hymn, Fräulein von Schlegel seemed to have a longing to turn people to the "Friend that sticketh closer than a brother" and never leaves nor forsakes us.

The German title of "Be Still, My Soul" is "Stille, mein Wille, dein Jesus hilft siegen." It was first published in *Neue Sammlung geistlicher Lieder* (1752). Fräulein von Schlegel received inspiration for the hymn from Psalm 46:10—"Be still, and know that I am God"—and I Thessalonians 4:17—". . . and so shall we ever be with the Lord."

Katharina von Schlegel wrote many lyrics, but "Be Still, My Soul" was the only hymn to be translated. Written in six stanzas, only five were translated into English and only three are in current use.

The translator of "Be Still, My Soul," Jane Laurie Borthwick (1813-1897), was as noted among translators of German hymns as was Miss von Schlegel among authors. Miss Borthwick was born in Edinburgh on April 9, 1813. Her father, James Borthwick, was manager of the British Insurance Company in Edinburgh. Jane Borthwick was a member of the Free Church of Scotland and was a strong supporter of missions.

The Borthwick sisters, Jane and Sarah (Mrs. Eric John Finlater), collaborated on translating from the German *Hymns from the Land of Luther* (four series: 1854, 1855, 1858, 1862). Under the initials H. L. L. (from *Hymns from the Land of Luther*), Miss Borthwick wrote and published numerous prose works, original poems, and translations of hymns. Hardly any hymnbook in England or America failed to include her original works and translations. Two of her best-known original hymns are "Come, Labour On" and "Rest, Weary Soul." Jane Borthwick died in Edinburgh on September 7, 1897.

FINLANDIA, the tune to which the hymn is sung, is an arrangement of the most popular and lyrical melody from the tone poem of that title composed by Finland's best-known and greatest composer, Jean Sibelius (1865-1957). The tune has been in American hymnals since 1933. Sibelius wrote FINLANDIA in 1897 as a patriotic tribute to his beautiful homeland. Sibelius was born in Tavastehus, Finland, in 1865. He visited America in 1914 and received a doctor of music degree from Yale University. Having ceased to compose after 1929, Sibelius died in Järvenpää, Finland, in 1957.

Hiding in Thee
1876

O safe to the Rock that is higher than I,
My soul in its conflicts and sorrows would fly;
So sinful, so weary, Thine, Thine would I be;
Thou blest "Rock of Ages," I'm hiding in Thee.

Refrain:

Hiding in Thee, Hiding in Thee,
Thou blest "Rock of Ages,"
I'm hiding in Thee.

In the calm of the noontide, in sorrow's lone hour,
In times when temptation casts o'er me its power;
In the tempests of life, on its wide, heaving sea,
Thou blest "Rock of Ages," I'm hiding in Thee.

How oft in the conflict, when pressed by the foe,
I have fled to my Refuge and breathed out my woe;
How often, when trials like seabillows roll,
Have I hidden in Thee, O Thou Rock of my soul.

—William O. Cushing

"Hiding in Thee" (or "Safe to the Rock") was written by William Orcutt Cushing in Moravia, New York, in 1876. According to the author, "it was the outgrowth of many tears, many heart conflicts, and yearnings of which the world can know nothing." Back of the hymn, he said, was "the history of many battles." However, he attributed the actual writing of the hymn to a request he received from Ira D. Sankey to "send me something new to help me in my gospel work." To Mr. Cushing, the request was a direct call from God. "As I waited," he said, "I began to think of the safety of being in Christ Jesus. 'Hiding in Thee' began to press to make itself known, and soon the poem was on its way to Mr. Sankey." Mr. Cushing was always quick to add that "it was Mr. Sankey's genius that gave the hymn wings." Its scriptural basis is Psalm 31:2— ". . . my strong rock, for an house of defence to save me."

William Orcutt Cushing, born in Hingham Center, Massachusetts, on December 31, 1823, entered the ministry. After many years as a preacher, he suffered a partial loss of speech. Not easily discouraged, Mr. Cushing prayed, "Lord, give me something to do for Thee," and the Lord graciously led him to write spiritual songs, especially for children. His works include "Ring the Bells of Heaven," "When He Cometh," "Under His Wings," "There'll Be No Dark Valley," and "Follow On."

One wonders if many of this godly man's songs are not autobiographical. Whatever came, he felt safe "Under His Wings." Beyond the "Dark Valley" of this world, his eye of faith saw the Lord's return and our eternal home. Therefore, he could "Follow On"—wherever the Lord might lead.

Mr. Cushing died on October 19, 1902.

Ira David Sankey (1840-1908) is one of the nineteenth century's best-known and best-loved gospel song writers— of both words and music. His work with Philip P. Bliss and Dwight L. Moody is legendary in the annals of gospel hymnody.

I Heard the Voice of Jesus Say
1846

I heard the voice of Jesus say,
  "Come unto Me and rest;
Lay down, thou weary one, lay down
  Thy head upon My breast."
I came to Jesus as I was,
  Weary, and worn, and sad;
I found in Him a resting place,
  And He has made me glad.

I heard the voice of Jesus say,
  "Behold, I freely give
The living water; thirsty one,
  Stoop down, and drink, and live."
I came to Jesus, and I drank
  Of that life-giving stream;
My thirst was quenched, my soul revived,
  And now I live in Him.

I heard the voice of Jesus say,
  "I am this dark world's Light;
Look unto Me, thy morn shall rise,
  And all thy day be bright."
I looked to Jesus, and I found
  In Him my Star, my Sun;
And in that Light of life I'll walk
  Till traveling days are done.

—Horatius Bonar

Horatius Bonar was born in Edinburgh, Scotland, on December 19, 1808. His grandfather was a noted minister and hymnist; his father was a God-fearing lawyer; and his mother was a devout woman who trained three sons for the ministry.

Ordained in the established Church of Scotland in 1837, Bonar later became a leader in the Free Church of Scotland. This denomination was formed in 1843 when nearly 500 ministers withdrew from the state church because Parliament refused to allow the church to govern itself. The Disruption, as it was known, was led by Thomas Chalmers, Bonar's former tutor. Bonar was a minister in Kelso at the time and stayed there to form a Free Church congregation that he pastored until 1866.

In 1843 Horatius married Jane Lundie, also a gifted writer and hymnist ("Fade, Fade, Each Earthly Joy"). The many sorrows that dotted their forty years together brought glory to God and widened their ministry. After five of their children died early in their lives, Horatius wrote, "Spare not the stroke; do with us as Thou wilt; let there be naught unfinished, broken, marred. Complete Thy purpose, that we may become Thy perfect image."

Dr. Bonar spent many hours each day in his study, praying aloud. A maid in his house was converted because she heard his earnest prayers. She explained, "If *he* needs to pray so much, what will become of me if I do not pray?"

Bonar's powerful intellect, his deep knowledge of Scripture, and his physical stature were balanced by a gentle and sympathetic nature and a childlike faith. He wrote 600 hymns and translated at least sixty psalms. So modest about his accomplishments was he, however, that it is difficult to find background material for his hymns.

Once when he was counseling a young man, Dr. Bonar found that the young man could not believe that the Lord would save him from his terrible sin. Dr. Bonar asked, "Which is of greater weight in the eyes of God—your sin, black as it is, or the Blood of Jesus, shed for sinners?" Joyfully the young man answered, "I am sure the Blood of Jesus weighs more heavily than even my sin." Writing "No, Not Despairingly," Dr. Bonar emphasized that the antidote to "crimson sin" is "the cleansing Blood of the Lamb of God."

Dr. Bonar loved young people and spent much time with them in mission and Sunday school work. When he observed in the young people a somewhat indifferent spirit toward the psalm singing at church but a jubilant spirit in their weekday songs, he decided to write sacred words for their joyful tunes. The experiment brought excellent results. A woman who had attended his Wednesday afternoon Bible class for girls recalled in later years, "We still cherish the hymn he wrote especially for us. It asked, 'Shall this life of mine be wasted? Shall this vineyard lie untilled? Then, no longer idly dreaming, Shall I fling my years away; But, each precious hour redeeming, Wait for the eternal day.'"

Bonar edited two magazines, published many books, and wrote hundreds of tracts. His tract *Believe and Live,* a favorite of Queen Victoria, sold a million copies.

One of Bonar's most popular hymns is, "I Heard the Voice of Jesus Say." Bonar published it in *Hymns Original and Selected* in 1846, though apparently it was written several years prior to that. David Breed calls the hymn "one of the most ingenious hymns in the language," pointing out that "each stanza divides equally between invitation and response." Stanza 1 suggests "a weary soul in search of rest from the heavy burden of sin and a heart that gladly responds to our Lord's invitation of Matthew 11:28." Stanza 2, which is based on the comforting promise of John 4:14, pictures "the restless soul striving after pleasure and excitement and finding satisfaction in drinking of the Water of Life." In stanza 3 "the traveler along life's dark way is inquiring for guidance and is told to look upward to the light that will lead him safely on." The inspiration is John 8:12.

In 1866 Bonar moved back to Edinburgh, laboring with much fruit as pastor of the Chalmers Memorial Church. In 1883 he was elected moderator of the Free Church. He died on July 31, 1889. His memorial service concluded with the singing of his hymn, "Ah! 'Tis Heaven at Last!"

"I Heard the Voice of Jesus Say" has had many appealing tunes. VOX DILECTI (John B. Dykes, 1823-1876) "perfectly balances the call of Jesus and the soul's response by using a minor key for the invitation and a major key for the response." Dykes composed this tune for this text in 1868. In many hymnbooks, however, the tune is "An English Air." THIRD MODE MELODY by Thomas Tallis (1567) is also very effective.

I Must Tell Jesus
1894

I must tell Jesus all of my trials;
I cannot bear these burdens alone;
In my distress He kindly will help me;
He ever loves and cares for His own.

Refrain:

I must tell Jesus! I must tell Jesus!
I cannot bear my burdens alone;
I must tell Jesus! I must tell Jesus!
Jesus can help me, Jesus alone.

I must tell Jesus all of my troubles;
He is a kind, compassionate Friend;
If I but ask Him, He will deliver,
Make of my troubles quickly an end.

Tempted and tried I need a great Saviour,
One who can help my burdens to bear;
I must tell Jesus, I must tell Jesus;
He all my cares and sorrows will share.

O how the world to evil allures me!
O how my heart is tempted to sin!
I must tell Jesus, and He will help me
Over the world the victory to win.

—Elisha Albright Hoffman

A woman in Lebanon, Pennsylvania, was on the bed of affliction. Her body was so racked with pain that her spirit seemed to be deflated, leaving her in deep despair. One day her pastor, the Reverend Elisha A. Hoffman, came to counsel with her. After she had rehearsed her trials, she asked, "What shall I do? Can you help me?" Pastor Hoffman prayed with her and read pertinent Scripture. Then he advised, "You must tell Jesus about your problems." When she had meditated on the suggestion for a few moments, she began to repeat over and over again— "Yes, I must tell Jesus."

As Pastor Hoffman was on his way home, the woman's happy words—"Yes, I must tell Jesus"—kept ringing in his heart and mind. Finally at home, he sat down and wrote the words to the song, "I Must Tell Jesus." First he stated the problem—"I must tell Jesus all of my trials. I cannot bear these burdens alone." Although this is good advice, more is needed than merely stating a problem. "In my distress," he continued, "He kindly will help me. He ever loves and cares for His own." Still he heard her repeating, "I must tell Jesus"; so he added a refrain to emphasize the phrase. Four times in four lines the minister repeats, "I must tell Jesus." He composed his own tune for the hymn, and they were published in *Pentecostal Hymns* in 1894. We use the same tune today.

Care-worn souls beyond number have been blessed by the instruction of this song. Women have happily sung it as they scrubbed their floors, laundered their clothes, and rocked their babies; and men have sung it at their work.

A woman inspired this song, and a man wrote it; therefore it is limitless in its outreach. Who in life—young or old, male or female, rich or poor, of high rank or low station—has not known trouble? And this hymn encourages all to cast their care upon Him for He cares for His own.

Elisha A. Hoffman was born in Orwigsburg, Pennsylvania, on May 7, 1839. Though originally connected with the Evangelical Association, a German Wesleyan denomination, he pastored the Benton Harbor Presbyterian Church in Michigan for thirty-three years. In his spare time, Elisha wrote more than 2000 hymns, the more familiar ones being such hymns as "Are You Washed in the Blood?" (words and tune) "Glory to His Name" (words only), and "Leaning on the Everlasting Arms" (words only). Elisha's main ministry centered on people from the so-called "other side of the track." He worked faithfully and lovingly with these people, and they felt deep appreciation for him. He died in 1929.

I Need Thee Every Hour
1872

I need Thee every hour,
   Most gracious Lord;
No tender voice like Thine
   Can peace afford.

Refrain:

I need Thee, O I need Thee;
Every hour I need Thee;
O bless me now, my Saviour,
I come to Thee!

I need Thee every hour,
   Stay Thou near by;
Temptations lose their power
   When Thou art nigh.

I need Thee every hour,
   In joy or pain;
Come quickly and abide,
   Or life is vain.

I need Thee every hour,
   Teach me Thy will;
And Thy rich promises
   In me fulfill.

I need Thee every hour,
   Most Holy One;
O make me Thine indeed,
   Thou blessed Son!

—Annie (Sherwood) Hawks

More than 400 hymns are attributed to Annie S. Hawks, but "I Need Thee Every Hour" is the only one remaining in common usage. Written in April 1872, its simple wording communicates the Christian's "ever present sense of needing divine help and guidance." It blends the voice, the will, the promises, the holiness, and the abiding presence of the One who is "able to do exceeding abundantly above all that we ask or think" (Ephesians 3:20).

"I Need Thee Every Hour" is based on John 15:4-5 and was first performed at the National Baptist Sunday School Convention in Cincinnati in November 1872. Soon the hymn was translated into many languages. It was featured at the World's Fair in Chicago and was made popular by the Moody-Sankey meetings.

Shortly before her death, Mrs. Hawks gave this background of the hymn:

> Whenever my attention is called to it I am conscious of great satisfaction in the thought that I was permitted to write the hymn, "I Need Thee Every Hour," and that it was wafted out to the world on the wings of love and joy, rather than under the stress of a great personal sorrow, with which it has so often been associated in the minds of those who sing it.
>
> I remember well the morning . . . when in the midst of the daily cares of my home . . . I was so filled with the sense of nearness to the Master that, wondering how one could live without Him either in joy or pain, these words, "I need Thee every hour," were ushered into my mind, the thought at once taking full possession of me . . .
>
> For myself the hymn was prophetic rather than expressive of my own experience at the time it was written, and I do not understand why it so touched the great throbbing heart of humanity. It was not until long years after, when the shadow fell over my way— the shadow of a great loss [supposed by some to be the death of her husband]—that I understood something of the comforting in the words I had been permitted to write and give out to others in my hours of sweet security and peace.

Annie Sherwood Hawks was born in Hoosick, New York, on May 28, 1835. At the age of fourteen she was writing poems for a newspaper. At twenty-four she was married to a very fine man and moved with him to Brooklyn, New York. There they joined a church pastored by Robert Lowry, the noted hymnist. Lowry recognized Mrs. Hawks' talent for writing and encouraged her to use it as a means of witnessing to the Lord's saving power and faithfulness. "If you will write the words," he challenged, "I will write the music." And he kept his promise. Mrs. Hawks' closing years were spent in Bennington, Vermont, with her daughter. On January 3, 1918, when she was almost eighty-two, Annie Hawks was called to be with the One who was the acknowledged need of her life.

Robert Lowry (1826-1899) was born in Philadelphia, March 12, 1826. Listed among his more familiar melodies are the tunes to "All the Way My Saviour Leads Me," "Saviour, Thy Dying Love," and "We're Marching to Zion." He is also noted for his hymn, "Shall We Gather at the River?" He collaborated with William H. Doane in preparing numerous collections. Lowry died at Plainfield, New Jersey, on November 25, 1899.

It Is Well with My Soul
1873

When peace, like a river, attendeth my way,
 When sorrows like sea-billows roll;
Whatever my lot, Thou hast taught me to say,
 "It is well, it is well with my soul."

Refrain:

It is well with my soul
It is well, it is well with my soul.

Though Satan should buffet, though trials should come,
 Let this blest assurance control,
That Christ hath regarded my helpless estate,
 And hath shed His own blood for my soul.

My sin—oh, the bliss of this glorious thought,
  My sin—not in part, but the whole,
Is nailed to the cross and I bear it no more,
  Praise the Lord, praise the Lord, O my soul!

And, Lord, haste the day when the faith shall be sight,
  The clouds be rolled back as a scroll,
The trump shall resound and the Lord shall descend,
  "Even so"—it is well with my soul.

—Horatio G. Spafford

Often in our hymn singing we tend to give more attention to the tune than to the message. Both are important, of course; but how much more worshipful our services would be if more Christians gave serious thought to singing "in your heart unto the Lord," and "with the understanding also" as Scripture instructs us to do (Ephesians 5:19; I Corinthians 14:15). Hymns do not merely happen; back of every hymn is an underlying theme that was, in many instances, prompted by some unusual circumstance in the life of the hymn writer. We need to catch a glimpse of the underlying motive as well as to study both the words and the music.

Connected with "It Is Well with My Soul"—directly or indirectly—are several disasters that claimed hundreds of lives. Tragedy preceded the writing of the words; tragedy followed the setting of the words to music.

Consider the calamitous background of the words of this song. Horatio G. Spafford was born in North Troy, New York, on October 20, 1828. He became a lawyer and was a teacher of medical jurisprudence in Chicago. In his early forties, Mr. Spafford suffered two misfortunes that greatly affected his life. The first was the Chicago fire of 1871. In this fire Mr. Spafford suffered heavy material losses. But this was minor when compared with the second tragedy of about two years later.

The Spaffords and their four young daughters were booked to sail for France on the *Ville du Havre*. Because of business commitments, Mr. Spafford had to delay his trip, but Mrs. Spafford and the children sailed as planned. At the last minute Mr. Spafford seemed to have a premonition that something might go wrong, for he changed his family's cabin arrangement to the starboard side of the vessel. In mid-ocean on November 22, 1873, the *Ville du Havre* collided with a large sailing vessel. The situation was critical. Gathering her children on deck, Mrs. Spafford knelt with them and asked God to spare them, if possible, or to make them ready to die, if that were His will. The children, having been converted in a meeting held by D. L. Moody in Chicago, were fully aware that the will of the Lord is the best thing for a Christian. Within half an hour, the *Ville du Havre* had sunk into the ocean; the Spafford children, along with about 220 other passengers, had perished.

Mrs. Spafford, after being tossed about in the waves for a while, was rescued by a sailor who was rowing over the spot where the ship sank; ten days later, she landed in Cardiff, Wales. From Cardiff she sent her husband a cablegram of two words—"Saved alone." When Mr. Spafford read the cablegram, he remarked to a friend, "I am glad to trust Christ when it costs me something."

Mr. Spafford sailed to England to be with his wife. There he was joined by D. L. Moody and Ira D. Sankey, who were holding a meeting in Scotland. The evangelist and his singer, both close friends of the Spafford family, felt that they might be of some comfort to the bereaved parents. Happily, however, the evangelistic duo found that the parents, though their hearts were aching, were manifesting great strength in the Lord and seemingly were feeling no bitterness of soul. The Spaffords' attitude—"It is well; the will of the Lord be done"—is reflected in the song "It Is Well with My Soul."

One hymnologist gives this version of the actual writing of this hymn:

When the ship on which Mr. Spafford was sailing to England arrived at the exact spot of the sinking of the *Ville du Havre,* the captain called Mr. Spafford on deck and pointed out to him the tragic spot. Mr. Spafford stood silently on deck a few moments; then he returned to his cabin and penned the words.

According to Mr. Sankey, however, the song was written three years after the tragedy at sea. Sankey says that he was in the home of the Spaffords at the time of the writing of the words, and that it was in commemoration of the third anniversary of the loss of his daughters and to voice his continuing submission to the divine will that Mr. Spafford wrote the words. Whichever version is correct, the words are thought-provoking and challenging, and the Lord has used them to bless the hearts of people beyond number.

As far as it is known, this hymn has never been sung to any tune other than the one composed for it in 1876 by P. P. Bliss (1838-1876), the evangelistic singer whose name appears on numerous tunes in our hymnbooks. In Mr. Bliss' tune for this song, one can hear the gentle ripple of the waves and the heavy swell of the ocean. Mr. Bliss not only wrote the music for this song; he was also the first person to sing it. He introduced the song at Farwell Hall, Chicago.

About a month later, Mr. Bliss and his wife left their two children with his mother and took a train trip to Chicago to begin new services. As the train approached Ashtabula, Ohio, a bridge gave way, plunging the train of seven cars into the icy river below. Many people were drowned; many others were caught in the wreckage and perished in the ensuing fire. Although Mr. Bliss could have escaped, according to the report of a survivor, he would not leave his wife. The circumstances of the wreck with the terrible fire made it impossible to determine how many lost their lives, but the number is usually estimated to be eighty or ninety, making it the worst train wreck up to that time. Friends who searched for days were never able to find a trace of the thirty-eight-year-old song leader and his wife.

The blessing of this hymn to thousands throughout many years is reflected in the remark made by a friend of Horatio Spafford. Repining under severe affliction, he read Spafford's song and remarked, "If Spafford could feel like that after suffering all he suffered, I will cease my complaints and will bravely bear my affliction."

In 1881, accompanied by his wife and another daughter, Spafford went to Jerusalem to live; he remained there until his death on October 16, 1888.

Peace, Perfect Peace
1875

Peace, perfect peace, in this dark world of sin?
The blood of Jesus whispers peace within.

Peace, perfect peace, by thronging duties pressed?
To do the will of Jesus, this is rest.

Peace, perfect peace, with sorrows surging round?
On Jesus' bosom naught but calm is found.

Peace, perfect peace, with loved ones far away?
In Jesus' keeping, we are safe, and they.

Peace, perfect peace, our future all unknown?
Jesus we know, and He is on the throne.

Peace, perfect peace, death shadowing us and ours?
Jesus hath vanquished death and all its powers.

It is enough: earth's struggles soon shall cease,
And Jesus call us to heaven's perfect peace.
—Edward Henry Bickersteth

Although many fanciful stories have been woven around the writing of this famous hymn, Dr. Bickersteth's son endorsed the story that follows:

On a Sunday morning in August 1875, Bishop Bickersteth was visiting the service of Canon Gibbon, vicar of Harrogate, whose text was Isaiah 26:3: "Thou wilt keep him in perfect peace, whose mind is stayed on thee: because he trusteth in thee." Bickersteth was greatly impressed by the canon's explanation that "in the original the words are 'peace, peace,' and in the 1611 translation they are 'perfect peace.'"

That afternoon Dr. Bickersteth visited an aged relative who was dying and who seemed to be deeply troubled. Dr. Bickersteth prayed, "O Lord, give me words of comfort for this dear saint." Suddenly the morning sermon flashed into his mind. Dr. Bickersteth had always been able to express himself well in verse; and he took from his pocket a piece of paper upon which he penned the words exactly as they are sung today. As he read the words to his dying relative, the bishop was pleased to see the face of this one at death's door brighten and his spirit become peaceful. If it could help one troubled soul, he thought, might it not help others?

Returning to his home, Dr. Bickersteth called his children for their usual Sunday afternoon tea and "hymn-reciting hour." "Children," he said, "I have written you a new hymn." And they listened, delightedly, to the freshly penned words.

Hymnologist C. S. Robinson points out that this hymn is perfect for antiphonal singing (that is, separate voices or choruses singing alternatively). Its structure involves a series of couplets, with the first line asking a question about some difficulty in life—daily pressures, surging sorrow, separation from loved ones, the future, death, and earthly struggle—and the second line giving the answer by employing the name of Jesus with some word of comfort. Even the tune (PAX TECUM) bears a plaintive tone for the questioner and a bright, vigorous tone for the answering promise from the words of the Lord.

Edward Henry Bickersteth (1825-1906) came from a family distinguished for its contributions in many fields—law, medicine, music, and the church. For example, his father, Edward Bickersteth, was a lawyer turned clergy-man who was known as a prominent Evangelical clergyman. He opposed the move to allow unitarians to participate in the work of the Bible Society. He also wrote books against the emerging Tractarian Movement, a group of Anglicans who favored instituting Romanist practices in the Church of England. Edward Bickersteth also compiled a hymnbook, *Christian Psalmody*, that went through fifty-nine editions in about seven years.

The son followed in his father's footsteps with his firm stand for evangelical truth and practical devotion. Born at Islington, England, on January 25, 1825, Edward Henry Bickersteth graduated with honors from Trinity College, Cambridge, in 1848. Having had a desire to enter the ministry since he was fourteen years old, he was ordained a short time later. After serving at Banningham and Tunbridge Wells, he became vicar of Christ Church, Hampstead, and served faithfully for thirty years. He later became dean of Gloucester, and, in 1885, bishop of Exeter.

Bickersteth took an active part in promoting mission-ary work. His father had been the first secretary of the Church Missionary Society, and the son served on its governing committee, made several visits to the field, and encouraged his church to contribute generously. He was also well known as a writer of prose and poetry. "Yesterday, Today, and Forever" (1866), a narrative poem about the afterlife in the tradition of Dante and Milton, sold 27,000 copies in England and 50,000 in America, respectable sales for that day. His pen produced numerous theological and devotional works that defended orthodoxy against the growing infidelity of the late 1800s.

Today we remember Bickersteth chiefly for his hymns, thirty of which came into common usage. Using his father's hymnbook as a foundation, he edited *The Hymnal Companion to the Book of Common Prayer* (1870), which in a brief period of time became the most popular collection for evangelical Anglicans.

Facts about PAX TECUM (Latin for "Peace be with you") are sparse. The tune was written by George T. Caldbeck

(1852-ca. 1912), an English musician, and was arranged by Charles John Vincent. Caldbeck was scholarly, though poor, and his many eccentricities made it difficult for anyone to work with him. He came to the place of having to sell tracts on the street. Arrested once for lacking a "peddler's license," he identified himself as the composer of PAX TECUM and was released. It is generally supposed that Caldbeck died in 1912.

The Sands of Time Are Sinking
1857

The sands of time are sinking,
  The dawn of heaven breaks,
The summer morn I've sighed for,
  The fair, sweet morn awakes:
Dark, dark hath been the midnight,
  But dayspring is at hand,
And glory, glory dwelleth
  In Immanuel's land.

Oh! Christ He is the fountain,
  The deep, sweet well of love!
The streams on earth I've tasted,
  More deep I'll drink above:
There, to an ocean fulness,
  His mercy doth expand,
And glory, glory dwelleth
  In Immanuel's land.

I've wrestled on towards heaven,
  'Gainst storm, and wind, and tide;
Now, like a weary traveler,
  That leaneth on his guide,
Amid the shades of evening,
  While sinks life's lingering sand,
I hail the glory dawning
  In Immanuel's land.

With mercy and with judgment
  My web of time He wove,
And aye the dews of sorrow
  Were lustered by His love.
I'll bless the hand that guided,
  I'll bless the heart that planned,
When throned where glory dwelleth
  In Immanuel's land.

Oh! I am my Beloved's,
  And my Beloved's mine!
He brings a poor, vile sinner
  Into His house of wine:
I stand upon His merit,
  I know no other stand,
Not e'en where glory dwelleth
  In Immanuel's land.

The bride eyes not her garment,
  But her dear bridegroom's face;
I will not gaze at glory,
  But on my King of grace;
Not at the crown He giveth,
  But on His pierced hand;
The Lamb is all the glory
  Of Immanuel's land.

—Anne Ross (Cundell) Cousin

"The Sands of Time Are Sinking" is taken from a poem that Anne Ross (Cundell) Cousin wrote in 1857. The original poem had nineteen double stanzas and was entitled "Glory Dwelleth in Immanuel's Land." Published first in tract form under the title of "The Last Words of Samuel Rutherford," it was sent all over the world; and from this poem have emerged two hymns—"His House of Wine" or "Oh! Christ He is the Fountain," and "Immanuel's Land" or "The Sands of Time Are Sinking." In spite of the title, the poem uses some phrases and ideas that the saintly Rutherford expressed at other times in his life.

Samuel Rutherford (1600-1661), the great Scottish preacher, theologian, and political theorist, had served well as minister and teacher in the face of severe persecution. In his well-known edition of Rutherford's *Letters,* Andrew Bonar, the brother of the hymn writer Horatius Bonar, gives the following account of Rutherford's dying words:

All that is told us of his deathbed is characteristic of the man. At one time he spoke much of "the white stone" and "the new name." When he was on the threshold of glory, ready to receive the immortal crown, he said, "Now my tabernacle is weak, and I would think it a more glorious way of going home to lay down my life for the cause, at the Cross of Edinburgh or St. Andrews; but I submit to my Master's will." . . . When asked, "What think ye now of Christ?" he replied, "I shall live and adore Him. Glory, glory to my Creator and Redeemer for ever. Glory shineth in Immanuel's land." The same afternoon he said, "I shall sleep in Christ; and when I awake, I shall be satisfied with His likeness. O for arms to embrace Him!" Then he cried aloud, "O for a well-tuned harp!" This last expression he used more than once, as if already stretching out his hand to get his golden harp, and join the redeemed in their new song. He also said on another occasion, "I hear Him saying to me, 'Come up hither.'" . . . To four of his brethren, who came to see him, he said, "My Lord and Master is chief of ten thousands of thousands. None is comparable to Him, in heaven or in earth. Dear Brethren, do all for *Him.* Pray for *Christ.* Preach for *Christ.* Do all for *Christ;* beware of men-pleasing. The Chief Shepherd will shortly appear." He often called Christ "his Kingly King." While he spoke even rapturously, "I shall shine! I shall see Him as He is! I shall see Him reign, and all His fair company with Him, and I shall have my large share"—he at the same time would protest, "I renounce all that ever He made me will or do as defiled or imperfect as coming from myself. I betake myself to Christ for sanctification as well as justification." Repeating I Corinthians 1:30, he said, "I close with it! Let Him be so. He is my all and all." "If He should slay me ten thousand times I will trust." . . . On the last day of his life, in the afternoon, he said, "This night will close the door, and fasten my anchor within the veil, and I shall go away in a sleep by five o'clock in the morning." And so it was. He entered Immanuel's land at that very hour, and is now (as himself would have said) "sleeping in the bosom of the Almighty," till the Lord come.

We may add his latest words. "There is nothing now between me and the Resurrection but 'This day thou shalt be with Me in paradise.'" He interrupted one speaking in praise of his painfulness in the ministry, "I disclaim all. The port I would be in at is redemption and forgiveness of sin through His blood." Two of his biographers record that his last words were, "Glory, glory dwelleth in Immanuel's land!" as if he had caught a glimpse of its mountain-tops.

Rutherford was educated in Edinburgh and taught Latin language and literature there. In 1627 he accepted a pulpit in the small parish of Anwoth, where he labored arduously for the souls of his parishioners. Though he did not have a pleasant sounding voice, he became well known as a preacher who constantly and forcefully dwelt on the glory and loveliness of the Saviour. A theological paper he wrote won him an offer of a professorship at Utrecht in the Netherlands, but he preferred his pastorate.

The established Church of Scotland, which was episcopal at this time, looked on Rutherford's theological treatise of 1636 with disfavor, and he was deprived of his charge in Anwoth. Later, when the Covenanters came into power, Rutherford was reinstated in the church. In 1639, he became professor at St. Andrews and principal of New College. In 1643 he received appointment to the Westminster Assembly in London. He may, in fact, have been the main author of the Shorter Catechism published by that body.

In 1660, after the restoration of Charles II, Rutherford received more severe persecution and was called to appear before the next Parliament to be tried for "high treason." Illness prevented his appearance at court, and Rutherford replied, "Tell them that I have a summons already from a superior Judge and judicatory, and I behove to answer my first summons; and, ere your day arrives, I will be where few kings and great folks come." When the Privy Council deprived him of his University offices, one man defended him, saying, "Ye have voted that honest man out of his College, but ye cannot vote him out of heaven."

Anne Ross Cousin, only daughter of Dr. David Ross Cundell, a surgeon in the British army, was born in 1824 in Leith, England. Her father died when she was only three years old. In 1847 she married the Reverend William Cousin, a Presbyterian minister in London who afterwards became a minister in the Free Church of Scotland.

Mrs. Cousin's hymns, besides appearing in many hymnbooks, were published along with some of her poems in a book that has been described as "107 meditations rather than hymns." Anne took great delight in Rutherford's dying words, which she read and reread. She was intrigued by *The Life and Letters of Samuel Rutherford*, and she borrowed from the work many of Rutherford's quaint expressions. For this reason, Rutherford must receive some of the honor for "The Sands of Time Are Sinking."

Mrs. Cousin died on December 6, 1906.

The tune to which "The Sands of Time Are Sinking" is usually sung is called appropriately RUTHERFORD. It has been attributed both to Chrétien Urhan (1790-1845) and to Edward Francis Rimbault (1816-1876). Apparently Urhan wrote the melody in 1834, and Rimbault arranged it in 1867 as we find it in hymnals today.

What a Friend We Have in Jesus
ca. 1855

What a Friend we have in Jesus,
  All our sins and griefs to bear!
What a privilege to carry
  Everything to God in prayer!
O what peace we often forfeit,
  O what needless pain we bear,
All because we do not carry
  Everything to God in prayer!

Have we trials and temptations?
  Is there trouble anywhere?
We should never be discouraged,
  Take it to the Lord in prayer.
Can we find a friend so faithful,
  Who will all our sorrows share?
Jesus knows our every weakness,
  Take it to the Lord in prayer.

Are we weak and heavy-laden,
  Cumbered with a load of care?
Precious Saviour, still our refuge—
  Take it to the Lord in prayer.
Do thy friends despise, forsake thee?
  Take it to the Lord in prayer;
In His arms He'll take and shield thee,
  Thou wilt find a solace there.

—Joseph M. Scriven

If Christians would study this hymn in depth, they would have a better understanding of how to deal with their problems and manifest a more radiant Christian spirit. An effective study plan would be to underscore key words, using different colors for words that signify the problems of life and those that relate to the solution of those problems. Glancing back over the underlined words, we could see that through prayer, all of our sins, griefs, sorrows, weaknesses, and cares are resolved in One who is not only our Friend, but also our Shield, our Peace, our Refuge, and our Solace.

"What a Friend We Have in Jesus" seems to have been the author's only attempt at hymn writing. In it he shows a deep knowledge of Scripture. Reference is made to Proverbs 18:24: "There is a friend that sticketh closer than a brother"; Psalm 55:22: "Cast thy burden upon the Lord, and he shall sustain thee"; I Peter 5:7: "Casting all your care upon him; for he careth for you"; and Philippians 4:6-7: "Be careful for nothing; but in everything by prayer and supplication with thanksgiving let your requests be made known unto God. And the peace of God, which passeth all understanding, shall keep your hearts and minds through Christ Jesus."

It was formerly generally accepted that "What a Friend We Have in Jesus" was written about 1855 and that it was occasioned by the tragic drowning of the author's fiancée on the eve of their wedding day. Certainly her death changed the tenor of his life; it led him to dedicate himself and all that he had to the service of the Lord and to the aid of poor people as the Lord should lead. But according to the author, the hymn was written to comfort his mother in Ireland in a time of sorrow, and he gave a copy to no one else but a friend's mother. This is the story that is now generally accepted. Whatever its inspiration, and however it got into print, for many years the hymn was ascribed erroneously to Dr. Horatius Bonar. When he disclaimed any connection with the hymn, it was marked "Author Unknown." Years later a friend who was attending Scriven during an illness found the words at his bedside and asked, "Joseph, did you write these words?" Mr. Scriven answered, "The Lord and I did it between us."

Joseph Scriven was born in 1819 or 1820 in Dublin, Ireland. He was educated at Trinity College, Dublin, and at the age of twenty-five moved to Canada. Although Scriven was eccentric, his friends and neighbors loved him and accepted his idiosyncrasies as "endearing qualities." It was not uncommon to see Scriven walking down the streets, his familiar saw and sawhorse on his shoulder, seeking someone in need. One day a man saw him and remarked to a companion, "I would like to have that man saw some wood for me." The companion answered, "You could never get him." "Why not?" asked the first man. The second man replied, "He never works for people who can pay; he *gives* his services to widows, sick people, and to any others who are unable to pay for help."

Scriven's death, like that of his sweetheart, was the result of tragedy. His body was found in a "water-run" near Lake Rice, Canada, on October 10, 1886. When friends erected a monument in his memory at Lake Rice, it read: "Four miles north, in Pengally's Cemetery, lies the philanthropist and author of this great masterpiece written at Port Hope, 1857." Accompanying the inscription were the stanzas of Scriven's immortal hymn.

The tune ERIE or CONVERSE, to which this comforting hymn was set, has been described as "having the merits of the gospel song without having its disadvantages." It was composed in 1868 by Charles Crozat Converse, LL.D. (1832-1918). Born in Warren, Massachusetts, Converse studied musical theory and composition at Leipzig, Germany, where he became acquainted with famous musicians such as Franz Liszt and Ludwig Spohr. Returning to America he obtained a law degree (1860) and began a practice in Erie, Pennsylvania, but throughout his life he was active in many areas besides law. He composed various types of music, including symphonies, cantatas, string quartets, and both serious and popular songs. He wrote on numerous topics, frequently under the pen name Karl Reden. He was also an inventor and an organ manufacturer. He attempted to introduce a new pronoun into English ("thon" in place of "he or she" and "him or her"), but the useful innovation died with him. Though most of his work has been forgotten, the tune to "What a Friend We Have in Jesus" lives on.

Guidance & Trust

All the Way My Saviour Leads Me
1874

All the way my Saviour leads me;
  What have I to ask beside?
Can I doubt His tender mercy,
  Who through life has been my Guide?
Heavenly peace, divinest comfort,
  Here by faith in Him to dwell!
For I know, whate'er befall me,
  Jesus doeth all things well.

All the way my Saviour leads me,
  Cheers each winding path I tread,
Gives me grace for every trial,
  Feeds me with the living bread.
Though my weary steps may falter,
  And my soul athirst may be,
Gushing from the Rock before me,
  Lo! a spring of joy I see.

All the way my Saviour leads me;
  Oh, the fullness of His love!
Perfect rest to me is promised
  In my Father's house above.
When my spirit, clothed immortal,
  Wings its flight to realms of day,
This my song through endless ages:
  Jesus led me all the way.

—Fanny J. Crosby

Most of Fanny Crosby's hymns were subjective. They were born out of personal experiences. "All the Way My Saviour Leads Me" is rooted in answered prayer.

One day in 1874 Miss Crosby (1820-1915) was in particular need of five dollars. Not having any idea where she could obtain the money, she prayed earnestly that the Lord would help her. Almost within minutes an admirer called at her home for a visit. As he left, he shook hands with her, leaving in her hand a five-dollar bill. He said, "I cannot account for bringing you this money, except to believe that the Lord sent me here." Later Miss Crosby said, "My first thought was that in a wonderful way the Lord had supplied my needs. So humbled was I by His goodness that thoughts of praise began to run through my mind; and soon the words to this hymn were clear to me."

Miss Crosby sent her new poem to Dr. Robert Lowry, and he composed a suitable melody, entitling it ALL THE WAY. Words and music were first published in *Brightest and Best*, a Sunday school collection compiled by Robert Lowry and William H. Doane (Chicago, 1875). The hymn was headed by the Scripture, "The Lord alone did lead him" (Deuteronomy 32:12).

Frances Jane Crosby was born on March 24, 1820, in Putnam County, New York. At the age of six weeks she was permanently blinded by a poultice that a doctor ignorantly applied to her eyes. Instead of bemoaning her affliction, she made up her mind—at the age of eight—to "store in her heart the little jewel of contentment."

Because of her blindness, Fanny memorized a wealth of Scripture. It is said that at ten she could recite the first five books of the Old Testament and the first four books of the New Testament.

At fifteen Fanny entered a school for the blind in New York City where she was a student seven years and a teacher eleven years. When notables visited the school, Fanny would recite some of her poems. In 1843 she accompanied some students to Washington to enlist the sympathy of Congress for the education of the blind. She moved the men to tears with her poems. In 1858 Miss Crosby married a blind teacher at the school, Alexander Van Alstyne. The scholarly Van Alstyne was an accomplished musician who took pride in his wife's genius, insisting that she retain her maiden name in connection with her work. Their only child died in infancy, and Van Alstyne died in 1902.

Fanny Crosby had the ambition to live to be 100 years old. She missed her goal by five years. On February 12, 1915, her "lamp all trimmed and burning bright," she entered "the palace of the King" to see her Saviour "face to face, and tell the story, 'Saved by grace.'"

The hymn makes it apparent that Miss Crosby knew trials and heartaches, but also that she viewed every experience of life in the light of divine love, mercy, grace, comfort, and joy. Her abiding faith told her that even at death she would still be singing, "Jesus led me all the way."

(For other hymns by Fanny Crosby, see pp. 148, 184.)

Blessed Assurance, Jesus Is Mine
1873

Blessed assurance, Jesus is mine!
Oh, what a foretaste of glory divine!
Heir of salvation, purchase of God.
Born of His Spirit, washed in His blood.

Refrain:

This is my story, this is my song,
Praising my Saviour all the day long.

Perfect submission, perfect delight,
Visions of rapture now burst on my sight;
Angels descending, bring from above
Echoes of mercy, whispers of love.

Perfect submission, all is at rest,
I in my Saviour am happy and blest;
Watching and waiting, looking above,
Filled with His goodness, lost in His love.

—Fanny J. Crosby

Fanny Crosby is one of the best-loved hymn writers of all time. Her hymns cover every aspect of salvation. "Jesus Is Calling" invites the sinner to Christ; "Pass Me Not" is the sinner's plea for salvation; "Blessed Assurance" and "I Am Thine" speak of the assurance of being an "heir of salvation"; "All the Way My Saviour Leads Me" expresses confidence in divine daily guidance that provides "grace for every trial" and feeds us with "the Living Bread"; "Rescue the Perishing" challenges believers to invite "the erring" and "fallen" to "Jesus the mighty to save"; and "Saved by Grace" and "Safe in the Arms of Jesus" are a foretaste of the believer's experience at death.

Not much is known of the actual writing of "Blessed Assurance," but Fanny Crosby (1820-1915) herself related this background: Mrs. Joseph Fairchild Knapp (Phoebe P. Knapp), wife of the organizer of the Metropolitan Life Insurance Company, went to visit Miss Crosby to get her opinion of a tune Mrs. Knapp had written. "What does it say to you, Fanny?" Mrs. Knapp asked. Miss Crosby answered, "Blessed assurance, Jesus is mine." And a few minutes later Miss Crosby handed to Mrs. Knapp the completed lyrics.

Fanny Crosby's hymns number more than 8000, although many of them have appeared under various pseudonyms.

That Fanny Crosby devoted herself to gospel songs is not surprising; her own conversion was rooted in a gospel song. In 1850 she heard a revival choir sing, "Alas, and Did My Saviour Bleed?" As they sang, "Here, Lord, I give myself away; 'Tis all that I can do," she went to the altar and dedicated herself and her talents to the Lord.

In later life Miss Crosby was told by a Scottish minister, "It is too bad that God, in His many wonderful gifts to you, did not include the gift of sight." Fanny answered, "If I had been given a choice at birth, I would have asked to be blind." "Why?" he asked. She replied, "The first face ever to gladden my sight will be when I get to heaven and behold the face of the One who died for me. The doctor who applied the fatal poultice might have blun-

dered, but God did not blunder. I verily believe that God
intended that I should live my days in physical darkness
so that I might be better prepared to sing His praise and
lead others from spiritual darkness into eternal light. With
sight I would have been too distracted to have written
thousands of hymns." Fanny prayed daily that she might
win a million souls to Christ; who can doubt that through
her gospel songs her prayer was answered?

The composer of the tune ASSURANCE, Phoebe Knapp
(1839-1908), was the daughter of a noted Methodist
evangelist, Walter C. Palmer. From childhood she had a
keen interest in music. Of the more than 500 tunes that
she wrote, ASSURANCE became the most famous. She
also wrote the music for Miss Crosby's Easter hymn,
"Open the Gates of the Temple." She died in Poland
Springs, Maine, on July 10, 1908.

(For other hymns by Fanny Crosby, see pp. 148, 182.)

Count Your Blessings
1897

When upon life's billows you are tempest-tossed,
When you are discouraged, thinking all is lost,
Count your many blessings, name them one by one,
And it will surprise you what the Lord hath done.

Refrain:

Count your blessings, Name them one by one;
Count your blessings, See what God hath done;
Count your blessings, Name them one by one;
Count your many blessings, See what God hath done.

Are you ever burdened with a load of care?
Does the cross seem heavy you are called to bear?
Count your many blessings, every doubt will fly,
And you will be singing as the days go by.

When you look at others with their lands and gold,
Think that Christ has promised you His wealth untold;
Count your many blessings, money cannot buy.
Your reward in heaven, nor your home on high.

So, amid the conflict, whether great or small,
Do not be discouraged, God is over all;
Count your many blessings, angels will attend,
Help and comfort give you to your journey's end.
—Johnson Oatman, Jr.

"**M**en sing it, boys whistle it, and women rock their babies to sleep to the tune." So said Gipsy Smith of this gospel song. And indeed it has been a perennial source of blessing, inspiration, and thanksgiving to many "over-burdened, weary hearts." One biographer points out that the cheery-hearted "Mrs. Wiggs of the Cabbage Patch" (Alice Hegan Rice) had a large part in making the song popular.

Stanza 1 views life as a sea that at times has such high billows that one tends to become discouraged, thinking all is lost. Oatman is saying, "Begin to count your blessings—not merely collectively, but also individually—and you will be surprised to see all that the Lord has done for you." Stanza 2 refers to the doubts that sometimes assail a person in times of heavy problems. Again he says, "Don't give in to the doubts. Count your blessings, and every doubt will disappear. Moreover you will find yourself singing as the days go by." Stanza 3 gives a warning against covetousness. "Instead of coveting the possessions of others," the author pleads, "set your mind and affection on eternal things that money cannot buy." Stanza 4 depicts life as a conflict—sometimes great and sometimes small. "Do not be discouraged," the author suggests, "God is over all, and He sends unnumbered blessings—His angels to help and comfort you to your journey's end." The refrain reemphasizes the counting of one's blessings, making doubly clear the fact that if one centers his thoughts on God rather than on self and circumstances, he will have a happier and more useful life.

We have little data with regard to the author of "Count Your Blessings." He was born "somewhere up East" (perhaps Lumberton, New Jersey), April 21, 1856. His father, a merchant in Lumberton, had a magnificent voice, and it is said that at church his son always chose a seat next to his father so that he might listen to the voice he admired so much. Perhaps the son's inability to sing well caused him to admire his father's talent even more.

When Oatman reached maturity, his father made him a partner in the family firm. But the heavy work schedule of merchantry interfered with the work Oatman wanted to do for the Lord. Eventually he relinquished his partnership in the business and entered the ministry. The Methodist Episcopal Church ordained him and assigned him to a church in the New Jersey Conference. Again his sphere of service seemed too restrictive, so he decided to travel from church to church, giving the gospel message. Though he was never a great preacher, Oatman did his best and won many souls to the Lord. Finally, at age thirty-six, he found an outlet that seemed to satisfy him: he could preach to millions by means of sermons in song.

More than 5000 song texts are attributed to this man. His works emphasized the greatness and saving power of Jesus Christ and urged people to live on a higher plane for the Lord. For most of his poems, it is said, he would accept only a nominal one-dollar payment for each. Other popular works of his include "Higher Ground" (1892) and "No, Not One" (1895).

In Norman, Oklahoma, September 25, 1922, Mr. Oatman "scaled the utmost height" to which he referred in "Higher Ground" and entered the ranks of the redeemed to join with them in the song of heaven.

The music for this song (BLESSINGS) was composed in 1897 by Edwin Othello Excell of Stark County, Ohio. Mr. Excell was a brick mason, a singing-teacher, a music publisher, and an evangelistic singer with both Sam Jones and Gipsy Smith. By the time he died while on a campaign

with Gipsy Smith in Louisville, Kentucky (June 10, 1921),
he was recognized as one of the greatest song leaders
of his day.

Great Is Thy Faithfulness, O God My Father
1923

"Great is Thy faithfulness," O God my Father,
  There is no shadow of turning with Thee;
Thou changest not, Thy compassions, they fail not;
  As Thou hast been Thou forever wilt be.

Refrain:

"Great is Thy faithfulness! Great is Thy faithfulness!"
  Morning by morning new mercies I see;
All I have needed Thy hand hath provided—
  "Great is Thy faithfulness," Lord, unto me.

Summer and winter, and springtime and harvest,
  Sun, moon, and stars in their courses above,
Join with all nature in manifold witness
  To Thy great faithfulness, mercy, and love.

Pardon for sin and a peace that endureth,
  Thine own dear presence to cheer and to guide;
Strength for today and bright hope for tomorrow,
  Blessings all mine, with ten thousand beside!

—Thomas O. Chisholm

The Old Testament prophet Jeremiah wrote, "It is of
the Lord's mercies that we are not consumed, because
his compassions fail not. They are new every morning:
great is thy faithfulness" (Lamentations 3:22-23). James,
a New Testament "servant of God and of the Lord Jesus
Christ," wrote, "Every good gift and every perfect gift is
from above, and cometh down from the Father of lights,
with whom is no variableness, neither shadow of turning"

(James 1:17). Centuries later Thomas Chisholm was reading these passages and felt inspired to put them into verse. First, he calls on all of nature to witness to God's faithfulness in all circumstances, in all seasons, and in all ages. He cites pardon for sin, peace that endures, the divine presence to cheer and to guide, and daily strength and hope. Feeling hopeless to enumerate all of God's blessings, he summarizes the rest in the words "and ten thousand other blessings besides." Chisholm ends his prayer-praise on a personal note: "Blessings all mine" and "Lord, unto me."

Thomas O. Chisholm was born on July 29, 1866, in Simpson County, Kentucky, near the town of Franklin. He was educated in a country school and at sixteen became a teacher at the school. At twenty-one Thomas accepted the post of associate editor of the *Franklin Favorite*, a weekly newspaper. In 1893, while attending a revival meeting conducted by Dr. H. C. Morrison, Thomas felt convicted of sin and was converted. Dr. Morrison was impressed with the young man's sincerity and talents, and he invited him to move to Louisville, Kentucky, and become manager and editor of Dr. Morrison's religious periodical, the *Pentecostal Herald.* At Louisville Thomas felt a call into the ministry and was ordained in the Methodist Church. His first pastorate was at Scottsville, Kentucky. Later, because of ill health, Thomas moved to Winona Lake, Indiana, to be near the Billy Sunday-Homer Rodeheaver headquarters. Even though his primary work was in the field of insurance, he preached as he was able. His next move was to Vineland, New Jersey, where he again combined the ministry and insurance business. In addition, Thomas took up a new work—writing hymns and religious verse. In 1953 the aged hymn writer entered a Methodist retirement home in Ocean Grove, New Jersey, remaining there until his death on February 29, 1960. His obituary in the March 2, 1960, issue of the *New York Times* shows the high esteem in which he was held.

Chisholm is credited with 1200 hymns and devotional poems. Only 800 hymns were published, and fewer were set to music. Two of the hymnist's more popular songs, in addition to "Great Is Thy Faithfulness," are "Living for Jesus" and "The Prodigal Son," both of which have been translated into several foreign languages.

At seventy-five Chisholm wrote to a friend, saying, "My income has not been large at any time due to impaired health in the earlier years which has followed me on until now. . . . I must not fail to record here the unfailing faithfulness of a covenant-keeping God and that He has given me many wonderful displays of His providing care, for which I am filled with astonishing gratefulness."

Chisholm mailed some of his poems to William M. Runyan, an accomplished musician at Moody Bible Institute and an editor at Hope Publishing Company. Mr. Runyan was deeply impressed with "Great Is Thy Faithfulness," and he prayed, "Lord, help me to write a tune that will help carry the message in a worthy way." The hymn's popularity proves that the musician's prayer was answered. Runyan's tune appeared first in *Songs of Salvation and Service* (1923). It was given the title of FAITHFULNESS in the *Baptist Hymnal* (1956).

Runyan was the son of a Methodist minister. He was born on January 21, 1870, in Marion, New York, and at fourteen moved to Kansas with his parents where he studied and also taught music until his ordination in 1891. For the next twelve years he served various pastorates before becoming associated with John Brown University at Sulphur Springs, Arkansas. In 1925, Runyan moved to Chicago and served as an editor at Moody Bible Institute and Hope Publishing Company. Because of his accomplishments in composing at least 300 gospel songs, editing magazines, and compiling and editing hymnbooks, Runyan was honored with the LL.D. degree by Wheaton College. Runyan died in Pittsburg, Kansas, on July 29, 1957.

Guide Me, O Thou Great Jehovah
1745

Guide me, O Thou great Jehovah,
  Pilgrim through this barren land;
I am weak, but Thou art mighty;
  Hold me with Thy powerful hand;
    Bread of heaven,
  Feed me till I want no more.

Open now the crystal fountain,
  Whence the healing stream doth flow;
Let the fire and cloudy pillar
  Lead me all my journey through;
    Strong Deliverer,
  Be Thou still my strength and shield.

When I tread the verge of Jordan,
  Bid my anxious fears subside;
Death of death, and hell's destruction,
  Land me safe on Canaan's side.
    Songs of praises,
  I will ever give to Thee.

Usually omitted:

Musing on my habitation,
  Musing on my heav'nly home
Fills my soul with holy longing,
  Come, my Jesus, quickly come:
    Vanity is all I see
  Lord, I belong with Thee.

—William Williams

"Guide Me, O Thou Great Jehovah" has been described as "the genuine heart song." For more than two centuries it has encouraged Christians around the world. Three women missionaries in China customarily sang this song each evening before retiring. One evening when their tent was surrounded by bandits, the women sang as though nothing unusual were happening. When they came to the words, "I am weak, but Thou are mighty," they felt an upsurge of comfort and courage. They said, "He is our 'strength and shield' and our 'Strong Deliverer.'" On a Christmas Day these women were in the clutches of robbers, having no nourishment except hard, dry bread and tea. They sang, "Bread of heaven, Feed me till I want no more," and felt secure. Like Paul and Silas, not even imprisonment could daunt their spirits and silence their voices of praise.

On April 2, 1865, General George E. Pickett wrote a letter to his wife, describing defeat at the Battle of Five Forks. He said, "I thanked the men for their bravery, and they responded with cheers and praise for me. In the midst of these cheers . . . old Gentry's voice began to sing the old hymn which the soldiers knew that I loved: 'Guide me, oh, thou great Jehovah. . . .' Voice after voice joined in till from all along the line the plea rang forth: 'Be my sword and shield and banner, Be the Lord my righteousness.'" [These words apparently come from one of the original stanzas usually omitted in today's hymnals.] General Pickett said that his eyes were brimming with tears as he had to say, "March!"

"Guide Me, O Thou Great Jehovah" opens with a plea for help, suggesting the need for stronger help than any man can give. Stanza 1 likens Christians to pilgrims "in a barren land," too weak to make it on their own. The stanza ends with the thought that God provides temporal, as well as spiritual, needs. Stanza 2 implores the "Great Jehovah" to send healing waters from "the crystal fountain" that flows freely and eternally. Citing the example of the "fiery, cloudy pillar" by which God led Israel from Egyptian bondage into the Promised Land, the petitioner pleads, "As Thou wast *their* strength and stay, Be Thou *my* strength and stay." Stanza 3 alludes to the swelling currents of the Jordan through which God led Israel on dry ground. In many hymnals since 1847 the words "Death of death and hell's destruction" have become "Bear me through the swelling current." The doxology "Songs of praises . . ." closes the stanza, and it usually ends the hymn. A fourth stanza, customarily omitted, longs for the heavenly home, requesting, "Come, my Jesus, quickly come. Everything here is vanity. I long to be with Thee."

Armin Haeussler (*The Story of Our Hymns*) points out that in every stanza and in almost every line of this hymn God's help to man in his earthly walk correlates with His help to Israel on their march to the promised land. "Bread of heaven" parallels "the manna in the wilderness." Haeussler also emphasizes the personal aspect of the hymn, as in the use of the personal pronoun.

"Guide Me, O Thou Great Jehovah" was written in 1745 by William Williams (1717-1791), the greatest Welsh hymn writer. The hymn has been translated into seventy-five languages. To Peter Williams (probably not related to William) goes the credit for the English translation of stanzas 1, 3, and 5 of the original five stanzas in Welsh in 1771. The author accepted Peter's translation and in 1772 made his own for stanzas 3 and 4, adding an additional stanza. (Some authorities attribute the translation of stanzas 3 and 4 to the son of William Williams— John Williams, principal of Trevecca College.)

William Williams was born near Llandovery, Wales, in 1717. His childhood desire was to be a medical doctor and so help ease physical suffering. Instead, he became an evangelist to point men to the Great Physician in whose shed blood is healing for the soul. At twenty William attended a Sunday morning service of an itinerant preacher, Howell Harris, who preached from a tombstone in a church cemetery in order to reach people as they left the church service. The self-styled "Tombstone Preacher" made a deep impression on Williams, and he decided to follow Harris' example of preaching in every possible place. For fifty years Williams traveled thousands of miles a year, preaching in all kinds of weather and with or without man's approval.

Williams became friendly with the Welsh Calvinistic Methodists, a group of Christians who favored Whitefield in his theological controversy with the Wesleys. (Wesleyan theology is classified as Evangelical Arminianism, while Whitefield and his followers were Calvinists.) This group challenged Williams to upgrade their hymns by writing some of his own, and "Guide Me, O Thou Great Jehovah" was his initial response. At twenty-eight Williams published a hymnbook, *Hallelujah* (1745), that quickly went into a third edition.

A powerful preacher and an accomplished vocalist, Williams was called "the Sweet Singer of Wales." He wrote approximately 800 hymns in Welsh and 100 in English. When he was denied advancement beyond the level of deacon in the Church of England because of his evangelistic methods, he said, "I have been disciplined too many times for preaching outside my parish. I look to the Lord, not to man for guidance." Like the Psalmist, Williams learned many spiritual lessons from nature. Williams' hymns, in their day, were a "mighty educational and cultural force." The hymns encouraged reading and also stirred men to action. Many illiterates who had always learned hymns by ear took reading lessons in order to learn the hymns more quickly.

In 1772 Williams published in leaflet form the four stanzas of "Guide Me, O Thou Great Jehovah." He headed the hymn with these words: "A Favorite hymn sung by Lady Huntingdon's young Collegians. Printed by the desire of many Christian friends. Lord, give it Thy blessing!"

Peter Williams (1722-1796), the translator of this hymn, was converted in a Whitefield revival in Wales. At Carmarthen College he was warned by a tutor not to attend the services of the "fanatical Whitefield." Ignoring the warning, Peter went with his friends to the meeting and was converted.

CWM RHONDDA, one of the finest Welsh hymn tunes, was composed by John Hughes (1873-1932) in 1907 for the annual singing festival (Cymânfau Ganu) at the Capel, Rhondda, Pontypridd, Wales. There already being a RHONDDA, he added CWM to distinguish his tune. (Pronounced "koom rrhawn-tha," the words mean "the valley of the Rhondda," referring to a river of that name in South Wales.) By 1932 the tune had celebrated 5000 festivals in Great Britain.

From the age of twelve Hughes was a hard worker. Music seemed to be especially easy for him, and he used his gift of music to the glory of the One who had given it to him. In addition to hymn tunes, Hughes wrote anthems and Sunday school marches. According to his widow, this tune was composed on a Sunday morning at Salem Chapel, a country church in Wales. The *Presbyterian Hymnal* of 1933 was apparently the first wedding of Hughes' tune to Williams' text.

He Leadeth Me, O Blessed Thought
1862

He leadeth me, O blessed thought!
O words with heavenly comfort fraught!
Whate'er I do, where'er I be,
Still 'tis God's hand that leadeth me.

Refrain:

He leadeth me, He leadeth me!
By His own hand He leadeth me!
His faithful follower I would be,
For by His hand He leadeth me.

Sometimes 'mid scenes of deepest gloom,
Sometimes where Eden's bowers bloom,
By waters still, o'er troubled sea,
Still 'tis His hand that leadeth me.

Lord, I would clasp Thy hand in mine,
Nor ever murmur nor repine;
Content, whatever lot I see,
Since 'tis my God that leadeth me.

And when my task on earth is done,
When, by Thy grace, the victory's won,
E'en death's cold wave I will not flee,
Since God through Jordan leadeth me.
—Joseph Henry Gilmore

The birthplace of this hymn was a brownstone dwelling in Philadelphia, Pennsylvania; the time was the evening of March 26, 1862. According to the author, Joseph Henry Gilmore, the background of the hymn is this:

I was invited to preach for two Sundays at the First Baptist Church of Philadelphia. At the mid-week service, on the 26th of March, 1862, I set out to give the people an exposition of the Twenty-third Psalm. I had given this exposition on three or four other occasions; but this time I did not get beyond the words "He leadeth me." So greatly impressed was I with the blessedness of divine guidance that I made this my theme.

It was the darkest hour of the Civil War. . . . It may subconsciously have led me to realize that God's leadership is the one significant fact in human experience, that it makes no difference how we are led, or whither we are led, so long as we are sure that God is leading us.

At the close of the mid-week meeting a few of us went to the home of my host, good Deacon Wattson. There we continued our discussion of divine guidance. While I was still talking and listening, I wrote on a piece of my exposition manuscript the words to this hymn. I handed the paper to my wife and more or less forgot the incident.

In 1865 I went to Rochester, New York, to preach a "trial sermon" at the Second Baptist Church. I picked up a church hymnal to see what songs they sang and was surprised to have the book fall open to the very song I had written three years earlier. To me this was an indication of divine leadership with regard to my acceptance of this pastorate.

When I returned home, I related this experience to my wife. "I do not understand it," I said. "My words had been set to music by Dr. William B. Bradbury; yet I had not given the words to anybody." My wife smiled and said, "I can explain it, Joseph. I felt that the words would bless the hearts of people in those troublesome times; so I sent the poem to *The Watchman and Reflector* [Boston]. I am glad to know that they have printed it." Later I found that Dr. Bradbury had read the poem in *The Watchman* and had felt that it should be set to music and published. I had written four stanzas and a two-line refrain; Dr. Bradbury had added only the last two lines of the refrain.

Joseph Gilmore was born in Boston, Massachusetts, on April 29, 1834. After graduating from Brown University and Newton Theological Seminary with honors, Gilmore served as pastor of Baptist churches in New Hampshire and New York. He taught Hebrew for a year at Rochester Theological Seminary and spent two years as private secretary to his father, who was governor of New Hampshire during the Civil War. In 1868 he became professor of logic, rhetoric, and English literature at the University of Rochester. Gilmore served forty years in the latter position; then he was made professor emeritus, an honor he held until his death on July 23, 1918.

William Batchelder Bradbury (1816-1868) was a native of York, Maine. He studied organ and voice in Boston and abroad and became an accomplished organist and choirmaster. His first position was at a small church that offered him twenty-five dollars per annum to play the organ. Upon assuming his duties he found that the type of organ owned by the church required that the musician depress the keys, then pull them up again to stop the sound. He promptly asked that his pay be doubled, since, as he told them, double work was required. Bradbury greatly enhanced church and choral music in America, publishing at least fifty-nine different hymn books.

The tune Bradbury wrote to go with "He Leadeth Me, O Blessed Thought" is called AUGHTON or HE LEADETH ME. It was published with Gilmore's text in Bradbury's *Golden Censor: a Musical Offering to the Sabbath Schools of Children's Hosannas to the Son of David*, 1864.

How Firm a Foundation
1787

How firm a foundation, ye saints of the Lord,
Is laid for your faith in His excellent Word!
What more can He say, than to you He hath said,
To you who for refuge to Jesus have fled?

"In every condition, in sickness, in health;
In poverty's vale, or abounding in wealth;
At home and abroad; on the land, on the sea,
As thy days may demand, shall thy strength ever be!

"Fear not, I am with thee, O be not dismayed,
For I am thy God, and will still give thee aid;
I'll strengthen thee, help thee, and cause thee to stand,
Upheld by My righteous, omnipotent hand.

"When through the deep waters I call thee to go,
The rivers of woe shall not thee overflow;
For I will be with thee thy troubles to bless,
And sanctify to thee thy deepest distress.

"When through fiery trials thy pathway shall lie,
My grace, all-sufficient, shall be thy supply;
The flame shall not hurt thee; I only design
Thy dross to consume, and thy gold to refine.

"E'en down to old age, all My people shall prove
My sovereign, eternal, unchangeable love;
And when hoary hairs shall their temples adorn,
Like lambs they shall still in My bosom be borne.

"The soul that on Jesus still leans for repose,
I will not, I will not desert to his foes;
That soul, though all hell should endeavor to shake,
I'll never, no never, no never forsake!"
—Anonymous ("K" in John Rippon's *Selection of Hymns*)

Fearful hearts, tired bodies, and confused minds by the thousands have been comforted by this "wonderful paean of faith in divine love and providence." Written to believers, it offers comfort to every age, in every condition. What Christian soul would not be buoyed by the two "nots" and three "nevers" of the last stanza? And who would not find comfort in the knowledge that whether one is at home or abroad, on land or sea, in sickness or health, in poverty or wealth, he has the assurance of the Lord's presence and of strength for the day's demands?

Andrew Jackson, in his last illness, said, "There is a beautiful hymn on the exceeding great and precious promises of God to His people. It was a favorite with my dear wife, and I would like to have you sing it now. The hymn is 'How Firm a Foundation.'" A favorite of Robert E. Lee, Theodore Roosevelt, and Woodrow Wilson, this hymn was sung at the funeral of each.

There is abundant Scripture upon which this anonymous hymn is based. Deuteronomy 33:25: "And as thy days, so shall thy strength be." Psalm 9:9: "The Lord also will be a refuge for the oppressed, a refuge in times of trouble." Isaiah 43:2: "When thou passest through the waters, I will be with thee; and through the rivers, they shall not overflow thee: when thou walkest through the fire, thou shalt not be burned; neither shall the flame kindle upon thee." II Corinthians 12:9: "And he said unto me, My grace is sufficient for thee: for my strength is made perfect in weakness." And Hebrews 13:5: "For he hath said, I will never leave thee, nor forsake thee."

Although many hymnbooks omit stanza 2 of this hymn, this practice does violence to the text. It leaves unanswered the important question of stanza 1: "What more can He say than to you He hath said, to you who for refuge to Jesus have fled?" Stanza 2 sets the stage, so to speak, for the many occasions described by the author as times of fleeing to Jesus for refuge. It is equally devastating to have stanzas 3 and 4 omitted, as is the practice of some hymnbooks. The ideal arrangement is every stanza in every hymnbook.

Who wrote this imperishable hymn? The exact authorship has been and still is uncertain. John Rippon, in his *Selection of Hymns from the Best Authors* (1787), identifies the writer only by the initial "K." Other hymnologists suggest George Keith (also spelled Kethe), a London bookseller and composer; Robert Keen, composer of the tune GEARD to which the hymn was originally sung; Caroline Keen; and a Mr. Kirkham, both a hymn writer and a publisher. Because the latter hymn writer, Mr. Kirkham, omitted the hymn from his compilation of hymns, most authorities would argue against his authorship in this instance.

Equally baffling is the identity of the composer of the old-time Southern melody, FOUNDATION (also BELLE-VUE or CONVENTION) to which this hymn is usually sung. It has been attributed erroneously by some to Anne Steele. The error was perpetrated when a poor page layout in a hymnal of 1889 caused it to appear that Anne Steele was the composer. Apparently the first printed version of this pentatonic melody, so typical of many Southern folk tunes, was in Joseph Funk's *Genuine Church Music* (Winchester, Virginia, 1832), where it is called PROTECTION.

Some hymnals use instead of or in addition to FOUNDATION the tune ADESTE FIDELES (sometimes called PORTUGUESE HYMN). This tune is discussed in connection with "O Come, All Ye Faithful" (page 83).

I Think When I Read That Sweet Story of Old
1841

I think when I read that sweet story of old,
  When Jesus was here among men,
How He called little children as lambs to His fold,
  I should like to have been with Him then.
I wish that His hands had been placed on my head,
  That His arms had been thrown around me,
And that I might have seen His kind look when He said,
  "Let the little ones come unto Me."

Yet still to His footstool in prayer I may go,
  And ask for a share in His love;
And if I thus earnestly seek Him below,
  I shall see Him and hear Him above,
In that beautiful place He has gone to prepare,
  For all who are washed and forgiven;
And many dear children are gathering there,
  For of such is the kingdom of heaven.

But the thousands and thousands who wander and fall
  Never heard of that heavenly home;
I should like them to know there is room for them all,
  And that Jesus has bid them to come.
I long for the joy of that glorious time,
  The sweetest, and brightest, and best,
When the dear little children of every clime
  Shall crowd to His arms and be blest.

—Jemima (Thompson) Luke

This popular children's hymn is a skillful blend of the past, the present, and the future. It embraces much Scripture and describes in few words our Lord's earthly ministry, His resurrection, His ascension and intercession, His preparation of our heavenly home that we gain by being "washed and forgiven," His desire that none should perish, and His Great Commission. The words "room for them all" suggests Scripture's "whosoever will."

"I Think When I Read That Sweet Story of Old" was written in 1841. Originally it contained two stanzas of eight lines each—stanzas embodying the thrill of knowing the Lord and of communing with Him. Much later, however, Mrs. Luke added a third stanza to challenge young people to help spread the gospel throughout the world.

The first writing of this hymn was on the back of an envelope. Jemima Thompson had been in attendance at Normal Infant School to "obtain knowledge of the system." As she had watched the teachers march around the room and had heard the marching tune—a Greek air, "Salamis"— she found herself intrigued with the melody and began a search for appropriate words. She said, "I searched several Sunday school hymnals for words to suit the measure, but in vain." One day while riding alone in a stagecoach, returning from a missionary trip of five miles, Jemima began to hum the haunting Greek air. Suddenly she became aware of lyrics that were forming in her heart and mind. And taking an envelope from her purse, she began to record the words. In her next class at home, she taught the words to her school children, who, on the following Sunday, sang the hymn at her father's church. So impressed with the song was the Reverend Mr. Thompson that he asked, "Who wrote that hymn?" The children happily replied, "Jemima wrote it." The next day "Proud Papa" sent a copy of the hymn to *The Sunday School Teachers' Magazine,* and they printed it immediately.

Jemima Thompson Luke was born near London on August 19, 1813. The daughter of an English philanthropist and minister, she was converted at the age of ten and at thirteen was writing anonymously for *The Juvenile Magazine.* Some time later she edited *The Missionary Repository,* which was the first missionary magazine ever published for children. Contributors to this magazine included Livingstone, Moffat, and James Montgomery. Jemima had signed up to go to India as a missionary to women, but ill health stood in her way. By means of her song, however, she has reached multitudes for the

Lord and has inspired hosts of children to answer God's call to the mission field.

In 1843 Jemima married the Reverend Samuel Luke, a Congregational minister. In 1851 she published *The Female Jesuit,* and in 1859 she published *A Memoir of Eliza Anne Harris.* For the most part, however, she is noted for her one hymn.

When her husband died in 1868, Jemima began to promote the building of parsonages in communities that were too poor to provide adequate housing for their ministers. In 1904, at the age of ninety-one, she was still actively testifying to the Lord's faithfulness.

Two years later, in 1906, Mrs. Luke's earthly ministry came to a close, but her challenge to children lives on in her immortal hymn.

The tune LUKE or, as it is sometimes known, SWEET STORY, was arranged in 1859 by William B. Bradbury from the Greek melody "Salamis." It reduces the original tune to half its size, so that each of the original stanzas is divided into two four-line stanzas.

Jesus, Lover of My Soul
1738

Jesus, Lover of my soul,
  Let me to Thy bosom fly,
While the nearer waters roll,
  While the tempest still is high:
Hide me, O my Saviour, hide,
  Till the storm of life is past;
Safe into the haven guide;
  O receive my soul at last!

Other refuge have I none;
Hangs my helpless soul on Thee;
Leave, ah! leave me not alone,
Still support and comfort me.
All my trust on Thee is stayed,
All my help from Thee I bring;
Cover my defenseless head
With the shadow of Thy wing.

Thou, O Christ, art all I want;
More than all in Thee I find;
Raise the fallen, cheer the faint,
Heal the sick, and lead the blind.
Just and holy is Thy name,
I am all unrighteousness;
False and full of sin I am,
Thou art full of truth and grace.

Here is the original stanza 3, which was omitted by Wesley himself (1753) and is rarely printed:

Wilt Thou not regard my call?
Wilt Thou not accept my prayer?
Lo, I sink, I faint, I fall—
Lo, on Thee I cast my care;
Reach me out Thy gracious hand,
While I of Thy strength receive,
Hoping against hope I stand,
Dying, and behold I live!

The original stanza 5, generally printed in most hymnals today as stanza 4, reads:

Plenteous grace with Thee is found,
Grace to cover all my sin;
Let the healing streams abound;
Make and keep me pure within.
Thou of life the fountain art;
Freely let me take of Thee:
Spring Thou up within my heart;
Rise to all eternity.

—Charles Wesley

This hymn has been called "the heart hymn of the ages." A famous preacher once said, "I would rather have written 'Jesus, Lover of My Soul' than to have the fame of all the kings that ever sat on earth. Kings will die. Thy hymn will go on until the last trump brings forth the angel band."

The writer of this hymn has been severely criticized for calling our Lord "Lover." He borrowed this term from a passage in the Apocrypha, Wisdom of Solomon 11:26, which says, "O Lord, Thou lover of souls." Still another criticism deals with "the author's emphasis on prayer for protection from life's storms when he should be asking for strength and courage to walk on the water." Actually the author is not praying to escape life's problems. He realizes that problems are inevitable. Rather he prays for courage to meet the problems aright. Most people see in this hymn a smooth transition from his prayer for protection to his confession of personal sin.

The stories of how this hymn came to be written are legion. Some hymnologists interpret it as an account of the conversion experience of Charles Wesley (1707-1788). Others describe it as an outgrowth of an incident in which Wesley, seated beside an open window, felt something hit his chest. It was a dove seeking refuge from a hawk. When the hawk had to fly away without its prey, Wesley said to himself, "That is the way it is with life: safety is to be found only in Jesus Christ." A third view says that the Wesley brothers were being hunted by a mob seeking to halt their meetings. The brothers took refuge in a springhouse; and Charles found a piece of lead, hammered it to a point, and wrote, "Hide me, O my Saviour, hide, Till the storm of life is past." One story is rooted in the thoughts of the author as he was in peril at sea. The calmness of Moravian shipmates impressed him so much that he prayed, "Oh, Thou who didst still the tempestuous sea for the disciples, Thou wilt provide the safety we need on this sea as well as on the sea of life." John Julian's *Dictionary of Hymnology* reminds us, however, that these stories, as interesting and dramatic as some of them are, have no foundation in fact. Julian says, "These charming stories must be laid aside until substantiated by direct evidence from the Wesley books; or from original manuscripts or printed papers as yet unknown."

Whatever prompted the lyrics, they are a vivid description of a soul that is deeply perplexed by spiritual problems and is crying for help. Finally, the soul comes to rest securely in its Father's arms. Although the figures of speech vary, the thought is the same. And as someone has suggested, "Every line parallels a passage of Scripture." For example, these verses correspond respectively to the lines of the first stanza: John 13:1, Psalm 143:9, Psalm 69:2, Psalm 55:8, Psalm 27:5, Isaiah 25:4, Psalm 107:30, Acts 7:59.

Although some hymnologists attribute the writing of this hymn to John Wesley, it is very unlikely that he was responsible for it, for, as some have pointed out, he "opposed terms of endearment when referring to the Lord." Such conjecture notwithstanding, the hymn is so simple that a child can understand it. Note that one-syllable words predominate.

Popular tunes to this hymn include HOTHAN by Martin Madan; ALMA, a variant of "Come Ye Disconsolate"; HOLLINGSIDE by John B. Dykes; ABERYSTWYTH by Joseph Parry; and REFUGE by J. P. Holbrook. By far the most familiar tune, however, is Simeon B. Marsh's MARTYN, which he wrote in 1834 to be used with one of Newton's hymns. Marsh (1798-1875), who had little formal musical training but made up for it by diligence, taught singing schools in the Albany Presbytery in New York. An active Presbyterian layman, he was also a newspaper editor.

(For other hymns by Charles Wesley, see pp. 41, 52, 58, 78, 101, 104, 271.)

My Faith Looks Up to Thee
1830

My faith looks up to Thee,
Thou Lamb of Calvary,
  Saviour divine!
Now hear me while I pray,
Take all my guilt away,
O let me from this day
  Be wholly Thine!

May Thy rich grace impart
Strength to my fainting heart,
  My zeal inspire;
As Thou hast died for me,
O may my love to Thee
Pure, warm, and changeless be,
  A living fire!

While life's dark maze I tread,
And griefs around me spread,
  Be Thou my Guide;
Bid darkness turn to day,
Wipe sorrow's tears away;
Nor let me ever stray
  From Thee aside.

When ends life's transient dream,
When death's cold, sullen stream
  Shall o'er me roll;
Blest Saviour, then, in love,
Fear and distrust remove;
O bear me safe above,
  A ransomed soul!

—Ray Palmer

There has never been a hymn of American origin translated into so many languages, used in so many hymnals, or sung so often as this song of consecration and faith. Written in the first person, it is the prayer of a soul who has entered into and has spent much time in the "secret place of the Most High."

Described by many as "the most famous hymn of modern times" and "a spiritual gem," this composition is appropriate for study at the beginning of a new year. As one writer has pointed out, the first stanza is a prayer of conversion and consecration, the second a prayer for perseverance, zeal, and love, and the fourth a prayer for sustaining grace and divine guidance.

Born in Little Compton, Rhode Island, on November 12, 1808, the gifted author of "My Faith Looks Up to Thee" was a descendant of William Palmer, who arrived on the ship *Fortune* at Plymouth in 1621, and of John and Priscilla Alden. A Boston dry-goods store was Ray Palmer's first place of employment, and during his years as a clerk he attended Park Street Congregational Church. Under the tutelage of Sereno E. Dwight, the pastor, Palmer was converted. Dwight inspired the young man to get an education, first at Phillips' Academy and later at Yale College.

Following graduation from Yale in 1830, Palmer went to New York for a year where he taught at a select school for young ladies. He then returned to New Haven, Connecticut, to teach in a girls' college. In 1835, Palmer was ordained to the ministry.

Palmer held two pastorates: he spent fifteen years in Bath, Maine, and fifteen more in Albany, New York. Returning to New York City, he became corresponding secretary of the American Congregational Union and within twelve years had assisted in erecting 600 church buildings. In 1878, forced to retire because of ill health, he moved to Newark, New Jersey, where he continued to write and act as a supply pastor. In 1887 Ray Palmer left this life to enter the Lord's presence.

According to Palmer, the circumstances of the writing of the hymn were these: he had just finished at Yale and was teaching in New York. The girls' school was headed by a godly woman whose family took young Palmer into their home. One evening he began to think how good the Lord had been to him, and with a prayerful heart he penned the words to the now famous song. As he reread the last phrase—"a ransomed soul"—he was so touched by the greatness of God's plan of redemption that he wept.

Palmer had not thought of other eyes seeing his words. But in Boston in 1833, he met Lowell Mason, an outstanding musician. Mason inquired about Palmer's health, and then said, "Mr. Palmer, Dr. Hastings and I are getting out a new hymnbook. Do you have something to contribute?"

Palmer reached into his pocket and took out the little morocco book in which he had written "My Faith Looks Up to Thee." He handed it to Mason, and asked, "What do you think of these words?"

Mason answered, "I would like to take a copy of the words to my home and think them over." So the two men went into a nearby store and had the words copied.

At home, Mason set the words to the tune OLIVET. A few days later the two men met again. "Mr. Palmer," Mason declared, "you may live many years and do many good things, but I think you will be best known to posterity as the author of 'My Faith Looks Up to Thee.'"

One inspiring story concerning Palmer's hymn is from the Civil War. A few soldiers met in a tent to pray together before going into a fierce battle. One of them suggested that they should put in writing something to leave behind, in case they did not return. One man took out a piece of paper, and from memory wrote the words of "My Faith Looks Up to Thee." He handed it to the other soldiers to sign. Only one of those men survived the battle, but he comforted the hearts of the bereaved families by sending them copies of the signed document.

Some historians have noticed a striking parallel between Palmer and another famous hymnist—Samuel F. Smith, who wrote "My Country, 'Tis of Thee." Both men were born in 1808; both were college graduates; both became ministers; both wrote their most famous hymn early in life; both hymns were in the same meter and were given to the world at nearly the same time—1830 and 1831. Today Ray Palmer and Samuel Smith are recognized as perhaps two of the greatest hymnists America has ever produced.

My Hope Is Built on Nothing Less
1834

My hope is built on nothing less
Than Jesus' blood and righteousness;
I dare not trust the sweetest frame,
But wholly lean on Jesus' name.

Refrain:

On Christ, the solid Rock, I stand;
All other ground is sinking sand.

When darkness veils His lovely face,
I rest on His unchanging grace;
In every high and stormy gale,
My anchor holds within the veil.

His oath, His covenant, His blood,
Support me in the whelming flood;
When all around my soul gives way,
He then is all my hope and stay.

When He shall come with trumpet sound,
Oh, may I then in Him be found;
Dressed in His righteousness alone,
Faultless to stand before the throne.

—Edward Mote

Hymnologists suggest I Corinthians 3:11 as the basis of this hymn: "For other foundation can no man lay than that is laid, which is Jesus Christ." Bishop Bickersteth, an outstanding hymnist, called it "a grand hymn of faith." In its original form, the hymn was composed of six four-line stanzas, the first of which began, "Nor earth, nor hell, my soul can move." Later, stanzas 1 and 2 were combined; and stanza 5, because it lessened the hymn's force, was deleted. The refrain presents in brief the message of the hymn and also the author's trust in Jesus Christ.

"The Solid Rock," as this hymn is also called, was written in 1834 and first published anonymously in leaflet form and in various papers. In 1836 it appeared in Mr. Mote's *Hymns of Praise* and was entitled "The Immutable Basis of a Sinner's Hope." When arguments began to arise about the authorship, Mr. Mote decided to acknowledge the words as his own.

The chorus and stanza 1 of the hymn came to Mr. Mote as he was on his way to work. He says,

> I began to meditate on "the gracious experience of a Christian." Soon the chorus, and then the first stanza, came into my mind. On the following Sunday, as I came out of Lisle Street meeting, Brother King invited me to his home to try to encourage his critically ill wife. I had early tea that day; then I went to the Kings' home. Mr. King said, "Before I go to a meeting, I always sing a hymn, read Scripture, and pray. Will you join me?" He searched in vain for a hymnbook. I said, "I have some verses in my pocket, Brother King. If you like, we can sing them." Mrs. King's heart responded to the words, and Mr. King asked me to leave a copy with her. Back at home I sat by the fireside, musing upon Mrs. King's reaction to the hymn; and soon the entire hymn was clear in my mind. I committed the words to paper, making a fresh copy for Mrs. King. Later the thought came to me that as these verses had met this dying woman's needs, perhaps they would help someone else. So I had a thousand leaflets printed for distribution.

Edward Mote was born in London on January 21, 1797. His background was far from Christian. So ignorant of spiritual matters was he that he did not even know that there was a God. His parents, keepers of a public house, sent their son to a school "where no Bible was allowed." On Sundays he and other wayward boys of the neighborhood played in the streets, giving no thought to church. When Edward became an apprentice to a cabinet maker, he found himself in regular attendance at church. The reason is not given. In 1813, at the age of sixteen, Edward heard the noted Reverend John Hyatt at Tottenham Court Road Chapel. The sermon made him "think on his ways," and two years later he yielded his heart to the Lord.

Shortly, Edward answered the call to preach and built a church. His congregation, through love, offered to deed the church to him as a gift. He answered, "I want not the church; I want only the pulpit. And if I cease to preach Christ, take even the pulpit from me."

By his words "in every high and stormy gale," Mote reminds himself and others that Christians are not exempt from trouble or temptation. But he goes on to explain that "dressed in His righteousness alone" (the righteousness of Jesus Christ) we can stand "faultless before the throne."

Assurance and security were constant companions of Edward Mote. In November 1874, his health began to fail, but he felt a renewed confidence in the merit of the precious blood of Christ that was shed at Calvary and through which men become children of God. He said, "I think I am nearing Port. But the truths I have preached I am living upon, and they will do to die upon. Ah! the precious blood! The precious blood which takes away all my sins; it is this which makes peace with God."

On November 13, 1874, Edward Mote was called to be with the Lord he had served so well. His grieving church erected near his pulpit a memorial plaque that included the words, "For twenty-six years the beloved pastor of this church, preaching Christ and Him crucified, as all the sinner can need, and all the saint can desire."

The tune SOLID ROCK was composed for this text in 1863 by William B. Bradbury (1816-1868), noted musician and promoter of musical instruction.

O God, Our Help in Ages Past
1719

O God, our help in ages past,
  Our hope for years to come,
Our shelter from the stormy blast,
  And our eternal home!

Under the shadow of Thy throne
  Thy saints have dwelt secure;
Sufficient is Thine arm alone,
  And our defense is sure.

Before the hills in order stood,
  Or earth received her frame,
From everlasting Thou art God,
  To endless years the same.

Thy Word commands our flesh to dust,
  "Return ye sons of men":
All nations rose from earth at first,
  And turn to earth again.

A thousand ages in Thy sight,
  Are like an evening gone;
Short as the watch that ends the night,
  Before the rising sun.

The busy tribes of flesh and blood
  With all their lives and cares
Are carried downwards by Thy flood,
  And lost in following years.

Time, like an ever-rolling stream,
  Bears all its sons away;
They fly, forgotten, as a dream
  Dies at the opening day.

Like flowery fields the nations stand
  Pleased with the morning light;
The flowers beneath the mower's hand
  Lie withering ere 'tis night.

O God, our help in ages past,
  Our hope for years to come,
Be Thou our guide while life shall last,
  And our eternal home.

—Isaac Watts

Based on Psalm 90, this hymn probably surpasses in grandeur all others that Watts wrote. It was written shortly before the death of Queen Anne while the people of England were in a state of anxiety over her successor. Watts sought, in the original nine stanzas of this hymn, to calm the fears of his countrymen by pointing out to them, in verse, that the same God who had been their help in the past was their hope for the future.

Born in 1674, Isaac Watts was the eldest son of a Christian educator who, for his strong Christian convictions, was twice imprisoned during Isaac's infancy. Often the mother—baby Isaac in her arms—could be seen sitting on a stone at the prison gate. So Isaac inherited strong convictions and "cut his teeth," so to speak, on biblical principles.

Family altar in the Watts household was a sacred time, and the children were always attentive and reverent. One night during family prayer, however, Isaac happened to glance up and see a mouse running up a bell rope by the fireplace. At the end of the prayer, the young lad surprised everyone by quoting a rhyme he had just made up:

A mouse, for want of better stairs
Ran up a rope to say his prayers.

By the age of eight, Isaac was studying Hebrew and Greek, as well as writing verse. Some friends offered him a free education if he would give up his high Christian standards, but he flatly refused the offer. Instead he went to a dissenters' academy (that is, one operated by those who dissented from the state church) where he received an excellent education.

Before his time, hymns were rarely sung in public

worship, as only crude versions of the Psalms were considered suitable. That type of music did not appeal to Watts; so one day, at the age of eighteen, he complained of it to his father. The father, aware of his son's interest in writing poetry, answered, "If you don't like our hymns, why don't you write some?" Isaac accepted his father's challenge and sat down and wrote, "Behold the Glories of the Lamb." By the end of his life Watts had written approximately 600 hymns. He is today regarded as "the creator of the modern English hymn."

At twenty-four, Watts preached his first sermon. This was the beginning of his prominence as a theologian. A few years later, in 1693, his health began to fail, leaving him a semi-invalid the rest of his life.

Not long after this, Sir Thomas and Lady Abney, both of dissenter backgrounds, invited Watts to visit their home. The visit lengthened into thirty-six years. The Abney home was conveniently situated near the church where Watts preached.

It was during his stay with the Abneys that Watts wrote most of his hymns. They run the gamut of Christian experience—majestic, doctrinal, simple, sweet, and appealing hymns. Sinners beyond number, including Fanny Crosby, owe their conversion to Watts' hymns.

Although Watts never married, he loved children and wrote many songs for them, the best-known ones being "Hush, my dear, lie still and slumber" and "Now I lay me down to sleep."

In addition to being a noted hymn writer and one of the foremost theologians of his day, Watts also wrote books, such as *Improvement of the Mind,* and textbooks on astronomy and geography. His sole aim in prose, poetry, and preaching was to edify Christians.

On November 25, 1748, at the age of seventy-five, Isaac Watts was called home to be with the Lord. By this time he was considered a national figure. He was buried at Bunhill Fields near John Bunyan's grave.

Most current hymnals include only five or six of Watts' original nine stanzas. John Wesley altered Watts' "Our

God" to "O God," and most hymnals print the hymn as Wesley liked it.

The hymn is usually sung to the tune ST. ANNE, named so at its first appearance in 1708 for St. Anne's Church in Soho where William Croft (1678-1727), who most likely wrote the tune, was organist. One should note, however, that the first line appeared in several other tunes in the seventeenth century.

(For other hymns by Isaac Watts, see pp. 81, 93, 129, 257, 298.)

O Love That Wilt Not Let Me Go
1882

O Love that wilt not let me go,
  I rest my weary soul in Thee;
I give Thee back the life I owe,
That in Thine ocean depths its flow
  May richer, fuller be.

O Light that followest all my way,
  I yield my flickering torch to Thee;
My heart restores its borrowed ray,
That in Thy sunshine's blaze its day
  May brighter, fairer be.

O Joy that seekest me through pain,
  I cannot close my heart to Thee;
I trace the rainbow through the rain,
And feel the promise is not vain
  That morn shall tearless be.

O Cross that liftest up my head,
  I dare not ask to fly from Thee;
I lay in dust life's glory dead,
And from the ground there blossoms red
  Life that shall endless be.

—George Matheson

Some hymnologists see in this hymn the feelings of a man who, because of physical blindness, had been rejected by the woman he loved. Others regard it as an outgrowth of the frustrations of blindness. According to the author, "It was the fruit of suffering, written when I was alone and suffering a mental anguish over something that no one else knew. I wrote the words in five minutes."

In stanza 1 the author acknowledges God as the Unfailing Love to whom he owes his life, his love, and his service. Stanza 2 seems to contrast physical sight, which fades, with divine light, which never fades but shines more and more until the perfect day. Stanza 3 portrays God as Abounding Joy, turning clouds into rainbows. Stanza 4 describes God as Eternal Life, providing on the cross, for all who will accept, "life that shall endless be." The author, seeing his personal cross enmeshed in a crown, triumphantly declares, in effect, "It is not proper to ask deliverance from this burden; I must rise above it."

George Matheson was born in Glasgow, Scotland, on March 27, 1842. The son of a prosperous merchant, he developed an eye problem that, by the time he entered the University of Glasgow at the age of fifteen, put him in total darkness. Undaunted by his blindness, Matheson finished college with honors at nineteen; then, aided by a sister who mastered Greek, Latin, and Hebrew in order to help him, he spent four years in theological studies. (This sister was also his "right arm" in his pastorates: Matheson would write his sermons in full, have her read them to him twice, and then would preach them from memory.)

Besides his astonishing powers of memory, Matheson had a brilliant and creative mind that he improved by diligent and methodical study. He had a wide knowledge of many subjects and was particularly known for his grasp of philosophy. His contemporaries speculated as to what he might have done were he not limited by his handicap, which, at any rate, he overcame so admirably. In this respect Matheson's own feeling was

> My life has been an obstructed and circumscribed life, but a life of boundless sanguineness, a life of quenchless hopefulness, and a life that has beaten persistently against the cage of circumstances and at the time of abandoned work has said not "Good night," but "Good morning."

Theologically, Matheson was a leader of the liberal wing of the Scottish Church, which, however, was a fairly conservative body. On the other hand, he rejected anti-supernaturalistic rationalism and many of the conclusions of higher criticism. Evolution, a subject that occupied his thinking, he was inclined to doubt, and that in a day when it was sweeping all before it. He was critical of the theology of Schleiermacher, who is often called the founder of modern religious liberalism. On the other hand, he adopted certain unbiblical positions, largely as a result of his attraction to Hegelian philosophy. He had no sympathy with the doctrine of verbal inspiration, saying, "The treasures are in earthen vessels. The thought is the main thing." He tended to emphasize elements of Christian truth that he found in other religions, maintaining that Christianity was reconciling and fulfilling these diverse fragments of divine revelation. To him, in spite of the Fall, all men were still sons of God by nature. Nevertheless, he was orthodox on many doctrines, and he was evidently a devout and spiritual pastor with a deep concern for his people.

Licensed as a Presbyterian minister in 1866, Matheson served as an assistant at a church in Glasgow for two years. His first pastorate was in Innellan, where he remained for eighteen years. While in Innellan, he received a summons to preach before Queen Victoria. So impressed was she with his preaching and prayers that she gave him a small bust of herself. Usually she presented the visiting preachers with a photograph of herself, but out of respect for Matheson's blindness she gave him the lovely sculpture. He later accepted a position at St. Bernard's

Parish Church, a congregation of nearly 2000 members in Edinburgh, where he served from 1886 to 1899. Besides his hymn writing, his theological work, and his preaching, he wrote several widely read devotional works.

On August 28, 1906, while on a much-needed holiday, Matheson was called to "the land of fadeless day" and was interred in his family's vault at Glasgow.

Much of the success of this hymn belongs to its tune, SAINT MARGARET. This tune was composed in 1884 by Dr. Albert L. Peace (1844-1912), organist of Glasgow Cathedral and musical editor of *The Scottish Hymnal* of 1885. Peace always carried in his pocket words for which tunes were needed; and when he would find the time or would feel a sudden inspiration, he would write a tune for one of the hymns. Inspiration for SAINT MARGARET came while he was sitting on the sands of Arron, a small island in Scotland. It was written especially for this text and for inclusion in the 1884 hymnal of which Peace was musical editor.

O Perfect Love, All Human Thought Transcending
1883

O perfect Love, all human thought transcending,
  Lowly we kneel in prayer before Thy throne,
That theirs may be the love that knows no ending,
  Whom Thou forevermore dost join in one.

O perfect Life, be Thou their full assurance
  Of tender charity and steadfast faith,
Of patient hope, and quiet, brave endurance,
  With childlike trust that fears nor pain nor death.

Grant them the joy which brightens earthly sorrow;
  Grant them the peace which calms all earthly strife,
And to life's day the glorious, unknown morrow
  That dawns upon eternal love and life.

—Dorothy Frances (Blomfield) Gurney

This popular wedding hymn was written in 1883. According to Mrs. Gurney, the hymn was written under these circumstances:

> It was Sunday evening and we were enjoying a time of hymn singing. A song that was particularly enjoyed by all of us was "O Strength and Stay," the tune to which was a favorite of my sister. As we finished singing this hymn, someone remarked, "What a pity the words of this beautiful song should be unsuitable for a wedding!" My sister turned to me and challenged, "What is the use of a sister who composes poetry if she cannot write new words to a favorite tune? I would like to use the tune at my wedding." I picked up a hymnbook and said, "If no one will disturb me, I will go into the library and see what I can do." Within fifteen minutes I was back with the group and reading the words I had jotted down. The writing of the words was no effort whatever after the initial idea came to me of the twofold aspect of perfect union, love and life. I feel that God helped me write this song.

Albert Edward Bailey, in *The Gospel in Hymns,* points out that "in this hymn the Lord Jesus Christ is given two titles that are of special significance in marriage—perfect love and perfect life. Embodied in these titles are two great ideals in motive and performance which, when neglected, will wreck the home, but when honored, will yield, as stanza 3 points out, joy instead of sorrow and peace instead of strife. This is another way of speaking of heaven." Certainly Mrs. Gurney incorporated in her prayer-hymn the truth that human love cannot begin to touch God's love, which "transcends all human thought."

Besides being sung at the wedding of Mrs. Gurney's sister, "O Perfect Love" was used at many fashionable London weddings and at the weddings of royalty. It was not until two or three years after the composition, however, that the hymn actually found its way into the hymn book, *Hymns Ancient and Modern.* In 1889 after Sir Joseph Barnby composed a new tune, SANDRINGHAM, for the hymn, it was sung at the wedding of Princess Louise of Wales (daughter of George V) to the Duke of Fife. Since that time, "O Perfect Love" has been translated into many languages and has attained worldwide fame. Its popularity continues to this day.

Mrs. Gurney was born at Finsbury Circus, London, October 4, 1858. She was the eldest daughter of F. G. Blomfield, rector of St. Andrew's Undershaft, London.

Mrs. Gurney was not only a composer of hymn lyrics, but also of other poetry. She authored a book of poems, *A Little Book of Quiet*, and two other volumes, each called *Poems*. Of all her verse, the piece remembered most is "God's Garden."

Upon her death in 1932 a brief, eulogistic piece appeared in the London *Times*: "Thousands of people at thousands of weddings must have sung, or heard sung, 'O Perfect Love' without knowing that Mrs. Gurney wrote the hymn. It was always to her a matter of amused regret that she did not get a royalty for each performance. . . . But it is not as an author that she will be best remembered by her many friends. . . . A wide circle of friends of every creed and class knew that they could take to her all their troubles, great or small, and come away with the burden of them lightened or removed."

Today the most popular tune to Mrs. Gurney's hymn is Barnby's SANDRINGHAM (also called O PERFECT LOVE). That the original melody should have been one by John B. Dykes is interesting, for Dykes was noted for refusing to allow his tunes to be joined to any hymns other than those for which he wrote them. Joseph Barnby (1838-1896), a distinguished English organist and choirmaster, was knighted in 1892. After serving at several churches in London, his last years were spent at Eton College and the Guildhall School of Music. His 246 hymns were published in one volume the year after his death.

Rock of Ages, Cleft for Me
1776

Rock of ages, cleft for me,
  Let me hide myself in Thee;
Let the water and the blood
  From Thy riven side which flowed,
Be of sin the double cure,
  Cleanse me from its guilt and power.

Not the labours of my hands
  Can fulfill Thy law's demands;
Could my zeal no respite know,
  Could my tears forever flow,
All for sin could not atone;
  Thou must save, and Thou alone.

Nothing in my hand I bring,
  Simply to Thy cross I cling;
Naked, come to Thee for dress;
  Helpless, look to Thee for grace;
Foul, I to the fountain fly;
  Wash me, Saviour, or I die.

While I draw this fleeting breath,
  When my eye-strings break in death,
When I soar through tracts unknown,
  See Thee on Thy judgment throne;
Rock of ages, cleft for me,
  Let me hide myself in Thee.

—Augustus Montague Toplady

Toplady first published this favorite hymn in his *Gospel Magazine*, March 1776, in four stanzas. A single stanza, comprised of portions of stanza 1 and another, had appeared the previous October. There have been numerous alterations to Toplady's original text. Most hymnals print only three stanzas, with the first and last more or less as Toplady wrote them and with the middle stanza being a conglomerate of phrases from Toplady's

original second and third stanzas. We print them above
as Toplady wrote them. Customary alterations, particularly in the fourth stanza, will be readily apparent to any
reader who knows this hymn.

Some hymnologists state that this hymn was inspired
by a severe thunderstorm from which Toplady had to seek
shelter in the cleft of two massive rocks at Burrington
Combe, Somerset, England. Although the author lived in
this area for several years and might have undergone such
an experience that later came to mind, he did not write
"Rock of Ages" until eleven years after he moved from
Somerset.

Many have maintained that "Rock of Ages" was
plagiarized from Wesley, citing the following paragraph:

> O Rock of Israel, Rock of Salvation, Rock struck and
> cleft for me, Let those two streams of Blood and water
> which once gushed out of Thy side, bring down pardon
> and holiness to my soul. And let me thirst after them
> now, as if I stood upon the mountain whence sprung
> this Water; and near the cleft of that Rock, the wounds
> of my Lord, whence gushed this sacred Blood.

Actually, these phrases are not by Wesley, but from a
sermon by Dr. Daniel Brevint. Charles Wesley *quoted* them
in his *Hymns on the Lord's Supper*, 1745. Plagiarism
or not, both men (Toplady and Wesley) had abundant
Scripture from which to draw their imagery. Exodus 33:22
refers to the "clift of the rock"; Exodus 17:6 "smite the
rock"; Deuteronomy 32:4 "the Rock"; and I Corinthians
10:4 "that Rock was Christ." Our Lord refers to "a rock"
in His Sermon on the Mount (Matthew 7:24-25) and to
"this rock" in conversation with Peter in Matthew 16:18.

Augustus Montague Toplady was born on November
4, 1740, in Farnham, England. A few months later his
father, a major in the British army, died at the siege of
Cartagena. Mrs. Toplady, who was a devout, intelligent,
and cultured lady, devoted much time in training her
"mentally and spiritually precocious son." At the age of

eleven he was writing in his diary mature thoughts of gratitude in recognition of the Lord's having kept him from evil. At twelve he was writing and preaching sermons, and at fourteen he was writing hymns, which he began to publish at the age of nineteen.

Toplady's conversion took place when he was sixteen. He and his mother had moved to rural Ireland. One day he was walking past a barn and heard some singing. Upon investigation he found a revival in progress: James Morris was preaching on the text, "But now in Christ Jesus ye who sometimes were far off are made nigh by the blood of Christ" (Ephesians 2:13). "I have been far off," Toplady confessed, "and I want to be made nigh by His Blood." Later he remarked, "Strange that I, who had so long sat under the means of grace in England, should be brought right unto God in an obscure part of Ireland, midst a handful of people met together in a barn, and by the ministry of one who could hardly spell his own name. Surely it was the Lord's doing and is marvellous."

Like many others of his day, Toplady battled tuberculosis, to which he succumbed on August 11, 1778, at the age of thirty-eight. In his final hours he remarked to a friend, "I cannot tell the comforts I feel in my soul; O, they are past expression. The consolations of God are so abundant that . . . my prayers are all converted into praise. I enjoy heaven already within my soul."

In English churches, as well as in many in America, "Rock of Ages" is sung to REDHEAD NO. 76 (also known as GETHSEMANE, AJALON, and PETRA). Some say that the composer, Richard Redhead (1820-1901), numbered his tunes as he wrote them rather than giving them names, but Haeussler insists that the tune is called REDHEAD NO. 76 because it was number seventy-six in *Church Hymn Tunes, Ancient and Modern*, which Redhead published in 1853. The alternate name PETRA is appropriate for music written specifically for "Rock of Ages," since in both Greek and Latin it means "rock." For a time in America the popular setting was RELIANCE, a tune composed by an English musician, John Henry

Gower (1855-1922), who was serving as an organist and choirmaster in Denver. Soon, however, TOPLADY became the familiar melody, and it has remained so. This tune was the work of an American, Dr. Thomas Hastings (1784-1872), and was written to accompany this hymn. Hastings first published TOPLADY, named for the author of the hymn, in *Spiritual Songs for Social Worship* (1831), which he edited with Lowell Mason.

The King of Love My Shepherd Is
1868

The King of love my Shepherd is,
  Whose goodness faileth never;
I nothing lack if I am His,
  And He is mine forever.

Where streams of living water flow,
  My ransomed soul He leadeth,
And, where the verdant pastures grow,
  With food celestial feedeth.

Perverse and foolish oft I strayed
  But yet in love He sought me.
And on His shoulder gently laid,
  And home rejoicing brought me.

In death's dark vale I fear no ill
  With Thee, dear Lord, beside me,
Thy rod and staff my comfort still,
  Thy cross before to guide me.

Thou spread'st a table in my sight,
  Thy unction grace bestoweth,
And O, what transport of delight
  From Thy pure chalice floweth!

And so through all the length of days
  Thy goodness faileth never:
Good Shepherd, may I sing Thy praise
  Within Thy house forever.
—Henry Williams Baker

We know nothing of the writing of this hymn except the date (1868), even though it is one of the finest paraphrases of the Twenty-third Psalm. Hymn writers of all nations and ranks have caught the spirit of the Shepherd Psalm and have poured out their love and affection to the One of whom the psalm speaks. Sir Henry Baker's paraphrase, however, has been labeled "the cream," "a gem of richest ore."

You will note in the hymn a skillful blend of Old and New Testament Scriptures. Stanza 1 introduces the Loving Shepherd, explaining that He shelters His own and supplies their needs. A prerequisite, of course, is abiding in Him. John 15:7: "If ye abide in me, and my words abide in you, ye shall ask what ye will, and it shall be done unto you." Philippians 4:19: "But my God shall supply all your need according to his riches in glory by Christ Jesus."

Stanza 2 suggests Calvary, where our Lord gave His life "a ransom for many" (Matthew 20:28). "Celestial food" is reminiscent of Israel's wilderness wanderings; yet it brings before us "the true bread from heaven" who "giveth life" and who promises, "he that cometh to me shall never hunger; and he that believeth on me shall never thirst" (John 6:32, 33, 35).

Stanza 3 hints of the parable of the lost sheep (Luke 15:4-7) and the resultant joy in being brought back by the Good Shepherd (John 10:11).

Stanza 4 offers comfort in death. It has the flavor of Psalm 116:15—"Precious in the sight of the Lord is the death of his saints"—and II Corinthians 5:8—"absent from the body . . . present with the Lord." Central, of course, is the cross.

From divine grace and the Lord's Supper in stanza 5 the author moves into stanza 6 with a repetition of the theme of never-ending goodness and calls for deepest praise on the part of those who abide under the Shepherd's care.

Sir Henry Williams Baker was the eldest son of Vice-Admiral Sir Henry Loraine Baker of the Royal Navy. He was born in London on May 27, 1821, and was educated at Trinity College, Cambridge. From 1851 until the time of his death he served as vicar of Monkland, Herefordshire, England. In 1859 he was knighted. Sir Henry was characterized by simplicity of language, earnestness of heart and mind, a deep knowledge of Scripture, and a plaintive quality in writing and composing. It is said that if a theme had both lights and shadows, he usually took comfort in the shadows.

In the mid-nineteenth century, during a time of strong emphasis on "Back to the Old Faith," hymnists were challenged to revamp the hymnals. Sir Henry served as chairman of the committee that prepared the monumental and highly influential work, *Hymns Ancient and Modern.* When the committee advertised for suggestions, replies came from more than two hundred leading clergymen. The committee pooled the suggestions, incorporating in the finished product the hymns that they judged to be of high literary and musical standards. Sir Henry was criticized for taking liberties in making changes in hymns without permission of the authors and for his rejection of hymns that he felt were "not of high quality." This brought against the book the sarcastic comment that the initials *H. A. and M.* actually stood for *Hymns Asked For and Mutilated.* In spite of these problems, however, between 1861 and 1912 the book reached a circulation of more than sixty million copies.

Sir Henry died on February 12, 1877. His last words were the third stanza of this hymn.

Of the several tunes that have been used with this hymn, the most popular one has been DOMINUS REGIT ME. Composed for the 1868 edition of *Hymns Ancient and Modern* by John Bacchus Dykes (1823-1876), it takes its name from the Latin title of the Twenty-third Psalm. The melody line follows the important syllables and words, making the hymn easy to sing. Dr. Dykes was criticized for writing so many tunes, about 300 going under his name. He answered, "I know so well the teaching power of hymns, if they are happily wedded, that I am very anxious to do my best (as far as God is pleased to help me) to add to the number of those useful unions. . . . My one desire is that each hymn be set to music (by whomsoever God wills to select for that purpose) that its power of influencing and teaching may be best brought out."

There Is a Name I Love to Hear
1855

There is a name I love to hear,
I love to sing its worth;
It sounds like music in mine ear,
The sweetest name on earth.

Refrain:

Oh, how I love Jesus,
Oh, how I love Jesus,
Oh, how I love Jesus,
Because He first loved me!

It tells me of a Saviour's love,
Who died to set me free;
It tells me of His precious blood,
The sinner's perfect plea.

It tells me of a Father's smile
That beams upon His child;
It cheers me through this little while,
Through deserts waste and wild.

It tells of One whose loving heart
  Can feel my deepest woe,
Who in each sorrow bears a part,
  That none can bear below.

It tells me what my Father hath
  In store for every day,
And though I tread a darksome path,
  Yield sunshine all the way.

It bids my trembling soul rejoice,
  And dries each rising tear;
It tells me in a still small voice,
  To trust and not to fear.

This name shall shed its fragrance still
  Along this thorny road,
Shall sweetly smooth the rugged hill
  That leads me up to God.

Jesus, the name I love so well,
  The name I love to hear;
No saint on earth its worth can tell,
  No heart conceive how dear.

—Frederick Whitfield

It was the breakfast hour in the Whitfield home, and every family member but Frederick was at the table. When he finally appeared, Frederick seemed somewhat glum. One of his sisters, aware that verse-writing always stimulated her brother and brought a sparkle to his eyes, said, "O Fred, there is a Name I love to hear." Very quickly he responded, "I love to speak its worth." Another sister added, "That sounds like music in my ear." Fred exuberantly exclaimed, "It is the sweetest name on earth." This joyful exchange of greeting forms stanza 1. Frederick added four additional stanzas. Hymn-menders of later date added the other stanzas, but most hymnbooks use only four or five of the eight stanzas.

"There Is a Name I Love to Hear" was first published

in leaflet form in 1855. Eventually, it was translated into several languages and has been included in numerous hymnbooks. Some say that Whitfield's repetition of "Oh, how I love Jesus" as the refrain was designed to acknowledge his sisters' collaboration on the hymn, while others claim that the refrain was not added until many years later by another hymn writer.

This simple song exalts the Lord Jesus Christ in an unusual way. Indirectly it exalts the written Word, for it is only through the study of the written Word that we gain knowledge of the Living Word. The hymn presents the Christian life from the standpoint of redemption and the Christian walk. Stanza 1 reflects the author's deep interest in music and his reverence for the Name of his Lord. Stanza 2 refers to redemption, saying that the precious blood of Jesus is the sinner's matchless plea. Stanzas 3 through 6 liken the Christian to a child who is encouraged by his Father's smile to face a cold, hard world with bravery and trust. Stanza 7 describes the Christian life as a thorny road and a rugged hill, suggesting that the Name of Jesus sheds fragrance on the road. The final stanza concludes that no saint on earth, however lofty his thoughts, can fully describe the value of the Name the author loves to hear.

Frederick Whitfield was born in Threapwood, Shropshire, England, on January 7, 1829. He was educated at Trinity College, Dublin. After his ordination in the Church of England he served various parishes and also as Secretary of the Irish Church Missions. He had more than thirty books of religious prose and verse to his credit. Whitfield died on September 13, 1904, in Croyden, England.

The tune BELMONT, to which this hymn reportedly was originally sung, without refrain, was first published in the first volume of *Sacred Melodies Adapted to the Best English Poets* (1812), a collection by William Gardiner (1770-1853). Though some have attributed the tune to Samuel Webb, Sr., Samuel Webb, Jr., and Mozart, the evidence points to Gardiner as the composer. The arrangement currently used dates from 1859 and was done by J. Bentley. BELMONT lends a serene dignity to the text, a loftiness that does not come across when the words are sung, as they usually are, to the traditional, anonymous tune OH HOW I LOVE JESUS. The latter, a lilting tune, typical of many nineteenth-century folksongs of the camp meeting type, has been sung with various texts, including Newton's "Amazing Grace" and Watts' "Alas, and Did My Saviour Bleed." These hymns, like "There Is a Name I Love to Hear," when sung to this tune, use the text of the refrain, "Oh, How I Love Jesus."

Commitment & Service

Jesus, and Shall It Ever Be
1765

Jesus, and shall it ever be,
A mortal man ashamed of Thee?
Ashamed of Thee, whom angels praise,
Whose glories shine through endless days?

Ashamed of Jesus! sooner far
Let evening blush to own a star;
He sheds the beams of light divine
O'er this benighted soul of mine.

Ashamed of Jesus! that dear Friend
On whom my hopes of heaven depend!
No; when I blush, be this my shame,
That I no more revere His name.

Ashamed of Jesus! yes, I may,
When I've no guilt to wash away;
No tear to wipe, no good to crave,
No fears to quell, no soul to save.

Till then, nor is my boasting vain,
Till then I boast a Saviour slain;
And O, may this my glory be,
That Christ is not ashamed of me!

—Joseph Grigg

"Jesus, and Shall It Ever Be" (or "Ashamed of Jesus") was published anonymously in 1765. The heading stated: "Shame of Jesus Conquered by Love. By a Youth of Ten Years." That a ten-year-old lad could write such a hymn is almost beyond belief. Yet authorities agree that Joseph Grigg (ca. 1720-1768) wrote the poem at the age of ten. The Reverend Benjamin Francis, who knew the boy and who later rearranged the hymn, settled the question of authorship and age.

Because of the humble surroundings of his youth, some hymnologists suggest that Grigg probably had help in polishing his hymn. Other hymnologists suggest that perhaps Joseph himself polished the hymn a bit later. In any case, Joseph, at a tender age, became thoroughly convinced that he was a sinner and that he needed the Lord Jesus Christ as Saviour.

"Jesus, and Shall It Ever Be" was written in seven stanzas and has been much and often altered. (Julian prints the entire original text in his *Dictionary of Hymnology*.) Some years later, stanza 1 was dropped, and a few words were altered. The hymn opens with a challenging question. In effect, it asks, "Shall it ever be that a mortal man could be ashamed of Thee—Of Thee whom angels praise and whose glories shine through endless days?" In stanzas 2 through 4 the writer exclaims, "Ashamed of Jesus! Unbelievable, especially when we consider who He is and what we are!" From that exclamation, he launches into a discussion of his opening question. He says that we may be ashamed of Jesus when we have no guilt to be washed away, no tears to be wiped, no fears to be quelled, and no soul that needs to be saved. Then he says, "Instead of our being ashamed of Jesus, let it be our shame that we do not revere the Name of such a dear Friend more." Grigg ends the poem with this challenge: "May our glory be that Jesus is not ashamed of us. Let us honor Him in our daily lives."

One marvels at a ten-year-old boy's ability to use such picturesque language as these words: "Let evening blush to own a star" and "midnight be ashamed of noon." Yet young Joseph wrote them. No doubt, he, like David the shepherd boy who became king of Israel, loved nature and spent much time in studying the beauties and changes of nature.

Until he was twenty-five, Joseph worked as a mechanic. Then he became an assistant Presbyterian minister and preached in London for four years. He met and married the wealthy widow of Colonel Drew, and she persuaded Joseph to devote his time to literary pursuits. Although Joseph continued to preach occasionally, his gift of writing took priority.

The hymn tune, FEDERAL STREET, was written in 1832 by Henry Kemble Oliver (1800-1885). It was named for a street in Salem, Oliver's hometown, and for a street in Boston where Oliver attended church. FEDERAL STREET graces a variety of hymns. It was popularized by Lowell Mason. It happened this way: Dr. Mason was conducting a singing school in Salem. One day he asked, "Does anybody have an original tune? If so, I shall be glad to consider it." Henry very timidly handed a tune to Dr. Mason, who adapted it to the poem, "So Fades the Lovely, Blooming Flower," which Anne Steele had written in memory of a child's death. Mason published the tune in *Boston Academy's Collection of Church Music* (1836).

Henry Kemble Oliver was born in Beverly, Massachusetts. He attended Harvard, but he was graduated from Dartmouth (1818). In 1862, Harvard, not wishing to be outdone, granted to Oliver the A.B. and M.A. degrees, listing his name in the class of 1818. Dartmouth conferred on him a Doctor of Music degree in 1883. Oliver was outstanding in public life. He served as adjutant-general of Massachusetts, as superintendent of the Atlantic Cotton Mills in Lawrence, as state treasurer during the Civil War, and as mayor of both Lawrence and Salem. Yet music exerted a strong pull on him. Although his father forbade him from making a career of music, Oliver found time enough to become proficient on a number of instruments. He served as organist to several churches in Salem and Lawrence, Massachusetts, during his lifetime. He published several hymn collections and founded the Salem Oratorio Society, the Salem Glee Club, and the Mozart Association. He died in Salem on August 12, 1885.

Jesus Calls Us
1852

Jesus calls us; o'er the tumult
  Of our life's wild, restless sea,
Day by day His sweet voice soundeth,
  Saying, "Christian, follow Me."

As of old, St. Andrew heard it
  By the Galilean lake,
Turned from home and toil and kindred,
  Leaving all for His dear sake.

Jesus calls us from the worship
  Of the vain world's golden store,
From each idol that would keep us,
  Saying, "Christian, love Me more."

In our joys and in our sorrows,
  Days of toil, and hours of ease,
Still He calls, in cares and pleasures,
  "Christian, love Me more than these."

Jesus calls us: by Thy mercies,
  Saviour, may we hear Thy call,
Give our hearts to Thine obedience,
  Serve and love Thee best of all.

—Cecil Frances Alexander

The basis of this hymn is Matthew 4:18-20, our Lord's call to Andrew and Peter. It was written especially for St. Andrew's Day (November 30), 1852, and was published the same year by the Society for Promoting Christian Knowledge. Like many other songs by Mrs. Alexander, "Jesus Calls Us" reveals the author's ability to view ordinary things as a means of expressing love for her Lord and of witnessing to His saving power.

Stanzas 1 through 4 are an appeal and an invitation or challenge. Stanza 1 views life—in part, at least—as a "wild, restless sea." Above this tumult, one hears the divine call, "Christian, follow Me." Stanza 2 reflects the Lord's call to Andrew and the admonition to put Him above houses, lands, and family. (It is unfortunate that so many hymnals omit this stanza, inasmuch as the hymn was written with the apostle Andrew particularly in mind.) Stanza 3 is a warning against worshiping the world and its allurements. Stanza 4 acknowledges that although life has its joys and its hours of ease, it also has its sorrows and toils. This stanza issues the strong challenge to love Jesus more than such experiences. Stanza 5 is in the vein of prayer. It is a plea for divine mercies by which one hears and obeys God's call, and it ends with the desire to serve and love Him "best of all."

Cecil Frances Alexander was born in 1818, the daughter of a noted landowner, John Humphreys, who also was a major in the Royal Marines. The Humphreys children had a wonderful home life. On Saturday nights Major Humphreys would gather the family in his study to discuss some of their writings and actions. Cecil, at a very early age, showed a remarkable ability for writing verse, but so stern was her father and so prone to criticize their works was he that she hid her poems under the rug. Imagine her surprise one Saturday evening to learn that he had discovered her hiding place and that he approved her writings! A family friend, hymn writer John Keble, admired her work and encouraged her to develop her talent.

In 1850, at age thirty-two, Cecil had two "serious suitors." She accepted William Alexander, a poor country minister who later became Archbishop and Primate of the Anglican Church of all Ireland. The new bride moved among the poor of her husband's parish with cheerfulness, sympathy, and helpful instruction. Her husband said, "From one poor home to another, from one bed of sickness to another, from one sorrow to another, she went. Christ was with her and in her, and hungry souls felt and appreciated her influence."

Mrs. Alexander was an ardent churchwoman who ably expressed her beliefs in "such vivid poetic form that the hearts of men were kindled to serve and to suffer for the Lord." Grieving hearts beyond number have found comfort in "The Pierced Hand" in which she says, "Only one hand, a pierced hand, Can heal the sinner's wound." Mrs. Alexander paraphrased many psalms and usually wrote a special song for every season.

Four hundred songs are credited to this dear Christian's pen. Many songs were written for children, the logic being that if she wrote simply so that children might understand, she would also meet the needs of the myriads of adults who were somewhat ignorant of Scripture. One day a little godson complained to Mrs. Alexander, "I don't understand the Apostles' Creed, and we have to memorize it." "That should not be," she thought; so she set herself to explaining the Creed in verse in order that the children might sing and understand the doctrines that were involved. "Suffered under Pontius Pilate, was crucified, dead and buried" inspired "There is a green hill far away, Without a city wall." Critics have argued against "a green hill," saying that it is unscriptural. She said, "When I went in and out of our city, I passed a grass-covered hill. For some reason, this hill reminded me of Calvary; so I wrote of Calvary as 'a green hill far away.'" It is said that she wrote "There Is a Green Hill Far Away" while sitting beside the sickbed of a Sunday school pupil and that the child always referred to the song as "my song." A Sunday school pupil asked, "Why was the green hill far away, and why didn't it have a city wall?" Immediately she changed "without" to "outside," though many publishers have rejected that change.

Two other Creed songs are "All Things Bright and Beautiful" and "I Believe in God the Father Almighty, Maker of Heaven and Earth." Mrs. Alexander's best-known poem is "The Burial of Moses," which received high praise from Alfred, Lord Tennyson. At thirty she published a book of hymns for children that for many years was unsurpassed.

Stopford Brooke described Mrs. Alexander's hymns as "charmingly simple and tender, clear in dogma, and of poetical beauty." He saw in them "the plainness of Watts" and a notable love for children. Dr. Benson notes that "she was one of the very few poets who disliked praise for her hymns." A friend of the poor and needy, she in no way sought praise or flattery. One notable exception was the occasion when someone would comment on having found the Lord by means of one of her hymns. This would thrill her beyond expression. All profits from her hymn writing went to the Irish School of Mutes.

Mrs. Alexander died in Londonderry on October 12, 1895. In tribute her husband said, "No matter what I may accomplish, I shall always be remembered as the husband of the woman who wrote 'There Is a Green Hill Far Away.'"

GALILEE (sometimes called JUDE), the tune to which "Jesus Calls Us" is usually sung, was composed for this text around 1887 by William Herbert Jude (1851-1922), an English organist, composer, editor, and lecturer.

More Love to Thee, O Christ
1856

More love to Thee, O Christ,
More love to Thee!
Hear Thou the prayer I make
On bended knee;
This is my earnest plea:
More love, O Christ, to Thee,
More love to Thee!

Once earthly joy I craved,
Sought peace and rest;
Now Thee alone I seek,
Give what is best;
This all my prayer shall be:
More love, O Christ, to Thee,
More love to Thee!

Let sorrow do its work,
  Send grief and pain;
Sweet are Thy messengers,
  Sweet their refrain,
When they can sing with me:
More love, O Christ, to Thee,
  More love to Thee!

Then shall my latest breath
  Whisper Thy praise;
This be the parting cry
  My heart shall raise;
This still its prayer shall be:
More love, O Christ, to Thee,
  More love to Thee!

—Elizabeth Payson Prentiss

In his *Life and Letters of Elizabeth Payson Prentiss,* the husband of Mrs. Prentiss gives the background of "More Love to Thee, O Christ": "It belongs probably as far back as the year 1856. Like most of her hymns, it is simply a prayer put into verse. She wrote it so hastily that the last stanza was left incomplete, one line having to be added in pencil when the hymn was printed."

Not even Mrs. Prentiss' husband knew of this hymn until thirteen years after its writing. The first printing was on a leaflet in 1869, and soon it was sweeping the country in revival meetings. Sales quickly reached 200,000 copies, and the hymn was translated into several languages.

Actually, "More Love to Thee, O Christ" is one of a pair of hymns. Mrs. Prentiss wrote "Press Close, My Child, to Me" as Christ's invitation or the Master's call and "More Love to Thee, O Christ" as the disciples' response.

The melody to which this hymn is usually set bears the same name as the hymn (MORE LOVE TO THEE). It was written by William Howard Doane (1832-1915), a wealthy manufacturer who composed a cantata and 2200 tunes and edited several compilations of hymns. Another

beautiful tune to which this hymn is sung is PROPIOR
DEO, which Sir Arthur Sullivan (1842-1900) composed
in 1872 for the hymn "Nearer, My God, to Thee."

Elizabeth Payson Prentiss was born in Portland, Maine,
on October 26, 1818. She was the youngest daughter of
a Presbyterian minister, the Reverend Edward Payson,
who was described as "so saintly that for many years after
his death hundreds of children were still being named
for him." The theme of Elizabeth's life was "more love
to Christ." Her literary ability was such that at the age
of sixteen she was furnishing short articles and poems
to the popular *Youth's Companion.* For a number of years
she taught school in Maine, Massachusetts, and Virginia.
In 1845 she married the Reverend George L. Prentiss,
who was a popular preacher and later became a professor
at Union Theological Seminary in New York.

From childhood Elizabeth suffered ill health. The year
1856 being a peak year of suffering, she prayed, "Let
sorrow do its work, Send grief and pain; Sweet are Thy
messengers . . . When they can sing with me, More love,
O Christ, to Thee." The more her body suffered, the more
"her spirit rose above pain and tribulation, daily growing
more radiant and beautiful." She said, "Much of my
experience in life has cost me a great price, and I wish
to use it for strengthening and comforting other souls."

To carry out her noble desire, Mrs. Prentiss wrote
Stepping Heavenward, a book somewhat autobiographical in thought. This book appeared in the same year as
"More Love to Thee, O Christ," and for years it remained
one of the most popular books for girls in the English
language. Another book, *The Flower of the Family,* also
met with wide success. In 1873 Mrs. Prentiss published
Religious Poems, containing 123 original poems. At least
four-fifths of her poems dealt with the subject of her Lord
and Master. In 1874 Mrs. Prentiss published *Golden
Hours or Hymns and Songs of the Christian Life.*

Dr. Theodore Cuyler, a family friend, said of this gifted
woman: "She was a very bright-eyed little woman, with
a keen sense of humor, who cared more to shine in her

own happy household than in a wide circle of society."

Mrs. Prentiss died on August 13, 1878, at her summer home in Dorset, Vermont. As she was being lowered into the grave, friends began to sing, "More love to Thee, O Christ. . . ." This dear woman was mourned around the world. A deeply touching condolence came from China. It was a fan on which was printed, in Chinese characters, the words of Mrs. Prentiss' famous hymn. Most touching, however, were these words that Dr. Prentiss found in her own handwriting:

One hour with Jesus! how its peace outweighs
The ravishment of earthly love and praise;
How dearer far, emptied of self to lie
Low at His feet, and catch, perchance, His eye,
Alike content when He may give or take,
The sweet, the bitter, welcome for His sake.

O Jesus, I Have Promised
   ca. 1866

O Jesus, I have promised
  To serve Thee to the end;
Be Thou forever near me,
  My Master and my Friend:
I shall not fear the battle
  If Thou art by my side,
Nor wander from the pathway
  If Thou wilt be my guide.

O let me feel Thee near me—
  The world is ever near;
I see the sights that dazzle,
  The tempting sounds I hear:
My foes are ever near me,
  Around me and within;
But, Jesus, draw Thou nearer,
  And shield my soul from sin.

O Jesus, Thou hast promised
  To all who follow Thee,
That where Thou art in glory,
  There shall Thy servant be;
And, Jesus, I have promised
  To serve Thee to the end;
O give me grace to follow,
  My Master and my Friend.

—John E. Bode

This stirring hymn of prayer and dedication was written around 1866 as "Hymn for the Newly Confirmed" in honor of the confirmation of the author's daughter and two sons. Originally it began, "O Jesus, *we* have promised. . . ." The Reverend Mr. Bode quizzed the young people; then he offered this compliment and challenge: "You have gladdened my heart. I wanted to be sure that you would understand what all of it meant, and knew what you were doing, according to your age and intelligence. In order to crystallize these thoughts in your minds, I have written a hymn containing all the important truths I want you to remember when you are finally confirmed. It contains six stanzas of eight lines each." After he had read the recently penned words to his children, he suggested that they select a suitable melody.

Probably because of the hymn's length, the following three stanzas are usually omitted from modern hymnals:

O let me hear Thee speaking
  In accents clear and still;
Above the storms of passion,
  The murmurs of self-will;
O speak to reassure me,
  To hasten or control;
O speak, and make me listen,
  Thou Guardian of my soul.

O let me see Thy features,
  The look that once could make

So many a true disciple
  Leave all things for Thy sake;
The look that beamed on Peter
  When he Thy name denied;
The look that draws Thy loved ones
  Close to Thy pierced side.

O let me see Thy foot-marks,
  And in them plant mine own;
My hope to follow duly
  Is in Thy strength alone;
O guide me, call me, draw me,
  Uphold me to the end;
And then in heaven receive me,
  My Saviour and my Friend.

The hymn first appeared in leaflet form in 1868 and then in *Hymns for Public Worship* (1869). The words of this beautiful hymn should prompt Christians to more faithful service to the Lord. In stanza 1 the writer, the singer, or the reader is challenged to be faithful "to the end." It begs the presence of the great "Master and Friend." Stanza 2 is a prayer that the Lord will shield the soul from falling prey to the dazzling sights of the world and from the attacks of foes without and within. Stanza 3 claims the divine promises of His presence and repeats the earlier promise of faithful service. It also asks for grace to follow our "Master and Friend."

John Ernest Bode, the faithful father who wrote these words, was born February 23, 1816, and was educated at Eton and Oxford. In 1841 he was ordained in the Church of England, serving six years as tutor in his college and from 1847 until 1860 as rector at Westwell, Oxfordshire. From 1863 until his death on October 6, 1874, Bode was rector at Castle Camps, Cambridgeshire, England. He published many literary works and was honored by being asked to deliver the Bampton Lectures at Oxford. Although he is credited with three volumes of poems, his fame derives from "O Jesus, I Have Promised."

The tune ANGEL'S STORY appeared in 1881. The name of the tune comes from the first line of the hymn for which it was composed, "I Love to Hear the Story Which Angel Voices Tell." It was written by Arthur Henry Mann (1850-1929), a native of Norwich, England. Mann was chorister at Norwich Cathedral under Dr. Zechariah Buck, and he also served as organist and choir director at various colleges and churches. Many musical works and books reaped the benefits of his editorship. Mann received a Bachelor of Music degree from Oxford in 1874 and a doctorate in music in 1882. He was acclaimed an authority on Handel and other composers. It is reported that he and Ebenezer Prout discovered the original wind parts of *The Messiah.*

Two other tunes often used with this hymn are LLANFYLLIN, a traditional Welsh melody published in 1865, and DAY OF REST by James William Elliott (1833-1915). Elliott's tune is first found in Sir Arthur Sullivan's *Church Hymns,* 1874, set to "O Day of Rest and Gladness." The tune may be older than 1874, however.

Spirit of God, Descend upon My Heart
pub. 1867

Spirit of God, descend upon my heart;
  Wean it from earth; through all its pulses move;
Stoop to my weakness, mighty as Thou art,
  And make me love Thee as I ought to love.

I ask no dream, no prophet ecstasies,
  No sudden rending of the veil of clay,
No angel visitant, no opening skies;
  But take the dimness of my soul away.

Hast Thou not bid me love Thee, God and King?
  All, all Thine own, soul, heart and strength and mind.
I see Thy cross—there teach my heart to cling:
  O let me seek Thee, and O let me find.

Teach me to feel that Thou art always nigh;
  Teach me the struggles of the soul to bear,
To check the rising doubt, the rebel sigh;
  Teach me the patience of unanswered prayer.

Teach me to love Thee as Thine angels love,
  One holy passion filling all my frame;
The baptism of the heaven-descended Dove,
  My heart an altar, and Thy love the flame.

—George Croly

"Spirit of God, Descend upon My Heart" is based on Galatians 5:25—"If we live in the Spirit, let us also walk in the Spirit"—and Matthew 3:16-17—"And Jesus, when he was baptized, went up straightway out of the water: and, lo, the heavens were opened unto him, and he saw the Spirit of God descending like a dove, and lighting upon him: And lo a voice from heaven, saying, This is my beloved Son, in whom I am well pleased." First entitled "Holiness Desired," the prayer hymn centers on the thought that if one is to *do* right, he must *be* right. Its first appearance was in Charles Rogers' *Lyra Britannica* (London, 1867), which was published seven years after the author's death. Each stanza was designed to express some longing of heart.

In stanza 1 the petitioner desires to be weaned from the earth and to love God as he should. It breathes of Paul's words to "set your affection on things above, not on things on the earth" (Colossians 3:2). Stanza 2, often omitted from hymnals, asks not for visions or dreams, but for clarity of soul. In stanza 3, also sometimes omitted, the petitioner acknowledges the divine commandment to love God "with all thy heart, and with all thy soul, and with all thy mind" (Matthew 22:37). Stanza 4 asks for patience to await God's time for answering prayer, and stanza 5 desires to love God as His angels love Him. One hymnist added the following stanzas as a closing to the hymn.

As some rare perfume in a vase of clay
  Pervades it with a fragrance not its own,
So then Thou dwellest in the human soul
  All heaven's sweetness seems about it thrown.

The soul alone like a neglected harp
  Grows out of tune and needs Thy hand divine.
Dwell Thou within it, time it, touch its chords,
  Till every note and string shall answer "Thine"!

Much controversy surrounds the authorship of this hymn, although in general the Reverend George Croly is considered to be the writer.

George Croly was born on August 17, 1780, in Dublin, Ireland. He received the M.A. degree from Dublin College in 1804, and in 1831 Dublin College honored him with the LL.D. degree. Croly took orders in the Church of Ireland and served in Dublin until 1810. Then he moved to London to begin service in a small church. In 1835 he accepted the challenge to reopen St. Stephen's Church, a London church that had been closed for more than a hundred years.

Croly drew large crowds to his church, but a contemporary said of him, "He was a man of vast power, was possessed of a mind of gigantic grasp, was prodigiously energetic, but was not a great preacher. Someone else points out that he was "a fundamentalist in theology, a fierce conservative in politics, and intensely opposed to all forms of liberalism." Yet with all of these glowing reports came the criticism that "as a rule, he preached over the heads of his audience. Instead of changing his terminology to his listeners' level of understanding, he expected them to leap to his level."

In London Croly also devoted much time to literary works. He was editor of a conservative weekly paper, *Britannia,* and contributed articles and poems to *Blackwood's Magazine, The Universal Review,* and *The Literary Gazette.* In 1854 he published a collection of hymns that he entitled *Psalms and Hymns for Public Worship.* He wrote three novels: *Tales of the Great St.*

Bernard, Marston, or The Soldier and Statesman, and *Salathiel. Salathiel,* a three-volume novel based on the legend of the wandering Jew, created quite a sensation; it was reprinted in 1901 in New York under the title of *Tarry Thou Till I Come.* In 1830 Croly published *The Life and Times of George IV.* In all, he is credited with at least forty volumes on varied subjects, including biography, history, and theology.

His ministry ended abruptly on November 24, 1860. While walking down a London street, he collapsed and died.

An early tune for "Spirit of God, Descend upon My Heart" was EMILIE by John Wesley Baume, popular violinist and music publisher of Chicago. But the most popular and enduring tune is MORECAMBE (formerly HELLESPONT), which was written in 1870 by organist Frederick Cook Atkinson (1841-1897) for use with Henry Francis Lyte's hymn, "Abide with Me."

Take My Life, and Let It Be
1874

Take my life, and let it be
Consecrated, Lord to Thee;
Take my hands, and let them move
At the impulse of Thy love.

Take my feet, and let them be
Swift and beautiful for Thee;
Take my voice, and let me sing
Always, only, for my King.

Take my silver and my gold,
Not a mite would I withhold;
Take my intellect, and use
Every power as Thou shalt choose.

Take my will and make it Thine,
It shall be no longer mine;
Take my heart, it is Thine own,
It shall be Thy royal throne.

Take my lips, and let them be
Filled with messages for Thee;
Take my moments and my days,
Let them flow in ceaseless praise.

Take my love, my God, I pour
At Thy feet its treasure store;
Take myself and I will be
Ever, only, all for Thee.

—Frances Ridley Havergal

This hymn of consecration is dated February 4, 1874. Miss Havergal recorded the following to explain its origin:

> I went for a little visit of five days. There were ten persons in the house, some unconverted and long prayed-for, some converted but not rejoicing Christians. He gave me the prayer, "Lord, give me *all* in this house!" and He just *did.* Before I left the house everyone had got a blessing. The last night of my visit I was too happy to sleep, and [I] passed most of the night in praise and renewal of my own consecration, and these little couplets formed themselves and chimed in my heart, one after another, till they finished with "ever, only, all, for Thee."

In this hymn of twelve couplets, the second through eleventh pairs, which involve possessions and parts of the body, melt into the first and last more general couplets, which beg, "Take my life" and "Take myself." Although most hymnals include this popular hymn, it is difficult to find two that arrange the couplets and/or stanzas the same way. Even hymnals that include six stanzas (and thus all the couplets) are at variance with regard to the arrangement of the couplets within the stanzas. It seems clear, however, from the author herself, what the first and last stanzas should be.

Frances Ridley Havergal was born at Astley, Worcestershire, on December 14, 1836. She was a precocious child who at seven could write verse and in her youth memorized the New Testament, the Psalms, Isaiah, and the minor prophets. At eleven Frances was warned of her mother's terminal illness. The child refused to believe it. Mrs. Havergal pleaded, "Fanny, dear, pray God to prepare you for all He is preparing for you." To the young poetess this meant believing in the Lord's preparing a Home for her at some future time. Later, however, Frances understood her mother's plea and made it her life prayer.

Surely no poetess ever had a more dedicated heart in using her talents for the Lord. Frances viewed all talents as divine gifts which should be used for God's glory. Because in her writing and singing she sought to win people to the Lord, she became known as an "Evangelist in Song." Miss Havergal knew several languages, including Hebrew and Greek, and did extensive study and witnessing, despite her frail health.

Of her talent Miss Havergal said,

> Writing is praying with me, for I never write a verse by myself; and [I] feel like a little child writing; you know how a child would look up at every sentence and say, "And what shall I say next?" That is just what I do. I ask at every line that He would give me, not merely thoughts and power, but also every *word*, even the very rhymes. I can never set myself to write verse. I believe my King suggests a thought, and whispers me a musical line or two, and then I look up and thank Him delightedly, and go on with it. That is how the hymns and poems come.

Although most of her life was spent in an invalid's chair, Miss Havergal maintained a happy spirit. Her hymns flow with words of praise, joy, victory, peace, and rest. Shortly before her death she wrote to her sister, "I had a great time early this morning. I seemed led to much more definite consecration than even when I wrote the hymn. When I came to the eleventh couplet—'Take my love'—I realized that these words had been unconsciously not filled up. The voice, silver, and gold were simple; but love? I shall go forward and expect Him to fill it up and let my life from this day answer to that."

On June 3, 1879, Miss Havergal was warned of impending death. "It is too good to be true!" she exclaimed. She looked heavenward, smiled, and began to sing, "Jesus, I will trust Thee." Her voice faltered on a high note, and she entered the abode of the One she loved so dearly. Carved on her coffin and monument, by her own request, were the words, "The blood of Jesus Christ his Son cleanseth us from all sin" (I John 1:7).

Fourteen tunes have graced this song. Miss Havergal's favorite was her father's PATMOS. The most popular church tune has been HENDON, composed by H. A. César Malan (1787-1864) in 1823.

Henri Abraham César Malan was a fervent evangelical Swiss preacher. Because he thundered against the spiritual deadness and growing Unitarianism of the state church in Geneva, he was forced to resign. Refusing to accept defeat, he preached for forty-three years in a chapel which he built in his own garden, and was also known for evangelistic tours of Great Britain, France, and Belgium. The University of Glasgow awarded him an honorary degree for his piety and faithful service to the cause of Christ. A man of many talents, Malan was not only a gifted preacher but also a poet, musician, artist, mechanic, blacksmith, printer, and carpenter. He wrote more than 1000 hymns and tunes, always providing tunes for his texts, and is considered "the greatest name in the history of French hymns," yet HENDON is the only contribution still in common use in the English-speaking world.

The anonymous tune YARBROUGH, once thought to have been composed by Bradbury, is set to "Take My Life, and Let It Be" in some hymnals.

Take the Name of Jesus with You
1870

Take the name of Jesus with you,
 Child of sorrow and of woe;
It will joy and comfort give you,
 Take it, then, where'er you go.

Refrain:

Precious name, Oh, how sweet!
Hope of earth and joy of heaven.

Take the name of Jesus ever,
 As a shield from every snare;
If temptations 'round you gather,
 Breathe that holy name in prayer.

Oh, the precious name of Jesus!
 How it thrills our souls with joy,
When His loving arms receive us,
 And His songs our tongues employ.

At the name of Jesus bowing,
 Falling prostrate at His feet,
King of kings in heav'n we'll crown Him,
 When our journey is complete.

—Lydia Baxter

Organist W. N. Burr was in the church after practicing his music when he noticed that an aged man had slipped in to listen to the majestic sounds. The visitor asked, "Won't you please play some more hymns?" And taking up a book of hymns, the man turned to the song, "Take the Name of Jesus with You." He placed it before the musician; "If you will play this song slowly," the stranger said, "I will try to sing it." Later Burr commented to a friend, "There was no music in the old man's voice, but his singing drew my soul a bit nearer to the Saviour."

This comforting hymn was written in 1870 by Mrs. Lydia Baxter. Set to music by William H. Doane, the song soon became well-known. There is, however, little information available about Mrs. Baxter's life and the writing of this hymn. She was born September 8, 1809, in Petersburg, New York. Through the influence of a Baptist home missionary, she was converted in her early years. The lovely hymnist became the wife of Colonel John C. Baxter, and they moved to New York City. Happily, she was able to lead her husband to the Lord Jesus Christ, and their home became a gathering place for ministers and other Christian workers to study God's Word.

Another of Mrs. Baxter's compositions, "There Is a Gate," was popular in the Moody-Sankey meetings in Britain in 1873-1874. A young woman, Maggie Lindsay of Aberdeen, Scotland, was impressed by the song and exclaimed during the service, "O heavenly Father, is it true that the gate is standing ajar for me? If it is, I will enter in." Maggie accepted the Lord that night, and the next day when she called on her pastor to tell him of her decision, she was told, "Go witness to your friends at school." She followed her pastor's advice and soon had the blessing of seeing a number of her friends saved.

In 1874 within a month of her conversion, Maggie was on a train bound for home. The train collided with another, and she was found in the wreckage, crushed and broken. In her hands she clutched a copy of *Sacred Songs and Solos* that was opened to her favorite song, "There Is a Gate." Rescuers carried her into a nearby cottage and provided careful nursing. Despite all their efforts, a few days later she was within those portals about which Mrs. Baxter had written.

Besides those mentioned above, the best-known of Mrs. Baxter's many hymns are "Go Work in My Vineyard," "In the Fadeless Springtime," and "One by One We Cross the River." In the latter she says,

One by one, with sins forgiven,
May we stand upon the shore,
Waiting till the blessed Spirit
Takes our hand and guides us o'er;
Till the loving, gentle Spirit
Leads us to the shining shore.

William Howard Doane (1832-1915), who wrote the tune PRECIOUS NAME (1871) and for whom Lydia Baxter wrote "Take the Name of Jesus with You," was, like Mrs. Baxter, a Baptist. He was one of the most popular composers of nineteenth-century gospel hymn tunes in America, collaborating most notably with Fanny Crosby (1820-1915), a Methodist.

Trust and Obey
   ca. 1887

When we walk with the Lord
In the light of His Word
   What a glory He sheds on our way!
While we do His good will
He abides with us still,
   And with all who will trust and obey.

Refrain:

Trust and obey, for there's no other way
To be happy in Jesus,
But to trust and obey.

Not a shadow can rise,
Not a cloud in the skies,
   But His smile quickly drives it away;
Not a doubt nor a fear,
Not a sigh nor a tear,
   Can abide while we trust and obey.

Not a burden we bear,
Not a sorrow we share,
   But our toil He doth richly repay;
Not a grief nor a loss,
Not a frown nor a cross,
   But is blest if we trust and obey.

But we never can prove
The delights of His love
  Until all on the altar we lay;
For the favor He shows,
And the joy He bestows,
  Are for them who will trust and obey.

Then in fellowship sweet
We will sit at His feet,
  Or we'll walk by His side in the way;
What He says we will do,
Where He sends we will go—
  Never fear, only trust and obey.

—John H. Sammis

This hymn shows that the basis of comfort and fellowship with God is trusting the Lord and obeying His Word. The hymn was inspired by a young man's testimony at a revival meeting led by D. L. Moody in Brockton, Massachusetts. The young man said, "I am not quite sure—but I am going to trust and I am going to obey." The words "trust" and "obey" impressed Mr. Moody's songleader, Daniel B. Towner, and he sent the story to a hymn writer, his friend J. H. Sammis, a Presbyterian minister. According to Mr. Sammis, the refrain was written first; then the stanzas seemed easy to write. Mr. Sammis sent the poem to Mr. Towner, who immediately sat down and sketched the tune. The first printed appearance of the hymn was in 1887 in *Hymns Old and New*.

John H. Sammis was born in Brooklyn on July 6, 1846. At twenty-three he moved to Logansport, Indiana, to pursue a business career. There he became involved in lay work, particularly with the YMCA. Soon the spiritual element overpowered his business interest, and he attended McCormick and Lane Theological Seminaries to prepare for the ministry. After his ordination in the Presbyterian church, Mr. Sammis served pastorates in Iowa, Indiana, Michigan, and Minnesota. The Los Angeles Bible Institute recognized the talents and sound faith of

Mr. Sammis, and he was invited to become a professor at that school. He held this position until the time of his death, June 12, 1919.

Daniel Brink Towner (1850-1919), who composed the tune TRUST AND OBEY, was born in Rome, Pennsylvania, on March 5, 1850. In addition to musical study with his father, he studied with John Goward, George F. Root, and George J. Webb. After serving as music director at a number of churches and working with Dwight L. Moody in his evangelistic campaigns, he became, in 1893, head of the music department of Moody Bible Institute. His honorary Doctor of Music degree was awarded by the University of Tennessee in 1900. He died while leading the music in an evangelistic campaign in Longwood, Missouri, October 3, 1919.

Warfare

Am I a Soldier of the Cross
ca. 1724

Am I a soldier of the cross,
A follower of the Lamb?
And shall I fear to own His cause,
Or blush to speak His name?

Must I be carried to the skies
On flowery beds of ease,
While others fought to win the prize,
And sailed through bloody seas?

Are there no foes for me to face?
Must I not stem the flood?
Is this vile world a friend to grace,
To help me on to God?

Sure I must fight, if I would reign;
Increase my courage, Lord;
I'll bear the toil, endure the pain,
Supported by Thy Word.

Thy saints, in all this glorious war,
Shall conquer, though they die;
They view [see] the triumph from afar,
And seize it with their eye.
[By faith they bring it nigh.]

When that illustrious day shall rise,
And all Thy armies shine
In robes of victory through the skies,
The glory shall be Thine.
—Isaac Watts

"**A**m I a Soldier of the Cross," with its soul-searching questions, its personal commitment, and its earnest petition for increased courage, was found among Isaac

Watts' sermons, not among his hymns. It concluded a discourse on "Holy Fortitude; or Remedies Against Fear." The text was I Corinthians 16:13—"Watch ye, stand fast in the faith, quit you like men, be strong"—and the original title was "Holy Fortitude." Watts read the poem— line by line—and led the congregation in singing it to a familiar tune. "Holy Fortitude" appeared in Volume III of *An Appendage to Watts' Sermons* (three volumes, published 1721-24).

Watts (1674-1748) was noted as "a master of simple language, using one-syllable words whenever possible." He was also a master at incorporating Scripture into his verse.

"Am I a Soldier of the Cross" appeared in Spurgeon's book, *Our Own Hymnbook; a Collection of Psalms and Hymns for Public, Social, and Private Worship* (1866), with stanzas 5 and 6 omitted. Another hymn collection changed the personal pronoun from the singular "Am *I* a soldier" to the plural "Are *we* the soldiers." One hymn mender changed the line, "And seize it with their eye" (stanza 5), to read, "By faith they bring it nigh." The hymn also began to appear regularly in Methodist hymnals around 1831 (although it had appeared in *The Methodist Pocket Hymn Book* of 1802).

Watts is credited with the first "true hymnbook in England." The title of the book was *Hymns and Spiritual Songs.* For many years Watts' hymns dominated hymnals. More recently, however, the number of Watts' hymns has decreased to about fifteen or twenty in most hymnals.

Some people object to Watts' use of warfare terminology with regard to the Christian life. His description, however, is biblically based. It should be noted that the author does not picture the Christian in a defeated position. Indeed, he looks forward to the day when "Thy saints . . . shall conquer, though they die [and] shall shine in robes of victory through the skies," with all glory going to the Lord.

ARLINGTON, the popular tune of "Am I a Soldier of the Cross" is taken from Thomas Arne's opera, *Artaxerxes*

(1762). It was arranged as a hymn tune by Ralph Harrison (1748-1810) for use in his *Sacred Harmonies* (1784).

Thomas A. Arne (1710-1778) is considered to be the eighteenth century's most famous native English composer. His father, a London upholsterer, sent his son to Eton College to study law. Thomas, however, secretly studied music. He became proficient on at least three instruments, muffling them at practice to keep his father from finding out about his musical endeavors. When Mr. Arne became aware of his son's interest in music, he was furious. After a serious argument, however, he consented to the change in his son's field of study.

Both Thomas and his sister had outstanding voices. So well did he coach his sister that she became noted in musical circles. Arne also directed bands in London at Drury Lane and Covent Garden, composed operas, and taught music. At forty-nine he received from Oxford University the Doctor of Music degree.

(For other hymns by Isaac Watts, see pp. 81, 93, 129, 214, 298.)

A Mighty Fortress Is Our God
1529

A mighty fortress is our God,
  A bulwark never failing;
Our helper He, amid the flood
  Of mortal ills prevailing.
For still our ancient foe
Doth seek to work us woe;
His craft and power are great,
And, armed with cruel hate,
  On earth is not his equal.

Did we in our own strength confide,
  Our striving would be losing,
Were not the right Man on our side,
  The Man of God's own choosing.
Dost ask who that may be?
Christ Jesus, it is He;
Lord Sabaoth His name,
From age to age the same,
  And He must win the battle.

And though this world, with devils filled,
  Should threaten to undo us,
We will not fear, for God hath willed
  His truth to triumph through us.
The prince of darkness grim—
We tremble not for him;
His rage we can endure,
For lo! his doom is sure,
  One little word shall fell him.

That word above all earthly powers—
  No thanks to them—abideth;
The Spirit and the gifts are ours
  Through Him who with us sideth.
Let goods and kindred go,
This mortal life also;
The body they may kill:
God's truth abideth still,
  His Kingdom is forever.
—Martin Luther

Whether sung as the dying words of martyrs, a pre-battle hymn of armies, words of comfort for discouraged individuals, or a church hymn of praise to God, this glorious testimony to the power of the Lord Jesus Christ is unsurpassed. Well does it deserve its many labels, such as "a spiritual tonic for the discouraged and distressed," "Luther in song," and "the Marseillaise of the Reformation." This hymn by Martin Luther (1483-1546) was written as a battle call for the Protestant Reformation against the Roman Church. James Moffatt refers to the hymn as "the greatest hymn of the greatest man in the greatest period of history." Dr. Louis Benson describes it as "an imperishable hymn, not polished and artistically wrought, but rugged and strong like Luther."

Based on Psalm 46—"God is our refuge and strength"— all stanzas of this hymn are interdependent. Stanza 1 offers the encouragement that, when under siege, God's children have an impregnable fortress against their "ancient foe," Satan (though Luther was also regarding the "foe" as the hierarchy of the Roman Church). Stanza 2 explains that human strength against the foe is doomed to failure, that the battle needs the strong arms of the Man of God's own choosing—even Christ Jesus our Lord and our victory. In stanza 3 the "prince of darkness" continues his evil works, though his doom is as certain as is our victory in Christ. This stanza ends with the thought that "one little word shall fell him." Stanza 4 picks up on "that word," assuring us that even though we may lose the things we own and love—and even our lives—His Word, eternal truth, shall prevail.

The date of "A Mighty Fortress" is uncertain. It has been suggested that the hymn was written by Luther on his way to the Diet of Worms or during his stay at Wartburg Castle. According to Luther's hymnbooks, the hymn seems to have been written later—perhaps in 1529. Luther loved "A Mighty Fortress"; often, when he was weary and somewhat despondent, he would say to his friend and companion, Philip Melanchthon, "Come, Philip, let us sing the forty-sixth Psalm."

By the year 1900 "A Mighty Fortress" had appeared in eighty translations in over fifty-three languages. In England the most popular version was that translated by Thomas Carlyle in 1831. In America today the most common is the 1852 translation by Frederick Henry Hedge.

Dr. Hedge was born in Cambridge, Massachusetts, on December 12, 1805. He traveled abroad with the historian George Bancroft and studied at schools in Hanover and

Saxony. After his graduation from Harvard in 1825, he held pastorates in Cambridge and Brookline, Massachusetts; Providence, Rhode Island; and Bangor, Maine. (He was ordained as a Unitarian minister in 1829.) In 1857 he accepted the professorship of ecclesiastical history at Harvard University, where later he was also professor of German; and he edited books even into his old age. Hedge died on August 21, 1890.

The tune, EIN' FESTE BURG, is also attributed to Luther. Typically for that day, the tune's name is derived from the hymn's opening line. This tune also forms the theme of Meyerbeer's opera, *Les Huguenots*, Mendelssohn's *Reformation Symphony*, Wagner's *Kaisermarsch*, Bach's Cantata 80, and Nicolai's *Fest Ouverture*. In the opinion of Robert Guy McCutchan *(Our Hymnody)*, the tune is "thrilling," possessing "a dignity, a solidarity, and an authority seldom equaled." Certain critics have insisted that the tune is "a patchwork of tunes which Luther sang as a monk." Julian—perhaps the outstanding authority on hymns—says that "Luther would still be the composer, for it requires much skill to weave fragments into a thing of beauty."

Martin Luther was born in Eisleben, Germany, on November 10, 1483. He was reared in modest circumstances by a gentle mother and a stern—almost cruel—father. From childhood Luther took great pleasure in music. His singing voice was outstanding, and his flute and lute playing were impressive. Music turned out to be a means of gaining an education for Luther. According to the custom of his day, Luther stood at the windows of wealthy people and sang for alms. So deeply impressed with his singing was one woman that she invited him to stay in her home during his school years.

To Luther music was "a divine grace and gift" that needed to be cultivated and used in God's service. Hymns, to Luther, were a sort of "miniature Bible." He said that "after theology, there is nothing that can be placed on a level with music. It drives out the devil and makes people cheerful. It is a gift that God gave to birds and to men.

Many Bible characters were especially gifted in music. Now we need to remove hymn singing from the domain of monks and priests and set the laity to singing. By the singing of hymns the laity can publicly express their love to the Almighty God."

Luther translated the Bible into German in order that the people, by reading the Word for themselves, might hear God speaking to them. Then through their singing of hymns they would speak to God.

Criticism has been leveled at Luther's "intemperate language toward his adversaries." A close look at his hymns reveals that he warred not against his own enemies, but against God's enemies. He felt constrained to follow the admonition of the apostle Paul to "fight the good fight of faith." Luther yearned for people to understand that "the just shall live by faith," and not by the traditions of a corrupt papal authority.

Luther died on February 18, 1546. Around the tower of the castle church where he is buried, there is a finely wrought mosaic that displays the words of his inspiring Reformation hymn. Whether in retrospect we view him as a monk in an Augustinian monastery, as a priest who sincerely desired to serve the Lord, as a musician, or as husband and parent, he has made an outstanding impact on the lives of Christians of all generations who have followed him.

Lead On, O King Eternal
1887

Lead on, O King Eternal,
  The day of march has come;
Henceforth in fields of conquest
  Thy tents shall be our home.
Through days of preparation
  Thy grace has made us strong,
And now, O King Eternal,
  We lift our battle song.

Lead on, O King Eternal,
  Till sin's fierce war shall cease,
And holiness shall whisper
  The sweet Amen of peace;
For not with swords loud clashing,
  Nor roll of stirring drums,
With deeds of love and mercy
  The heavenly kingdom comes.

Lead on, O King Eternal,
  We follow, not with fears;
For gladness breaks like morning
  Where'er Thy face appears;
Thy cross is lifted o'er us;
  We journey in its light;
The crown awaits the conquest;
  Lead on, O God of might.

—Ernest Warburton Shurtleff

Created in 1887 for the commencement exercise at Andover Theological Seminary, this spirited prayer-hymn, with its "day of march," "days of preparation," "journey," "conquest," and "crown," is appropriate for the graduation season.

One of the candidates for degree that year was Ernest Warburton Shurtleff. When the class of '87 met to discuss ways of making their commencement distinctive, someone suggested that Ernest write a special hymn for the class to sing as they marched in to receive their degrees. Ernest, a young man who already had two volumes of poetry to his credit, met the challenge with willingness and capability. "Lead On, O King Eternal" was the result.

Such words as "march," "fields of conquest," "tents," and "battle song" make it clear that the theme of this song is the Christian's victory. Many believers look upon "Lead On, O King Eternal" as their favorite expression of this theme of victory. The author's description of the consecrated Christian as an obedient soldier of the cross echoes Paul's admonition to Timothy in II Timothy 2:1-3:

"Thou therefore, my son, be strong in the grace that is in Christ Jesus ... endure hardness, as a good soldier of Jesus Christ."

Ernest Warburton Shurtleff was born in Boston on April 4, 1862. He was educated at Harvard and Andover. While at Andover he played the organ and sang for Sunday services.

In addition to holding pastorates in widely separated parts of the United States, Shurtleff also organized an American church at Frankfurt, Germany, in 1905. At the Academy Vitti in Paris (1906-1912), he had charge of the Students' Atelier Reunions. Because of his outstanding contributions to music and preaching, he was awarded the honorary degree of Doctor of Divinity by Ripon College.

When World War I began, Shurtleff and his wife, Helen, devoted themselves to relief work. This was Shurtleff's last field of service. Though he died in 1917, his testimony has lived on. Men have said of him, "He was not only a talented man; he was also a kind man—a goodwill ambassador for the Lord."

Henry Smart (1813-1879) wrote LANCASHIRE, the tune to which "Lead On, O King Eternal" is usually sung. He had spent four years studying law before he decided to abandon the bar for the organ bench. His family was not at all surprised when he joined their rich musical heritage. Smart descended from a long line of musicians— his father was a noted violinist, and his uncle was one of England's best-known and best-loved organists and composers.

Smart composed LANCASHIRE in 1835 for a festival in celebration of the tricentennial of the Reformation in England. For that occasion it was set to the words of Reginald Heber's missionary hymn, "From Greenland's Icy Mountains." Apparently this tune was first used with Shurtleff's "Lead On, O King Eternal" in *The Methodist Hymnal* of 1905.

Despite Smart's limited formal training, his personal studies enabled him to make great strides in music, and his accomplishments won high praise from music critics.

He also designed and supervised the building and installation of organs.

For the last fifteen years of his life, Mr. Smart was completely blind. This affliction would have stopped many lesser men, but Smart's remarkable memory enabled him to continue his work. In fact, some of his best work was the fruit of these years, including the tune to "Angels, from the Realms of Glory." He played the organ from memory, dictated new compositions to his daughter, and continued to supervise the installation of organs.

"Lead On, O King Eternal" is indeed a zealous rallying theme. The men graduating at Andover, like all men, had no hope of winning the crown they longed for unless they realized the commitment the song implies. One must be a dedicated follower, totally given over to the winning of the battle, before he dare cry, "Lead on!" It is vital that one who gives himself to be a soldier of Christ dwell in the tents of his Lord and follow Him not in "the spirit of fear; but of power, and of love, and of a sound mind" (II Timothy 1:7).

Onward, Christian Soldiers
1864

Onward, Christian soldiers,
  Marching as to war,
With the cross of Jesus
  Going on before:
Christ the royal Master
  Leads against the foe;
Forward into battle,
  See, His banners go.

Refrain:

Onward, Christian soldiers,
  Marching as to war,
With the cross of Jesus
  Going on before.

At the sign of triumph
  Satan's host doth flee;
On, then, Christian soldiers,
  On to victory!
Hell's foundations quiver
  At the shout of praise;
Brothers, lift your voices,
  Loud your anthems raise.

Like a mighty army
  Moves the Church of God;
Brothers, we are treading
  Where the saints have trod;
We are not divided,
  All one body we,
One in hope and doctrine,
  One in charity.

What the saints established
  That I hold for true;
What the saints believed
  That believe I, too.
Long as earth endureth,
  Men that Faith will hold—
Kingdoms, nations, empires,
  In destruction rolled.

Crowns and thrones may perish,
  Kingdoms rise and wane,
But the Church of Jesus
  Constant will remain;
Gates of hell can never
  'Gainst that Church prevail;
We have Christ's own promise,
  And that cannot fail.

Onward, then, ye people,
  Join our happy throng;
Blend with ours your voices
  In the triumph song;
Glory, laud, and honor
  Unto Christ the King;

This through countless ages
  Men and angels sing.
—Sabine Baring-Gould

"**O**nward, Christian Soldiers" is Baring-Gould's most famous hymn. To some hymnologists, it is "the most famous Christian marching hymn in the English language." A song of battle, of victory, of inspiration, and of praise, it has been used for political and war victories as well as for church services. It is said to have been "the battle song of Roosevelt's Progressive Campaign of 1912" and "a prime favorite in World War I." Stanza 4 is usually omitted, and in many hymnbooks other stanzas have been altered or omitted.

The motivation for this hymn—to march and to encourage other Christians to join in honoring the Lord—is suggested by the word "marching" in stanza 1 and by the invitation of stanza 6 to participate "in the triumph song." It was Whitmonday, the day after Whitsunday or Pentecost (the seventh Sunday after Easter, which in the Victorian Era initiated several festival days in commemoration of the descent of the Holy Ghost at Pentecost). Customarily on this day, Sunday school children in England marched to nearby villages, singing hymns as they went. The march concluded with a feast. In 1864 the festival convened at Horbury Bridge, near Wakefield, Yorkshire, the new parish of the Reverend Sabine Baring-Gould. Feeling that the march would be more effective if the children sang a more spirited marching song, the thirty-year-old bachelor minister stayed up late on Sunday evening, searching for something suitable. Failing to find a hymn to his liking, he set himself to writing one. The hymn was completed in less than fifteen minutes and was titled "Hymn for Procession with Cross and Banners." This title was chosen because the children marched behind an elevated cross and carried various Christian banners. The Sunday school children were delighted to know that they had been the inspiration of the new hymn, and they sang more heartily than ever. Thirty years later Baring-Gould expressed surprise at the hymn's popularity, saying, "It was written in great haste, and I am afraid that some of the lines are faulty."

Years later Baring-Gould was humbled, but thrilled, to know that on a certain May Sunday his hymn would be sung in more than 100 languages in Sunday schools around the world. No other hymnist seems to have been accorded this honor.

Sabine Baring-Gould (1834-1924) was born in Exeter, England, on January 28, 1834. He was the eldest son of the wealthy Edward Baring-Gould of Lew-Trenchard, an estate in Exeter, North Devonshire. In 1856 he received his M.A. degree at Clare College, Cambridge, and in 1864 he took holy orders in the Church of England, being installed as curate at Horbury (near Wakefield, England). His special charge was the Horbury Bridge Mission; there he remained until 1867.

At Horbury, Baring-Gould became interested in Grace Taylor, daughter of a mill worker. Reportedly he saved Miss Taylor from drowning; then he asked permission of the parents to send her away to school. Upon her graduation in 1868, they were married, with Baring-Gould performing the ceremony. Mrs. Baring-Gould was "wife, friend, companion, and assistant rolled into one"; and when she died, Baring-Gould had engraved on her tombstone the Latin words meaning, "Half of my soul."

In 1881 Edward Baring-Gould died, leaving to his son Sabine the family estate. Sabine moved to Lew-Trenchard and was rector, squire, lord of the manor, and author. Religious and outspoken, the Reverend Mr. Baring-Gould lived by the principle that "if I start a task, I keep with it until it is finished. It would never do to wait from day to day for some moments which seem favorable for work."

This versatile and prolific writer wrote numerous books of biography, history, poetry, hymns, fiction, and religion. His largest work, *Lives of the Saints,* in fifteen volumes, was placed on the Roman Catholic *Index,* an indication of the author's attitude toward Romanism. His hymns include the evening hymn, "Now the Day Is Over." Baring-Gould pioneered in collecting English folk songs and was a noted translator of hymns. He was also master of several choir schools, including London and Hurst Pierpont College, Sussex. All of his ninety-three works were written in longhand, without aid of a secretary. Baring-Gould died at Lew-Trenchard on January 2, 1924.

Originally this hymn was sung to the tune of the slow movement of Haydn's *Symphony in D*, No. 15. In 1871 a new tune, ST. GERTRUDE, was written by a twenty-nine-year-old organist, Arthur Seymour Sullivan (1842-1900), the Sir Arthur Sullivan of "Gilbert and Sullivan" fame. Sullivan was visiting the Clay-Ker-Seymers family at Hanford, Dorsetshire. According to Mrs. Gertrude Clay-Ker-Seymers, he was on one of many lengthy visits to their home when he wrote the tune and dedicated it to her (thus, ST. GERTRUDE). "We went into our private chapel," she explained, "and sang the new tune, with Sir Arthur accompanying us on the harmonium." Majestic and stirring, the tune is "charged with the spirit of hope and triumph." H. Augustine Smith (*Lyric Religion*) describes it as an excellent tune for modulating, stanza by stanza, into higher keys—D, E flat, E, and F. Sullivan was born in London on May 13, 1842. He was a prolific writer of sacred and secular tunes, his best-known secular works being probably the operettas *H.M.S. Pinafore* and *The Mikado*. He received a Mus.D. at Cambridge in 1876 and at Oxford in 1879. Because of his musical achievements, Sullivan was knighted in 1883. Sir Arthur died in London on November 22, 1900.

Those who insist on writing trivial words and frivolous tunes for children to sing, while neglecting the great wealth of excellent hymns that have been written for children, would do well to remember that this great hymn of the church was written for Sunday school children.

Soldiers of Christ, Arise
1749

Soldiers of Christ, arise,
And put your armor on,
Strong in the strength which God supplies
   Through His eternal Son;
   Strong in the Lord of hosts,
   And in His mighty power,
Who in the strength of Jesus trusts
   Is more than conqueror.

Stand, then, in His great might,
   With all His strength endued,
And take, to arm you for the fight,
   The panoply of God;
   That, having all things done,
   And all your conflicts past,
Ye may o'ercome, through Christ alone,
   And stand entire at last.

Leave no unguarded place,
   No weakness of the soul;
Take every virtue, every grace,
   And fortify the whole.
   From strength to strength go on,
   Wrestle and fight and pray;
Tread all the powers of darkness down,
   And win the well-fought day.

—Charles Wesley

Charles Wesley (1708-1788) knew much about the
Christian life as a war, but he also knew that every conflict
ends with victory in Christ Jesus. He endured bitter
persecution, yet he stood without flinching. The story is
told of an officer who boasted around his town that he
was going to "brandish a sword at the Reverend Charles
Wesley's breast and let the people watch Wesley faint."
The officer brandished the sword, but Wesley did not faint.
Instead, he very calmly handed the officer one of John

Wesley's tracts, "Advice to a Soldier." Many times John and Charles Wesley were abused, even to the point of being dragged through the streets. Not once, however, did the Wesleys trim their preaching. They continued to preach the full counsel of God's Word.

The original version of "Soldiers of Christ, Arise" was published in 1749 in *Hymns and Sacred Poems.* There were sixteen stanzas, and the title was "The Whole Armour of God, Ephesians VI." Beginning with John Wesley's *Collection of Hymns for the People Called Methodists,* of 1780, twelve of the stanzas appeared as three separate hymns. Not until 1847 did the hymn appear in a three-stanza version.

Percy Dearmer described "Soldiers of Christ, Arise" as exhibiting "mastered simplicity, . . . faultless technique, [and] sagacity in the use of imperfect rhymes." William T. Stead said of the hymn, "It is as inspiring as is the blast of the bugle."

The popular tune DIADEMATA was written for "Crown Him with Many Crowns," ca. 1868, by George Job Elvey (1816-1893). Its name comes from Revelation 19:12, where the Greek word for *crowns* is *diademata.*

(For other hymns by Charles Wesley, see pp. 41, 52, 58, 78, 101, 104, 204.)

Stand Up, Stand Up for Jesus
1858

Stand up, stand up for Jesus,
  Ye soldiers of the cross;
Lift high His royal banner,
  It must not suffer loss;
From victory unto victory,
  His army shall He lead,
Till every foe is vanquished
  And Christ is Lord indeed.

Stand up, stand up for Jesus,
The trumpet call obey;
Forth to the mighty conflict,
In this His glorious day.
"Ye that are men, now serve Him,"
Against unnumbered foes;
Let courage rise with danger,
And strength to strength oppose.

Stand up, stand up for Jesus,
Stand in His strength alone;
The arm of flesh will fail you—
Ye dare not trust your own;
Put on the gospel armor,
Each piece put on with prayer;
Where duty calls, or danger,
Be never wanting there.

Stand up, stand up for Jesus,
The strife will not be long;
This day the noise of battle,
The next, the victor's song;
To him that overcometh,
A crown of life shall be;
He with the King of glory
Shall reign eternally.
—George Duffield, Jr.

This hymn of strength and service challenges Christians to march on courageously for Jesus. Its determined spirit was inspired by the life and courageous death of George Duffield's friend, Dudley A. Tyng.

Tyng, an Episcopalian, and Duffield, a Presbyterian, were two young ministers outstanding in Christian work in Philadelphia. Philadelphia, like many other cities of America, was experiencing a time of great revival in 1857-1858. Because of certain convictions, Tyng had resigned his formal pulpit and was holding services in Jaynes' Hall. On an April Sunday afternoon in 1858 Tyng preached to 5000 men, using as his text: "Go now ye that are men, and serve the Lord" (Exodus 10:11). An estimated 1000 men publicly responded to the invitation.

On the following Wednesday, young Tyng (he was about thirty years of age) left his study and went to the barn to check a corn-shelling machine that was powered by a mule. When Tyng reached over to pat the tired animal, the sleeve of his silk study gown fell into the cogs, causing his arm to be pulled into the wheel. The machine severed his arm at the shoulder.

Days of intense pain followed. Finally Tyng heard the doctor say, "There is no hope. He cannot get well." Without comment on the doctor's verdict, Tyng asked, "Doctor, are you a Christian? I have loved you as a friend, and I long to have you as a brother in Christ. Let me entreat you to come to Jesus." Tyng explained the plan of salvation; then he turned to a group of ministers in the room and cried, "Sing, sing. Can you not sing?" Tyng himself started singing the words, "Rock of Ages, cleft for me; Let me hide myself in Thee," but he could not finish even one stanza. Tyng's father leaned over his dying son and asked, "Do you have a farewell message for your friends?" The son whispered, "Tell them to stand up for Jesus."

On the Sunday following the funeral, Duffield held a memorial service for his colleague. The text of his sermon was Ephesians 6:14: "Stand therefore, having your loins girt about with truth, and having on the breastplate of righteousness." At the conclusion of his tribute, Duffield read the lyrics quoted above—lyrics which he had written upon his return from Tyng's funeral and which use the dying words of his revivalist friend. The second stanza repeats Tyng's last text: "Ye that are men now serve Him."

Duffield was the son, the grandson, and the father of Presbyterian ministers. Born in Carlisle, Pennsylvania, on September 12, 1818, he was educated at Yale and at Union Theological Seminary. He pastored churches in New York, New Jersey, Pennsylvania, Michigan, and Illinois. Duffield died in 1888.

Although choirs and congregations often use Adam

Geibel's tune for this hymn, it is usually sung to WEBB, a tune composed by George J. Webb twenty-eight years before the hymn was written. Born in England on June 24, 1803, Webb studied piano and violin as a child and, before he was twenty, was proficient on the organ. In 1830 Webb moved to America where, in 1836, in cooperation with Dr. Lowell Mason, he founded the Boston Academy of Music. He died in Orange, New Jersey, October 7, 1887. The alternative tune, GEIBEL, was written specifically for this text in 1901 by the blind composer Adam Geibel (1885-1933). Born in Germany, Geibel was brought as a child to America. Improper medication for an eye infection caused the loss of his sight. Despite his handicap, he became a good organist and conductor as well as a prolific composer of both sacred and secular music. The Adam Geibel Music Company, which he founded, became eventually the Rodeheaver Hall-Mack Company.

The Son of God Goes Forth to War
1812

The Son of God goes forth to war,
  A kingly crown to gain;
His blood-red banner streams afar:
  Who follows in His train?
Who best can drink His cup of woe,
  Triumphant over pain,
Who patient bears His cross below,
  He follows in His train.

The martyr first, whose eagle eye
  Could pierce beyond the grave,
Who saw his Master in the sky,
  And called on Him to save:
Like Him, with pardon on his tongue,
  In midst of mortal pain
He prayed for them that did the wrong:
  Who follows in his train?

A glorious band, the chosen few,
  On whom the Spirit came:
Twelve valiant saints, their hope they knew,
  And mocked the cross and flame:
They met the tyrant's brandished steel,
  The lion's gory mane;
They bowed their necks the death to feel:
  Who follows in their train?

A noble army, men and boys,
  The matron and the maid,
Around the Saviour's throne rejoice,
  In robes of light arrayed:
They climbed the steep ascent of heaven
  Through peril, toil, and pain;
O God, to us may grace be given
  To follow in their train.

—Reginald Heber

The general acceptance of modern hymnody in the Church of England was in large measure the result of Reginald Heber's joyful and triumphant hymns. One of his most popular hymns is "The Son of God Goes Forth to War." It's popularity was enhanced by Mrs. Juliana Horatia Ewing's *Story of a Short Life,* in which she referred to the hymn as the "Tug-of-War Hymn, a favorite hymn in the barracks." *Story of a Short Life* centers on an accident victim, the son of an officer, who spends most of his life as a hopeless cripple. When death seems imminent, the young cripple requests that someone sing "The Tug-of-War Hymn." Very quickly a group of soldiers gather under his window and begin to sing. When they come to the lines that speak of "a noble army, men and boys," they see a hand lower the blind at the window, signifying that the sufferer has gone.

David R. Breed regards "The Son of God Goes Forth to War" as the "finest of martial hymns." The hymn was published posthumously, though not by design. Heber

(1783-1826) had pleaded with Archbishop Manners Sutton and later with the bishop of London to authorize the publishing and the public use of his hymns. Heber's chief argument said, "Other churches are making their singing a powerful engine for religious good. These hymns are entering the Episcopal congregation, and I feel that the use of such hymns should be regulated." His request was ignored.

"The Son of God Goes Forth to War," a hymn of conflict and victory, was written in 1812 (although not published until 1827) to be used on St. Stephen's Day (the day after Christmas), when the church honors the first Christian martyr. Although many people decry the hymn's imagery of war, it harmonizes with Scripture.

"The Son of God Goes Forth to War" was written in eight four-line stanzas, but it is printed in hymnals today as four eight-line stanzas. Based on Acts 7:54-60 (the account of Stephen's martyrdom) and Matthew 23:24, it opens with a picture of our Lord's suffering. Stanza 1 depicts Jesus Christ "as a Warrior-Conqueror who someday will be crowned as King." In His army are all "who best can drink His cup of woe [His suffering on the Cross]." "His blood-red banner streams afar" refers to the shedding of His blood on the Cross. From stanza 2, which alludes to Stephen, the first Christian martyr, Heber moves to "the chosen few, on whom the Spirit came" (on the Day of Pentecost), and then to twelve valiant saints (the apostles), and then to martyrs of all ages (Revelation 7:9-17). The following suggestions have been offered for the singing of this hymn as it appears in most hymnals. Stanza 1, with its military air, demands a good march tempo. Stanza 2, a word-picture of the first martyr, should be interpreted with reverential awe. Stanzas 3 and 4, which depict the growth of the church from the original Twelve to "the noble army," should be steadily increased in volume.

In the original manuscript, line 1 of this hymn read, "The Son of God *is gone* to war." Line 1 of stanza 3 spoke of "a *noble* band" instead of "a *glorious* band." In line

4 of stanza 3 "the torch of flame" has become "the cross and flame."

"The Son of God Goes Forth to War" in no way paves the Christian road with ease. Indeed, it uses the solid warning of our Lord that "strait is the gate and narrow is the way" and Paul's terminology of life as a race, a battle, and a warfare. The hardness of the Christian life is tempered, however, with the thought of the "ever-watchful eye of our loving Heavenly Father." This hymn challenges Christians to endure pain, woe, martyrdom, and the grave, and to keep the eye of faith on the eternal rejoicing of the future. At the heart of the hymn is the searching question, "Who follows in His train?"

Heber wrote numerous hymns, including several missionary hymns. His work and that of Sir Robert Grant, Heber's friend, have been described as "exalted of language, faultless of rhythm, possessed of a startling grandeur of imagery, and having lines 'as perfectly chiseled as a cameo and as clear as a trumpet call.'"

Much credit for this hymn's popularity must go to its tune, ALL SAINTS' NEW, which Henry S. Cutler (1824-1902) wrote in 1872 especially for this hymn. Because another tune bore the title of ALL SAINTS, Cutler added the word "New" to set his tune apart.

Henry Stephen Cutler, Mus.D., was born in Boston on October 13, 1824. He was educated in America, Germany, and England, after which he became an organist, first at Boston's Grace Episcopal Church and later at the Church of the Advent. There he organized a choir of men and boys, the first surpliced choir in America. Cutler became famous for this innovation, but his fame, in part, was due to the criticism he received for using robes at a church service, which some people considered overly formal. In 1858 Cutler moved to New York to become organist-choir master at Trinity Church. Again he innovated, bringing his choir into the chancel wearing cassocks and cottas, this time to honor the visit of the Prince of Wales. And again it caused quite a stir. It is possible that the situation cost Cutler his position at

Trinity, for while he was on a concert tour, the church "voted him out," supposedly for being "A.W.O.L." Undaunted, Cutler moved on to serve churches in Brooklyn, Providence, Philadelphia, and Troy. He died December 5, 1902, in Boston, where he had lived in retirement since 1885.

(For another hymn by Reginald Heber, see p. 10.)

Church & Kingdom

Blest Be the Tie That Binds
  1772

  Blest be the tie that binds
  Our hearts in Christian love;
The fellowship of kindred minds
  Is like to that above.

  Before our Father's throne
  We pour our ardent prayers;
Our fears, our hopes, our aims are one,
  Our comforts and our cares.

  We share our mutual woes,
  Our mutual burdens bear;
And often for each other flows
  The sympathizing tear.

  When we asunder part,
  It gives us inward pain;
But we shall still be joined in heart,
  And hope to meet again.

  This glorious hope revives
  Our courage by the way;
When each in expectation lives,
  And longs to see the day.

  From sorrow, toil, and pain,
  And sin, we shall be free;
And perfect love and friendship reign
  Throughout eternity.
—John Fawcett

The story of "Blest Be the Tie That Binds" is locked into the events of the author's life. John Fawcett was born in 1740 in Lidget Green, Yorkshire, England. He was orphaned at the age of twelve, and at thirteen he began a six-year apprenticeship (actually an enslavement) to a London tailor. John was required to work from six in the morning to eight in the evening daily. At night, when he retired to his attic room, the lad would lie on the floor and read *Pilgrim's Progress.* His reading light was a candle that he hid under "an earthen bushel."

Pilgrim's Progress afforded John his first experience with spiritual matters. At fifteen or sixteen he attended a meeting conducted by the Reverend George Whitefield in a large field with twenty thousand people in attendance. John was soundly converted. He joined the Baptist church in Bradford in 1758, and, having answered the call to the ministry, he was ordained a Baptist minister in 1763.

John's first pastorate was at a small church in Wainsgate, Yorkshire. Wainsgate was "less than a village." When Fawcett and his bride, who was five years his senior, arrived in Wainsgate, they found only a few houses on a barren hill. There being no parsonage, they had to "board around." Wainsgaters were described as "uneducated, pagan, and hot-tempered." Their meeting place was a small, damp house, which had a seating capacity of 100 people. The congregation had to sit on stools, for there were no benches.

The Wainsgate Baptist Church grew so rapidly that the men of the church had to add a balcony to the meeting place; later the church's growth forced them to build a larger church, the property for which was donated by a local farmer.

John Fawcett earned only $200 (25 pounds) a year, and part of that amount was in potatoes and wool. In 1772, possibly because of his meager salary and his increasing family (four children in five years), Pastor Fawcett accepted a call to succeed the noted John Gill at Carter Lane Baptist Church in London. No doubt Fawcett reasoned that in London he would be able to "reach more people for the Lord."

The following traditional and touching, though unauthenticated, story of this hymn was first told in 1869 in Josiah Miller's *Singers and Songs of the Church.* A similar account had appeared earlier, however, in John Gadsby's *Memoirs of the Principal Hymn Writers and Compilers of the 17th, 18th, and 19th Centuries* (London, 1861).

Fawcett's farewell sermon was preached on a Sunday in 1772. The next day he and his family emerged from their dwelling place to walk to the dray that would take them and their meager belongings to London. How surprised they were to see around the dray their parishioners who had come to say good-bye. The Fawcetts looked upon the smiling, but tear-stained, faces of their friends, and they felt a stirring of heart. "How can I leave these people?" thought Mr. Fawcett. "They love the Lord, they love our family, and they need our ministry." Mrs. Fawcett sensed her husband's thoughts, and she asked, "John, do you think that we should leave these people?" "No," he answered. "We *should* not leave, and we *shall* not leave." And turning to the men of his church, he said, "Men, start unloading our belongings. I shall notify the London church that I cannot come."

In honor of his people's devotion, Pastor Fawcett penned a poem that he entitled "Brotherly Love" (later known as "Blest Be the Tie That Binds"). He finished the poem at midnight on Saturday night, and on Sunday he read it to his congregation. Again the people wept. This time, however, their tears were tears of joy for being able to have their beloved pastor and his family a while longer.

A while longer, indeed! Fawcett's time at Wainsgate stretched to fifty-four years. During this time he founded a training school for young ministers, wrote many theological books and commentaries, and composed numerous hymns (166 of which were included in his *Hymns Adapted to the Circumstances of Public Worship and Printed Devotion*, published in 1782). Appearing as number 104 in Fawcett's publication of 1782, although it may have been written as early as 1772, "Blest Be the Tie That Binds" consisted of the six four-line stanzas printed above. Most hymnals print only the first four stanzas.

Fawcett's *Essay on Anger* impressed King George III to offer to the author "any benefit he could confer." The minister answered, "Thank you, but I live among a people who love me. The Lord has blessed my labors among these people, and I need nothing that a king can supply."

In 1811, Brown University in Providence, Rhode Island, recognized Fawcett's accomplishments by conferring upon him the honorary Doctor of Divinity degree. Fawcett died of a stroke on July 25, 1817.

The tune DENNIS, to which this hymn is most often sung, was possibly composed by Johann (Hans) Georg Nägeli (1773-1836), a musician and publisher at Wetzikon, Switzerland. He published many works of Beethoven, Clementi, and Cramer and was a pioneer music educator. Lowell Mason, who arranged and introduced this tune in 1845, was greatly influenced by Nägeli's educational methods and applied them in American schools.

Faith of Our Fathers!
1849

Faith of our fathers! living still
In spite of dungeon, fire, and sword:
O how our hearts beat high with joy
Whene'er we hear that glorious word!

Refrain:

Faith of our fathers, holy faith!
We will be true to thee till death!

Our fathers, chained in prisons dark,
Were still in heart and conscience free:
How sweet would be their children's fate,
If they, like them, could die for thee!

Faith of our fathers! we will love
Both friend and foe in all our strife:
And preach thee, too, as love knows how,
By kindly words and virtuous life:
—Frederick W. Faber

An angry farmer was threatening some young men for trespassing. So smoothly and convincingly did one of the young men apologize that the farmer's wife said to her husband, "Ye must let them gan, Maister; the young gentleman has sic a pratty tongue." The young man of "sic a pratty tongue" was Frederick William Faber, who later became a prolific writer and "a preacher of persuasive voice and charming personality."

Faber was born on June 28, 1814, at the vicarage at Calverley, Yorkshire, near his famous theologian uncle— George Stanley Faber. The atmosphere of young Faber's home, since the family was of Huguenot stock, was one of "strict Calvinism." His church was the Church of England. Faber was educated at Balliol and University colleges, Oxford. When he announced his decision to enter the ministry, William Wordsworth said, "I admire your choice, but I grieve at the loss of such a good poet."

After his graduation, Faber was ordained in the Church of England (1837). After touring Europe in 1841, he was assigned to a very corrupt area, and he is credited with effecting "a moral revolution." Eventually, two influences—his travels and his admiration for John Henry Newman (author of "Lead, Kindly Light"), whom he had met at college—led him into the Roman Catholic Church. This was surprising, for in college Faber had written anti-Catholic tracts. Newman and Faber seemed to have kindred spirits, and their ministry became intertwined.

In 1848 Newman established a community connected with the Oratory of St. Philip Neri, which Faber joined. An oratory is an organization of secular priests not under vows who devote themselves to prayer, preaching, and the celebration of the sacraments. The word itself comes from the Latin *oratorium* ("a place of prayer") and has given us the word *oratorio*, a type of sacred choral music that developed from the musical devotions of the Oratory. In 1849 Newman sent Faber to London to establish another branch of the Oratory.

Dr. David R. Breed (*The History and Use of Hymns and Hymn Tunes*) states that "few hymnists have been more often quoted than F. W. Faber. Many single lines have become almost proverbial, though many who make use of them are ignorant of their origin." Some examples of Faber's pithy lines are the following:

For right is right, since God is God, and right the day must win.
Every moment of resistance to temptation is a victory.
The surest method of arriving at a knowledge of God's eternal purposes about us is to be found in the right use of the present moment. Each hour comes with some little fagot of God's will fastened upon its back.
We cannot resist the conviction that this world is for us only the porch of another and more magnificent temple of the Creator's majesty.

Some hymnologists date the writing of some of Faber's hymns to the period before his conversion to Roman Catholicism. Others insist that all of his hymns were written after his defection. They were, at least, published after he entered the Roman Church. Although critics have described the language of his hymns as too extravagant, incongruous, sentimental, and obscure in meaning, they praise Faber's vivid imagination. They cite "There's a Wideness in God's Mercy" in which Faber likens God's mercy to "the wideness of the sea" and "Hark, Hark, My Soul" in which he uses the imagery of "bells at evening pealing" and "the voice of Jesus sounding o'er land and sea."

"Faith of Our Fathers!" is from Faber's *Jesus and Mary or Catholic Hymns for Singing and Reading* (London, 1849). Originally the third stanza said:

Faith of our fathers! Mary's prayers
Shall win our country back to thee;
And through the truth that comes from God
England shall then indeed be free.

This stanza was altered to read:

Faith of our fathers! We will strive
To win all nations unto thee,
And through the truth that comes from God
Mankind shall then be truly free.

Many hymnals omit this stanza.

Protestants who sing "Faith of our fathers! living still/ In spite of dungeon, fire, and sword" envision the heroes of faith as recorded in Hebrews chapter 11 or the martyrs of the early Church before the rise of Romanism. Faber's references, however, are to the Fathers of the Roman Catholic faith.

Faber wrote his initial hymns to follow the pattern of some of his favorite hymn tunes. "Faith of Our Fathers!" was set to ST. CATHERINE (called TYNEMOUTH in England), a tune by Henri Frederick Hemy (1818-1888). The tune was composed in 1864 for a hymn that opened with the words, "Sweet Saint Catherine [a fourth-century martyr of Alexandria], Maid most pure, Teach us to meditate and pray." It was adapted by James G. Walton (1821-1905). Hemy was born at Newcastle-upon-Tyne and eventually taught music there. An accomplished organist and arranger, he compiled many books on sacred music. His original tunes, though few, and his arrangements appeared in *Crown of Jesus Music*, which was popular in the Roman Catholic churches of England.

Faber died on September 26, 1863, leaving to posterity 150 hymns (numbered to correspond to the number of the Psalms). He felt that in some measure he had met his goal—to write for Roman Catholics some inspiring hymns such as the hymns of Newton, Cowper, and the Wesleys that were important to him in his youth.

For All the Saints
1864

For all the saints who from their labors rest,
Who Thee by faith before the world confessed,
Thy name, O Jesus, be forever blest.
Alleluia! Alleluia!

Thou wast their rock, their fortress and their might;
Thou, Lord, their captain in the well-fought fight;
Thou, in the darkness drear, their one true light.
Alleluia! Alleluia!

For the Apostles' glorious company,
Who, bearing forth the cross o'er land and sea,
Shook all the mighty world, we sing to Thee.
Alleluia! Alleluia!

For the Evangelists, by whose blest word,
Like fourfold streams, the garden of the Lord
Is fair and fruitful, be Thy name adored.
Alleluia! Alleluia!

For Martyrs, who, with rapture-kindled eye,
Saw the bright crown descending from the sky,
And died to grasp it, Thee we glorify.
Alleluia! Alleluia!

O may Thy soldiers, faithful, true, and bold,
Fight as the saints who nobly fought of old,
And win, with them, the victor's crown of gold.
Alleluia! Alleluia!

O blest communion, fellowship divine!
We feebly struggle; they in glory shine.
Yet all are one in Thee, for all are Thine.
Alleluia! Alleluia!

And when the strife is fierce, the warfare long,
Steals on the ear the distant triumph song,
And hearts are brave again and arms are strong.
Alleluia! Alleluia!

The golden evening brightens in the west;
Soon, soon to faithful warriors cometh rest;
And sweet the calm of Paradise, the blest.
Alleluia! Alleluia!

But lo! there breaks a yet more glorious day;
The saints triumphant rise in bright array;
The King of Glory passes on His way.
Alleluia! Alleluia!

From earth's wide bounds, from ocean's farthest coast,
Through gates of pearl stream in the countless host,
Singing to Father, Son, and Holy Ghost.
Alleluia! Alleluia!

—William Walsham How

"For All the Saints" is one of the lengthiest and most popular works of William Walsham How (1823-1897). Dr. Charles S. Robinson, in *Annotations Upon Popular Hymns*, describes this hymn as having been "praised by the best critics, accepted by the highest authorities, and introduced in nearly all the compilations over the world."

"For All the Saints" is a "skillful blend of the past, the present, and the future." The original title read, "For All *Thy* Saints," with a reference to Hebrews 12:1. The hymn was first published in *Hymns for Saints' Days, and Other Hymns*, 1864.

"For All the Saints" was written in eleven three-line stanzas, each stanza ending with "Alleluia! Alleluia!" Eventually, three stanzas were removed and published as a separate hymn, and the remaining stanzas were used in varying numbers and arrangements.

It is to be noted that "For All the Saints" is somewhat in the vein of prayer. It addresses the Lord Jesus Christ as our Rock, our Fortress, our Might, our Captain, our Lord, and the King of Glory, and it expresses hope that all soldiers of the Cross shall "earnestly contend for the faith," even as did the saints of old. The hymn does not minimize the ferocity, the length, and the noise of the battle. Rather, it sees these elements as overpowered by eventual and eternal victory in Christ Jesus. The hymn closes with a picture of "a countless host" streaming through "gates of pearl and singing praise to Father, Son, and Holy Ghost."

A number of hymnologists point out that the emphasis of this hymn is faith. They regard line 2—"Who Thee by faith before the world confessed"—as being the most important line in the hymn, with all other lines "serving as background and scenery."

William Walsham How, who wrote this hymn in 1864, authored a total of fifty-four hymns. Among these are "Jesus! Name of Wondrous Love," "O Word of God Incarnate," "O Jesus, Thou Art Standing," and "We Give Thee But Thine Own." Bishop How was known as "the children's bishop" and "the poor man's bishop" because of his legendary deeds of kindness in the poor districts of London. He thought so little of ecclesiastical attainment that he even neglected to tell his family when he received an offer to become bishop of Durham and refused it. Though not a brilliant intellect and somewhat liberal in his theology, How was a shining example of selfless service for the needy. He received an honorary Doctor of Divinity degree from the Archbishop of Canterbury in 1879, and a similar honor from Oxford University in 1886. He was born in Shrewsbury, Shropshire, England, December 13, 1823, and died while on vacation in Ireland, on August 10, 1897.

The first tune for this hymn was SARUM (sometimes called ST. PHILIP or FOR ALL THE SAINTS), which was composed for this text in 1869 by Sir Joseph Barnby (1838-1896). Sir Joseph was highly regarded in musical circles and for many years served well as director of music at Eton College and principal of the Guildhall School of Music. Sir Joseph also served as musical editor of five hymnals.

SARUM was popular in Britain, but in America Ralph Vaughan Williams' SINE NOMINE (1906) became the favored tune. Many hymnologists have pointed out that

SARUM is less well suited rhythmically to the words than is SINE NOMINE. For instance, line 1 with SARUM would read, "*For all the saints who from . . . .*" Haeussler comments regarding SINE NOMINE, "The accents in the music coincide with those in the text and the melody and harmonization move forward with the strides of a victorious faith." Actually, either tune fits quite well, but Vaughan Williams' tune is definitely more majestic and exuberant.

Ralph Vaughan Williams (1872-1958) was born in Down Ampney, Gloucestershire, England, October 12, 1872. His formal training took place at Trinity College, Cambridge; Royal College of Music, London; and with well-known musicians such as Max Bruch and Maurice Ravel. Among Vaughan Williams' accomplishments were his teaching at Royal College and his editing and coediting outstanding hymnals (such as the *English Hymnal,* 1906, and the *Oxford Book of Carols,* 1928). An enthusiastic collector of folksongs, Vaughan Williams used these tunes in many of his compositions, which ranged from simple hymns to major symphonies. He died in St. Marylebone, England, August 26, 1958. He is regarded as Britain's greatest composer since Henry Purcell (1659-1695).

(For other hymns by William Walsham How, see pp. 140, 146.)

Glorious Things of Thee Are Spoken
1779

Glorious things of thee are spoken,
* Zion, city of our God;*
He whose word cannot be broken
* Formed thee for His own abode;*
On the Rock of Ages founded,
* What can shake thy sure repose?*
With salvation's walls surrounded,
* Thou mayst smile at all thy foes.*

See, the streams of living waters,
  Springing from eternal love,
Well supply thy sons and daughters,
  And all fear of want remove.
Who can faint, while such a river
  Ever flows their thirst to assuage?
Grace which, like the Lord, the Giver,
  Never fails from age to age.

Round each habitation hovering,
  See the cloud and fire appear
For a glory and a covering,
  Showing that the Lord is near!
He who gives us daily manna,
  He who listens to our cry,
To Him raise the glad hosanna,
  Rising to His throne on high.

Blest inhabitants of Zion,
  Washed in the Redeemer's blood!
Jesus, whom their souls rely on,
  Makes them kings and priests to God;
'Tis His love His people raises
  Over self to reign as kings;
And as priests, His solemn praises
  Each for a thank offering brings.

Saviour, if of Zion's city
  I, through grace, a member am;
Let the world deride or pity,
  I will glory in Thy Name:
Fading is the worldling's pleasure;
  All his boasted pomp and show;
Solid joys and lasting treasure,
  None but Zion's children know.

—John Newton

To many people this glorious paean of praise, this hymn of optimism that is laced with Scripture and is prophetic of a glorious future for the church of God, is one of John Newton's (1725-1807) greatest hymns. Based on Isaiah 33:20-21, it bespeaks Zion in the future and promises peace and quiet in the eternal presence of "the glorious Lord." Originally, the hymn was entitled "Zion; or, The City of God." The present title and the hymn's opening words are an arrangement of Psalm 87:3— "Glorious things are spoken of thee, O city of God." Apparent in the hymn is Newton's belief in the eternality of both the Written Word and the Living Word of God and his confidence in having eternal life through Christ Jesus.

"Glorious Things of Thee are Spoken" first appeared in five stanzas in the *Olney Hymns* (1779). Later, stanzas 4 and 5 were dropped from some hymnals. The last four lines of stanza 3 originally went:

Thus deriving from their banner,
  Light by night, and shade by day,
Safe they feed upon the manna
  Which He gives them when they pray.

In 1905 another editor replaced these same lines with the first four lines of stanza 1.

Stanza 1 embodies Revelation 21 and 22 and suggests the endurance and strength that flow from the Rock of Ages, the Lord Jesus Christ. To Newton the walls of protection in the city are salvation.

Stanza 2 expresses Revelation 22:1—"And he shewed me a pure river of water of life, clear as crystal, proceeding out of the throne of God and of the Lamb." It reflects safety and provision, with all fear of want removed. That a Christian could have before him "streams of living waters, Springing from eternal love" and grow weary and faint is beyond Newton's comprehension. This water, he explains, "like the Lord, the Giver, Never fails from age to age." Stanza 2 also draws on Psalm 46:4: "There is a river, the streams whereof shall make glad the city of God, the holy place of the tabernacles of the most High."

In stanza 3 Newton recalls the pillar of cloud by day and the fire by night that God used to guide Israel to the Promised Land (Exodus 13:22). The author interprets this Old Testament incident as a symbol of the New Jerusalem in which neither sun nor candle is needed, "for the Lord giveth them light." The manna that was miraculously supplied to Israel in the wilderness pre-figures the fruit of the Tree of Life in Revelation 22:2 that will yield "twelve manner of fruits . . . every month." The analogy is that every need will be provided eternally.

The closing lines of stanza 4 suggest the priesthood of each believer, making it possible for us to come before the throne of God with boldness.

The "glorious things" conclude with a sharp contrast of the worldling's "fading pleasure," his "boasted pomp and show," and the Christian's "solid joys" and "lasting treasures" that are provided in Christ Jesus. Newton's attitude in this stanza is reminiscent of the attitude of the apostle Paul, who said, "The Lord shall deliver me from every evil work, and will preserve me unto his heavenly kingdom: to whom be glory for ever and ever" (II Timothy 4:18). Newton says, "Let the world deride and pity me, I will glory in Thy Name."

The tune AUSTRIA (also called CHEADLE, HAYDN, VIENNA, EMPEROR'S HYMN, and AUSTRIAN HYMN) was a favorite of its composer, Franz Joseph Haydn (1732-1809). It may have been the last tune he ever played. The French were attacking Vienna, and the aged Haydn asked to be taken to his harpsichord so that he might play this tune. Five days later he was dead.

AUSTRIA was written for use with "Hymn to the Emperor" ("Gott, erhalte Franz, den Kaiser," whose text was by Lorenz Hauschka) and was first performed on February 12, 1797, at a birthday celebration for Emperor Franz II. The inspiration for the tune was a Croatian folksong, "Vjutro rano se ja vstanem." The first three measures are identical. AUSTRIA is also the theme of the slow movement (with variations) in Haydn's String Quartet in C (Opus 76, No. 3). Used for a time as the Austrian national hymn, this tune was taken over for use as the Nazi hymn of Germany during the World War II era and sung to the text, "Deutschland, Deutschland über Alles"

("Germany, Germany above all"). Today it is still sung as the West German national anthem, but with the more noble words, "Einigkeit, und Recht, und Freiheit, für das Deutsche Vaterland" ("Unity, Right, and Freedom, for the German Fatherland.") The most familiar usage of the tune in America, however, is with "Glorious Things of Thee Are Spoken" to which it was set in 1805. One authority recounts an interesting sidelight to this tune. He says that a stocking manufacturer, William Gardiner (*Sacred Melodies*, 1812), gave the famous Haydn a pair of stockings on which were woven the opening bars of his EMPEROR'S HYMN.

Franz Joseph Haydn was born in Rohrau, Austria, on March 31, 1732. He died in Vienna on May 31, 1809. As a boy he lived with a cousin who taught him music, and then as a teenager he became a choir boy at St. Stephen's Cathedral in Vienna. Life was hard, but he slowly struggled out of poverty and want. Haydn learned composition by his own effort, greatly influenced by Johann Joseph Fux and Carl Philipp Emanuel Bach, and was finally honored with an honorary Mus.D. from Oxford University. He epitomized Christian joy. He said, "When I think of God, my heart dances within me, and my music has to dance, too." Haydn accepted his musical talent as a treasure from God. Many compositions were prefaced with the words, *In nomine Domini* ("In the Name of the Lord"), and closed with the words, *Laus Deo* ("Praise to God").

(For another hymn by John Newton, see p. 96.)

I Love Thy Kingdom, Lord
1801

I love Thy kingdom, Lord,
The house of Thine abode,
The Church our blest Redeemer saved
With His own precious blood.

I love Thy Church, O God!
Her walls before Thee stand,
Dear as the apple of Thine eye,
And graven on Thy hand.

For her my tears shall fall;
For her my prayers ascend;
To her my cares and toils be given,
Till toils and cares shall end.

Beyond my highest joy
I prize her heavenly ways,
Her sweet communion, solemn vows,
Her hymns of love and praise.

Jesus, Thou friend divine,
Our Saviour and our King,
Thy hand from every snare and foe
Shall great deliverance bring.

Sure as Thy truth shall last,
To Zion shall be given
The brightest glories earth can yield,
And brighter bliss of Heaven.
—Timothy Dwight

The lyrics of this hymn are based on Psalm 137:5-6: "If I forget thee, O Jerusalem, let my right hand forget her cunning. If I do not remember thee, let my tongue cleave to the roof of my mouth; if I prefer not Jerusalem above my chief joy." This is probably the earliest American hymn to remain in common usage today. In order to understand the writing of these words, it is helpful to know some of the background of American hymnology.

The first hymnbook (in fact, the first book of any kind) to be printed in colonial America was *The Bay Psalm Book* of 1640. This book took its name from its place of publication, the Massachusetts Bay Colony. Isaac Watts' *Hymns and Spiritual Songs* appeared in England in 1707, and his *Psalms of David Imitated* in 1719. Although some of the books found their way to America, they did not find immediate acceptance. It was not until the spiritual awakening fired by the preaching of Jonathan Edwards in 1734 and strengthened by the visit of George Whitefield to New England in 1740 that the joyful and challenging hymns of Watts began to be sung in American churches.

In 1785 the General Association of Congregational Churches asked Joel Barlow, Revolutionary War chaplain, to "revise Watts' works, purging them of their British flavor." When Barlow's revision proved unsuitable, they asked Dr. Timothy Dwight, president of Yale and a grandson of Jonathan Edwards, to take over the project. Dr. Dwight's revision appeared in 1801 and included many hymns of other writers as well as thirty-three of his own paraphrases. Eventually some of Dwight's paraphrases became independent hymns. The most notable, of course, and the only one to survive, is "I Love Thy Kingdom, Lord."

Timothy Dwight was born at Northampton, Massachusetts, on May 14, 1752. Some chroniclers have likened his life to "an imagined romance." At the age of four he could read the Bible. At six he could read Latin. At seventeen he was graduated from Yale, and at nineteen he became a tutor there. So popular was he in the latter capacity that by the time he was twenty-five, he was the subject of a petition, unanimously signed by the students, to have him made the president of Yale. Timothy declined the honor, however, in favor of becoming a chaplain in the Continental Army.

Dwight was popular as a chaplain too. Officers and enlisted men alike enjoyed his made-to-order patriotic songs, and George Washington considered him a personal friend. But his career as a chaplain was cut short by the death of his father. After a year he had to return home to manage the family farm and support his mother and brothers and sisters.

In 1783, after a short session in the Massachusetts legislature, Mr. Dwight was called to the Congregational church at Greenfield, Connecticut. His salary being too meager for the needs of his family, he founded an academy and became a teacher.

At the age of forty-three, in 1795, Mr. Dwight accepted the presidency of his alma mater. A noted church historian says,"When he became the head of Yale, no more than four or five students were professing Christians. But after listening to his chapel messages, the students experienced a spiritual awakening that spilled over to Amherst, Dartmouth, and Williams." Thus, what is known as the Second Great Awakening may be said to have begun under Dwight's leadership. His chapel sermons were later published and widely circulated under the title *Theology Explained and Defended.*

Dwight lived a useful life in spite of serious handicaps. Because he strained his eyes through long hours of reading by candlelight, by the time he was twenty-five he could stand no more than fifteen minutes of reading at one sitting. Much of his work was accomplished laboriously with the help of others who read to him. The literary historian Moses Coit Tyler wrote of Dwight's life that "it was almost never exempt from severe bodily pain, but pervaded throughout by singular activity, power, and productiveness, and challenging the public admiration, then and since then, by its breadth, versatility, and robust sense; its brilliance, its purity, its dignity of tone, its moral aggressiveness, its many-sided and benign achievement." Dwight died in New Haven, Connecticut, on January 11, 1817, bequeathing to society a deep inspiration and challenge.

The tune to which Dwight's hymn is usually sung is ST. THOMAS. It is a portion of an earlier tune called HOLBORN, which first appeared in London in 1763 in the second edition of Aaron Williams' *Universal Psalmodist.* The fragment that forms the present ST. THOMAS appeared in the fifth edition of this collection (1770) and in the same year appeared also in Isaac Smith's *Collection of Psalm Tunes.*

Jesus Shall Reign Where'er the Sun
1719

Jesus shall reign where'er the sun
Does his successive journeys run;
His kingdom stretch [spread] from shore to shore,
Till moons shall wax and wane no more.

Behold! the islands, with their kings,
And Europe, her best tribute brings;
From North to South the princes meet
To pay their homage at His feet.

There Persia, glorious to behold,
There India shines in Eastern gold,
And barbarous nations, at His Word
Submit, and bow, and own their Lord.

To Him shall endless prayer be made,
And endless praises crown His head;
His name like sweet perfume shall rise
With every morning sacrifice.

People and realms of every tongue
Dwell on His love with sweetest song,
And infant voices shall proclaim
Their early blessings on His name.

Blessings abound where'er He reigns;
The prisoner leaps to loose his chains;
The weary find eternal rest,
And all the sons of want are blest.

Where He displays His healing power,
Death and the curse are known no more;
In Him the tribes of Adam boast
More blessings than their father lost.

Let every creature rise and bring
Peculiar honors to their [our] King;
Angels descend with songs again,
And earth repeat the loud Amen!

—Isaac Watts

It was Whitsunday, about 150 years after the writing of "Jesus Shall Reign." Approximately 5000 South Pacific Islanders were listening intently to their king—King George the Sable—who was reading a new charter of government. At the conclusion, the new charter declared that the islands, which formerly had been known as heathen islands, now would be called a Christian nation. Suddenly all of the chiefs and warriors and people—young and old—burst into singing, "Jesus shall reign where'er the sun/ Does his successive journeys run. . . ."

A careful reading of this hymn reveals a striking resemblance to Psalm 72, which seems to be a paraphrase of David's prayer for his son Solomon and his prophecies of the glories and peace of Solomon's kingdom. David longed for his son's understanding of the divine judgments and righteousness in order that he might judge God's people "with righteousness" and "the poor with judgment." David saw beyond Solomon's reign to the righteous reign of the Lord Jesus Christ.

Isaac Watts (1674-1748) read this passage and became intrigued with the psalmist's imagery of nature—"rain upon the mown grass" and "showers that water the earth." It thrilled him to think that the name of his Lord should be "continued as long as the sun," and that "all nations shall call him blessed." Such thoughts prompted him to pen the verses that later received the label, "the pioneer missionary hymn."

As originally written, "Jesus Shall Reign" contained eight stanzas, although most modern hymnals use only four, five, or six. Omitting stanzas 2, 3, 7, and 8, they combine some of the thoughts of these stanzas to form new stanzas. The revision of "Jesus Shall Reign" makes it much more effective, which provides a strong argument for hymn revisions in general.

This "first positive missionary pronouncement" predates by at least sixty years the missionary endeavors of William Carey. "Jesus Shall Reign" was written in 1719, and William Carey's efforts were launched in 1779.

DUKE STREET, the hymn's popular tune (also known

as ST. HELEN'S and WINDLE), was composed by John Hatton (1790?). Its first known printing was in 1793 in Henry Boyd's *Select Collection of Psalm and Hymn Tunes.* Boyd, a teacher of psalmody in Glasgow, headed the tune, "Addison's Nineteenth Psalm," omitting the composer's name. It was to be sung to Addison's hymn, "The Spacious Firmament on High." The second printing was in William Dixon's *Euphonia* (1805), which lists both the tune name and composer. In this country the tune was called NEWRY in *The Methodist Harmonist,* 1821 (the first official tunebook of American Methodists). Composer Hatton was born at Warrenton, near Liverpool, but very few pertinent facts of his life are known. His latter years are described as having been spent on Duke Street, St. Helen's district, township of Windle, which inspired the three names of his only known tune. Hatton is said to have lost his life in a stagecoach accident in 1793.

(For other hymns by Isaac Watts, see pp. 81, 93, 129, 214, 257.)

The Church's One Foundation
1866

The Church's one Foundation
  Is Jesus Christ her Lord;
She is His new creation,
  By water and the word:
From heaven He came and sought her
  To be His holy bride;
With His own blood He bought her,
  And for her life He died.

Elect from every nation
  Yet one o'er all the earth,
Her charter of salvation,
  One Lord, one faith, one birth;

One holy name she blesses,
Partakes one holy food,
And to one hope she presses,
With every grace endued.

The Church shall never perish!
Her dear Lord to defend,
To guide, sustain, and cherish,
Is with her to the end;
Though there be those that hate her,
And false sons in her pale,
Against the foe or traitor
She ever shall prevail.

Though with a scornful wonder
Men see her sore opprest,
By schisms rent asunder,
By heresies distrest;
Yet saints their watch are keeping,
Their cry goes up, "How long?"
And soon the night of weeping
Shall be the morn of song.

'Mid toil and tribulation,
And tumult of her war,
She waits the consummation
Of peace forevermore;
Till with the vision glorious
Her longing eyes are blest,
And the great Church victorious
Shall be the Church at rest.

So, Lord, she stands before Thee,
Forevermore Thine own;
No merit to her glory,
Her boasting this alone:
That she who did not choose Thee
Came, chosen, at Thy call,
Never to leave or lose Thee,
Or from Thy favour fall.

For Thy true Word remaineth;
  No creature far or nigh,
No fiend of hell who reigneth
  In hell or haunted sky;
No doubting world's derision
  That holds her in despite,
Shall hide her from Thy vision,
  Shall lure her from Thy light.

Thine, Thine! In bliss or sorrow,
  As well in shade as shine;
Of old, today, tomorrow,
  To all the ages, Thine.
Thine in her great commission,
  Baptized into Thy Name,
And in her last fruition,
  Of all her hope and aim.

Yet she on earth hath union
  With God the Three in One,
And mystic sweet communion
  With those whose rest is won:
O happy ones and holy!
  Lord, give us grace that we,
Like them, the meek and lowly,
  On high may dwell with Thee.

—Samuel John Stone

In 1860, the year after the world had been introduced to Darwinism by the publication of *The Origin of Species*, a volume entitled *Essays and Reviews* brought the controversy over higher criticism before the English public. The authors of the book questioned the historical accuracy of Scripture and taught liberal views on certain doctrines. More fuel was added to the fires by *The Pentateuch and Book of Joshua Critically Examined* (1862-63) by John William Colenso (1814-1883), bishop of Natal in South Africa. This book attacked the Mosaic authorship of the Pentateuch, called Joshua a myth and the books of Chronicles fictitious, and even disputed the accuracy of Christ's statements about Moses. Many responded that such a man was not fit to be a leader of the Church.

Bishop Gray of Cape Town, South Africa, supported by forty other bishops, deposed Colenso for his heresy. Upon his refusal to submit, he was brought to court and the deposition confirmed. Colenso appealed, however, to a secular court under the Crown, the Judicial Committee of the Privy Council, and he was reinstated. The result was a schism in the South African church until after Colenso's death.

One of Bishop Gray's strongest supporters in the controversy was the Reverend Samuel John Stone, curate at Windsor. Stone was already concerned about the perfunctory manner in which some of his parishioners were quoting the Apostles' Creed. They seemed to have no understanding of the words they spoke. So, after much prayer, Stone decided to write twelve hymns in explanation of the Creed and also in defense of the inspiration of the Bible. "The Church's One Foundation" explains the ninth article of the Creed—"I believe in the Holy Catholic [Universal] Church; the Communion of Saints." The overtones of the Colenso-Gray controversy are apparent throughout the hymn, especially in stanzas 3 and 4 (usually omitted from hymnals). To Stone, headship of the Church was vested in Jesus Christ, not in man and man's whims.

The collection of Stone's twelve creedal hymns was printed in *Lyra Fidelium* ("Lyre of the Faithful") in 1866. "The Church's One Foundation" was written originally in seven stanzas. In 1868 a revised form in five stanzas was prepared for *Hymns Ancient and Modern,* and that is the form which is still in general use. Later (1885) it was expanded to ten stanzas in order to make it appropriate for an ecclesiastical processional in Salisbury Cathedral. Though Stone was only twenty-seven when he wrote the hymn, it shows that he was well grounded in the faith. Stone's hymns have been described as expressing "a manly faith" and being "rhythmic, vigorous, scriptural." John Julian labels "The Church's One Foundation" as "magnificent." Others have viewed it as "The National Anthem of the Churches."

Samuel John Stone was born on April 25, 1839, at Whitmore, Staffordshire, England. His father, a minister to humble people, instilled in his son an awareness of the worth and needs of poor people. No doubt he prayed that someday his son would join him in his ministry to the poor.

Stone was educated at Oxford. There he distinguished himself in books and in athletics, especially in boating. He was strong physically, as well as mentally and spiritually. One day he saw a small girl being mistreated by some bullies. He came to her defense and bested the hoodlums, who ran away badly bruised.

Samuel Stone's sight was set on the army as a career. God, however, had other plans for him: He wanted him in the ministry. After serving at Windsor for eight years, he succeeded his father at his church in the poorer section of London. He built numerous churches, many of which he financed from his own pocket. It was his belief that poor people deserved to have beautiful churches in which to worship.

An outstanding work of this minister was that of opening the church at 6:30 in the morning to accommodate early commuters—many of them poor working girls who arrived an hour ahead of their work schedule. Dr. Stone would hold a brief service, have prayer, and then allow the girls to rest, to read, or to sew. The commuters were touched by his thoughtfulness, and soon he was affectionately called "the poor man's pastor."

Although many people admired Stone's strong defense of Scripture, other people criticized his efforts. To them he was "the most tyrannical priest in East London." Why? He argued against public schools. He felt that public schools would conflict with his parochial schools and might deprive the children of the religious training that they needed. He was a strong advocate of "the old order."

Samuel Stone wrote seven books of verse and felt privileged to serve on the committee that compiled the 1909 edition of the standard *Hymns Ancient and Modern.*

Stone gave twenty years of faithful service at St. Paul's, Haggerston, London, and in 1890 moved to All-Hallows-on-the-Wall, also in London. On November 19, 1900, Stone's earthly life came to an end. He is buried at Haggerston.

AURELIA (from the Latin *aureus,* which means "golden") was written by Samuel Sebastian Wesley (1810-1876), son of Samuel Wesley, a leading musician of London, and the grandson of the famous hymn writer, Charles Wesley. Samuel Sebastian Wesley was named for his father and for Johann Sebastian Bach, the great musician his father so deeply admired. From the age of nine to seventeen, Samuel served as a choirboy at the Royal Chapel and then became its organist. Later his fame grew so much that he was known as one of the most prominent organists of England. It is said that Wesley's fingers and feet moved so swiftly as he played that people would crowd around the organ just to watch him play. At twenty-nine he received both his Bachelor of Music degree and a doctorate in music from Oxford. In 1872 he published *The European Psalmist,* a collection of 733 hymn tunes including 130 of his own composition. He died in London on April 19, 1876.

Originally the tune AURELIA, to which we sing "The Church's One Foundation," was written for "Jerusalem the Golden" (1864). However, at a thanksgiving service for the recovery of the Prince of Wales (February 27, 1872) held at St. Paul's Cathedral, the tune became linked to Stone's famous hymn "The Church's One Foundation." Shortly thereafter one critic called the tune "secular twaddle," hardly worthy to be joined with a hymn. Its popularity has made it plain, however, that most people like it. The words and music have been together for over a hundred years and are well accepted.

Nation

Battle Hymn of the Republic
1861

Mine eyes have seen the glory of the coming of the Lord;
He is trampling out the vintage where the grapes of wrath
  are stored;
He hath loosed the fateful lightning of His terrible swift
  sword:
  His truth is marching on.

Refrain:

Glory, glory, Hallelujah! Glory, glory, Hallelujah!
Glory, glory, Hallelujah! His truth is marching on.

I have seen Him in the watch-fires of a hundred circling
  camps;
They have builded Him an altar in the evening dews and
  damps;
I can read His righteous sentence by the dim and flaring
  lamps;
  His day is marching on.

I have read a fiery gospel, writ in burnished rows of steel;
"As ye deal with My contemners, so with you My grace shall
  deal";
Let the Hero, born of woman, crush the serpent with His heel;
  Since God is marching on.

He has sounded forth the trumpet that shall never call
  retreat;
He is sifting out the hearts of men before His judgment seat;
O be swift, my soul, to answer Him! be jubilant, my feet!
  Our God is marching on.

In the beauty of the lilies Christ was born across the sea,
With a glory in His bosom that transfigures you and me:
As He died to make men holy, let us die to make men free,
  While God is marching on.

—Julia Ward Howe

Julia Ward Howe (1819-1910) was one of the foremost American women of the nineteenth century. Her list of accomplishments includes numerous books, a prominent role in the movement to abolish slavery, her advocacy of women's suffrage, and her persistent efforts in behalf of various charitable causes. Yet today she is remembered chiefly for "The Battle Hymn of the Republic."

Born on May 27, 1819, in New York City, Julia Ward grew up in an atmosphere of culture, wealth, and Christian orthodoxy. However, she began reading current European authors such as Goethe and mingling in the fashionable literary circles, which were largely dominated by Unitarians and Transcendentalists such as William Ellery Channing, Ralph Waldo Emerson, and Margaret Fuller. These influences soon led her away from her Christian upbringing. She married Samuel Gridley Howe, a pioneer in education for the blind and also of Unitarian sympathies. Later on, she often preached in Unitarian pulpits. Be that as it may, "The Battle Hymn of the Republic" does not strongly reflect her heretical theology, so that few people who sing the song today realize the author's background. It is a stirring song of patriotism that reminds us that a righteous cause will eventually triumph. It has often galvanized our armies into courageous action in defense of our country.

In the fall of 1861 Mrs. Howe and her husband, accompanied by their pastor, Dr. James Freeman Clarke, and their close friend, Governor John A. Andrews of Massachusetts, traveled to Washington. There they watched a "grand review" of McClellan's Army of the Potomac. When news was received of a surprise move by the Southern troops, the review had to disband. As the Howe party watched the boys march back into Washington and heard them sing "John Brown's Body," Dr. Clarke commented, "That is a good marching tune, Julia. Why don't you write better words for it?" She replied, "I have often prayed that I might, Pastor."

That night Mrs. Howe went to bed and slept soundly for awhile. But in the early morning she awoke to find her mind filled with thoughts of "a hundred circling camps" that were visible from her hotel window and the sound of "the trumpet that shall never call retreat." To her these things were a reminder of the battle of Armageddon and the Lord's return. Slipping out of bed, she set down on paper the immortal words that she felt suited the prescribed tune as well as the times.

Returning to Boston, Julia showed her poem to the editor of *The Atlantic Monthly.* He paid her five dollars (some say four dollars) for it and suggested its appropriate title.

The popularity of "Battle Hymn of the Republic" is attributed to Charles C. McCabe, "the Singing Chaplain" of the 122nd Ohio Volunteer Infantry. Chaplain McCabe had read the poem in *The Atlantic Monthly* and memorized it. In 1863 he was captured by the Confederates in Winchester, Virginia, and imprisoned in Libby Prison at Richmond. One evening the prisoners at Libby received the distressing news that their Union troops had lost 40,000 men in a battle. How happy they were later to learn that the report had been in error and that their forces had instead been victorious. Chaplain McCabe began to sing "Mine eyes have seen the glory of the coming of the Lord," and the other prisoners joined in the chorus, "Glory, glory, Hallelujah!"

Following his release from prison, McCabe went to Washington to speak before the Christian Commission. There he recounted his prison experience and sang "Battle Hymn of the Republic." The audience applauded; then President Lincoln, the tears streaming down his face, requested, "Please sing it again." McCabe was honored later to sing the hymn at several memorial services for Lincoln.

Mrs. Howe received many honors for her literary efforts and for her work in behalf of women's suffrage, the celebration of Mother's Day, and other causes. On June 16, 1909, she received an honorary degree at Brown University, Rhode Island; and on October 5, 1910, at the age of ninety-one, she received an honorary degree from

Smith College. As she was wheeled onto the platform at Smith she was given a standing ovation. When the presentation was finished, the organ pealed a chord, and everyone stood and sang "Mine eyes have seen the glory of the coming of the Lord . . ."

Although many tunes were composed for "Battle Hymn of the Republic," Mrs. Howe preferred the spirited air of "John Brown's Body." The source of this tune (now called BATTLE HYMN) is debatable. Some people attribute it to William Steffe of Richmond, saying that he composed it for use in a camp meeting in Georgia. Some say that it originated in South Carolina. Whatever its source, the tune has been considered "undignified" by many musicians; some have refused to play it, but thousands have cheered it.

God of Our Fathers, Whose Almighty Hand
1876

God of our fathers, whose almighty hand
Leads forth in beauty all the starry band
Of shining worlds in splendor through the skies,
Our grateful songs before Thy throne arise.

Thy love divine hath led us in the past,
In this free land by Thee our lot is cast;
Be Thou our Ruler, Guardian, Guide, and Stay,
Thy Word our law, Thy paths our chosen way.

From war's alarms, from deadly pestilence,
Be Thy strong arm our ever sure defense;
Thy true religion in our hearts increase,
Thy bounteous goodness nourish us in peace.

Refresh Thy people on their toilsome way,
Lead us from night to never-ending day;
Fill all our lives with love and grace divine,
And glory, laud, and praise be ever Thine.

—Daniel C. Roberts

In 1876, Brandon, Vermont, like many other towns
and cities, was planning a Fourth of July celebration in
honor of the centennial of American independence. A new
Episcopal minister in town, Daniel Crane Roberts, often
wrote poetry, and the celebration committee approached
the young minister about writing a special hymn for the
occasion. Mr. Roberts graciously accepted the challenge.
Soon he handed to the committee "God of Our Fathers,
Whose Almighty Hand." The hymn came to the attention
of numerous newspaper publishers, and within a short
time it was being featured at other centennial celebrations. The success of his hymn deeply humbled the young
minister, and he answered numerous requests for personal history, saying, "My personal history is of little
account. I remain a country parson, known only within
my own small world."

When the General Convention of the Episcopal Church
appointed a commission to revise its hymnal, Mr. Roberts
sent his hymn anonymously, promising to send his name
were the hymn accepted. It was accepted and printed
anonymously in the report to the commission. Before the
hymnal was printed, however, Roberts' hymn was honored
by being selected for the centennial celebration of the
adoption of United States Constitution (1892). A member
of the Centennial Committee, Mr. George William Warren,
composed a tune for the still anonymous text.

Born on November 5, 1841, in Bridgehampton, Long
Island, Daniel Crane Roberts entered Kenyon College,
Gambier, Ohio, in 1857. He later volunteered for service
in the Civil War, entering as a private in 1862, and became
a member of the 84th Ohio Volunteers. In 1865 Mr.
Roberts was ordained as a deacon, and in 1866 he began
his ministry at Christ Church, Montpelier, Vermont. From
Montpelier he went to serve churches in Lowell, Massachusetts, and Brandon, Vermont. In 1885 the Reverend
Mr. Roberts received from Norwich University the honorary Doctor of Divinity degree. He began in 1878 a thirty-
year ministry at St. Paul's Episcopal Church in Concord,
New Hampshire, where he died on October 31, 1907.

Originally, "God of our Fathers, Whose Almighty Hand" was sung to Alexis Lvov's tune RUSSIAN HYMN (1833). According to Louis F. Benson, Daniel Roberts had RUSSIAN HYMN in mind when he wrote the hymn. The familiar tune—NATIONAL HYMN—was composed for this hymn in 1892 by George William Warren (1828-1902), organist at St. Thomas' Church, New York City. The tune's opening trumpet fanfare enhances its martial tone; and the closing phrase bears strong resemblance to RUSSIAN HYMN.

George William Warren was born in Albany, New York, on August 17, 1828. He served as organist in churches in Albany and Brooklyn prior to his service in New York City.

In 1888 Mr. Warren published *Warren's Hymns and Tunes As Sung at St. Thomas' Church.* His alma mater—Racine College, Racine, Wisconsin—conferred on him the honorary degree of Doctor of Music.

Warren died in New York City on March 17, 1902. Surprisingly, his funeral, which was attended by thousands, was without musical sound. "Not even the best of organists was worthy to preside at the console that day."

My Country, 'Tis of Thee
1831

My country, 'tis of thee,
Sweet land of liberty,
   Of thee I sing:
Land where my fathers died,
Land of the pilgrim's pride,
From every mountain side
   Let freedom ring!

My native country, thee,
Land of the noble free,
   Thy name I love:
I love thy rocks and rills,
Thy woods and templed hills;
My heart with rapture thrills,
   Like that above.

Let music swell the breeze,
And ring from all the trees
   Sweet freedom's song:
Let mortal tongues awake;
Let all that breathe partake;
Let rocks their silence break,
   The sound prolong.

Our fathers' God, to Thee,
Author of liberty,
   To Thee we sing:
Long may our land be bright
With freedom's holy light;
Protect us by Thy might,
   Great God, our King!

—Samuel F. Smith

Hymnists have described "My Country, 'Tis of Thee" as "having easy grace, directness, simplicity, zealous patriotism, fervent piety, and an insistent note of liberty." Oliver Wendell Holmes, Samuel Smith's classmate at Harvard, praised the use of the personal pronoun, saying, "Smith's use of 'My' instead of 'Our' gives the song a joyous ring and makes it seem personal to every individual. Long after I and my works are forgotten, Smith's song will still be popular."

Stanza 1 of the hymn addresses our nation as "sweet land of liberty" and acknowledges that this liberty was purchased by the lives of the fathers and the pilgrims. Stanza 2 refers to certain beauties of the land whose very name the author loves. Stanza 3 challenges all people and all of nature to join in "sweet freedom's song"; and stanza

4 invokes the protection of the "Author of liberty" and the "Great God, our King." A fifth stanza, because of its "anti-British sentiments," was soon dropped. The hymn was first performed publicly on July 4, 1831. The occasion was a children's concert at Boston.

The hymn had its critics, of course. Harvard's President Eliot exclaimed, "Did ever a piece of doggerel win a man such fame!" Other critics labeled the hymn "too New Englandish"; and Dr. Henry Van Dyke, in an effort to remedy the problem, wrote:

I love thine inland seas,
Thy groves of giant trees,
  Thy rolling plains;
Thy mighty rivers' sweep,
Majestic canyons deep,
Thy mountains, wild and steep,
  All thy domains.

Thy silver eastern strands,
Thy Golden Gate that stands
  Fronting the West;
Thy flowing southland fair,
Thy sweet and crystal air—
O land beyond compare,
  Thee I love best.

Samuel Francis Smith, D.D., was born in Boston on October 21, 1808. From childhood he was keenly interested in language study, and eventually he became proficient in fifteen languages. Smith was graduated from Harvard and from Andover Theological Seminary. At Andover he wrote two outstanding hymns—a missionary hymn, "The Morning Light Is Breaking," and "My Country, 'Tis of Thee."

The patriotic hymn was written within half an hour late one afternoon. Samuel Smith was sitting in a worn chair in a poorly furnished house. His feet were propped on a woodbox near the stove, and he was leafing through a German hymnbook. Dr. Lowell Mason had asked him to translate some of the children's hymns or to write new words to old tunes. Suddenly Smith's attention was drawn to a spirited tune that he thought had a patriotic ring. He did not realize that the tune belonged to "God Save the King," and soon he had written his famous words to the tune.

In 1832 Samuel Smith married Mary White, and they had six children. Their son Dan was a missionary to India and for forty years was president of Karen Baptist Theological Seminary at Rangoon. Samuel Smith held several New England pastorates, and also served as Professor of Modern Languages at Waterville College (now Colby College) in Maine.

On November 16, 1895, at the age of eighty-seven, Dr. Smith boarded a train to go to a speaking engagement in a Boston suburb. He greeted a friend on the train; then he gasped and was in the presence of the One to whom he attributed America's greatness. Smith left to posterity the legacy of 150 original hymns.

The well-known tune AMERICA is anonymous, though it is apparently of English provenance. The first printings were apparently in *Thesaurus Musicus* (1744) and *Gentleman's Magazine* for October 1745.

Appendixes

Comparative Chart of Hymns

This chart summarizes the information presented in the book in simplified form. For example, only the most common tunes are listed. Tune names are in capital letters. The page number where the hymn and its story may be found in the book is given after the title. The following abbreviations are used:
ad.—adapted by; arr.—arranged by; att.—attributed to; c.—century; harm.—harmonized by; st.—stanza(s); tr.—translated (by); *—approximate date; @—date published.

Date	Author or Composer	Birth/Death	Nationality
Abide with Me: Fast Falls the Eventide *(153)*			
1847	Henry Francis Lyte	1793–1847	Scottish
EVENTIDE			
1861	William Henry Monk	1823–1889	English
Alas! and Did My Saviour Bleed *(93)*			
1707	Isaac Watts	1674–1748	English
AVON			
1800*	Hugh Wilson	1764–1824	Scottish
All Hail the Power of Jesus' Name *(25)*			
1779	Edward Perronet (st. 1–8)	1726–1792	English
1789	John Rippon (st. 9)	1751–1836	English
MILES LANE			
1779	William Shrubsole	1760–1806	English
CORONATION			
1793	Oliver Holden	1765–1844	American

Date	Author or Composer	Birth/Death	Nationality

DIADEM
1838   James Ellor   1819–1899   English

All People That on Earth Do Dwell   *(1)*
1561   William Kethe   –1594   Scottish
OLD HUNDREDTH
1551   Louis Bourgeois   1510*–1561*   French

All the Way My Saviour Leads Me   *(182)*
1874   Fanny Jane Crosby   1820–1915   American
ALL THE WAY
1875   Robert Lowry   1826–1899   American

Amazing Grace   *(96)*
1779   John Newton (st. 1–6)   1725–1807   English
XIX c. Anonymous (st. 7)
AMAZING GRACE
1831@   Early American tune

Am I a Soldier of the Cross   *(257)*
1724*   Isaac Watts   1674-1748   English
ARLINGTON
1762   Thomas Augustine Arne   1710-1778   English

A Mighty Fortress Is Our God   *(259)*
1529   Martin Luther   1483-1546   German
1831   tr. Thomas Carlyle   1795-1881   English
1852   tr. Frederick Henry Hedge   1805-1890   American
EIN' FESTE BURG
1529   att. Martin Luther   1483-1546   German

And Can It Be That I Should Gain   *(101)*
1738   Charles Wesley   1707-1788   English
FILLMORE
1869@   att. Jeremiah Ingalls   1764-1828   American
SAGINA
1825*   Thomas Campbell   1777-1844   Scottish

Angels, from the Realms of Glory   *(73)*
1816   James Montgomery   1771-1854   Scottish
REGENT SQUARE
1867   Henry Thomas Smart   1813-1879   English

Away in a Manger   *(75)*
1885*   anonymous (st. 3)

Date	Author or Composer	Birth/Death	Nationality
1892*	anonymous (st. 1, 2)		

MUELLER

1887	James Ramsey Murray	1841-1905	American

CRADLE SONG

1895	William James Kirkpatrick	1838-1921	Irish/ American

Battle Hymn of the Republic *(306)*

1861	Julia Ward Howe	1819-1910	American

BATTLE HYMN (or JOHN BROWN'S BODY)

early XIX c.	att. William Steffe		American

Be Still, My Soul *(156)*

1752	Katharina von Schlegel	1697-	German
1855	tr. Jane Laurie Borthwick	1813-1897	Scottish

FINLANDIA

1897	Jean Sibelius	1865-1957	Finnish

Blessed Assurance, Jesus Is Mine *(184)*

1873	Fanny Jane Crosby	1820-1915	American

ASSURANCE

1873	Phoebe Palmer Knapp	1839-1908	American

Blest Be the Tie That Binds *(280)*

1772	John Fawcett	1740-1817	English

DENNIS

	Johann (Hans) Georg Nägeli	1773-1836	Swiss
1845	Lowell Mason	1792-1872	American

Bob Jones University Hymn *(134)*

1945*	Bob Jones (st. 1, 2, 3, 7, 8)	1911-	American
1961	Bob Jones (st. 4, 5, 6)	1911-	American

BACCALAUREATE

1945	Harriette Stollenwerck Parker	1913-1946	American

Break Thou the Bread of Life *(137)*

1877	Mary Artemisia Lathbury (st. 1, 2)	1841-1913	American
1913@	Alexander Groves (st. 3, 4)	1842-1909	English

BREAD OF LIFE

1877	William Fiske Sherwin	1826-1888	American

Date	Author or Composer	Birth/Death	Nationality

Christ the Lord Is Risen Today *(104)*
1739 Charles Wesley   1707-1788   English
EASTER HYMN
1708@ Anonymous

Come, Thou Almighty King *(29)*
1757* anonymous
ITALIAN HYMN
1769 Felice de Giardini   1716-1796   Italian

Come, Thou Fount of Every Blessing *(32)*
1758 Robert Robinson   1735-1790   English
NETTLETON
1813* Anonymous
WARRENTON
1844* Anonymous

Come, Ye Thankful People, Come *(62)*
1844 Henry Alford   1810-1871   English
ST. GEORGE'S WINDSOR
1858 George Job Elvey   1816-1893   English

Count Your Blessings *(186)*
1897 Johnson Oatman, Jr.   1856-1922   American
BLESSINGS
1897 Edwin Othello Excell   1851-1921   American

Crown Him with Many Crowns *(35)*
1851 Matthew Bridges   1800-1894   English
1874 Godfrey Thring   1823-1903   English
DIADEMATA
1868 George Job Elvey   1816-1893   English

Doxology *(64)*
1695 Thomas Ken   1637-1711   English
OLD HUNDREDTH
1551* Louis Bourgeois   1510*-1561*   French

Fairest Lord Jesus *(4)*
1677@ *Münster Gesangbuch* (st. 1, 3)
1842 *Schlesische Volkslieder* (st. 2)
SCHÖNSTER HERR JESU
1677@ Unknown origin
CRUSADER'S HYMN
1842@ Silesian folksong

Date	Author or Composer	Birth/Death	Nationality

Faith of Our Fathers! *(283)*

1849	Frederick William Faber	1814-1863	English
ST. CATHERINE			
1864	Henri Frederick Hemy	1818-1888	English

For All the Saints *(287)*

1864	William Walsham How	1823-1897	English
SARUM			
1869	Joseph Barnby	1838-1896	English
SINE NOMINE			
1906	Ralph Vaughan Williams	1872-1958	English

Glorious Things of Thee Are Spoken *(290)*

1779	John Newton	1725-1807	English
AUSTRIA			
1797	Franz Joseph Haydn	1732-1809	Austrian

God of Our Fathers, Whose Almighty Hand *(309)*

1876	Daniel Crane Roberts	1841-1907	American
RUSSIAN HYMN			
1833	Alexis Feodorovich Lvov	1799-1870	Russian
NATIONAL HYMN			
1892	George William Warren	1828-1902	American

Great God of Wonders! *(8)*

1769@	Samuel Davies	1723-1761	American
SOVEREIGNTY			
1769	John Newton	1725-1807	English

Great Is Thy Faithfulness, O God My Father *(189)*

1923	Thomas Obadiah Chisholm	1866-1960	American
FAITHFULNESS			
1923	William Marion Runyan	1870-1957	American

Guide Me, O Thou Great Jehovah *(192)*

1745	William Williams (tr. st. 2, 3, 4)	1717-1791	Welsh
1772	tr. Peter Williams (st. 1, 3, 5)	1722-1796	Welsh
CWM RHONDDA			
1907	John Hughes	1873-1932	Welsh

Date	Author or Composer	Birth/Death	Nationality

Hail, Thou Once-Despised Jesus! *(107)*
1757	John Bakewell	1721-1819	English
AUTUMN			
1796*	François Hippolyte Barthélémon	1741-1808	French
PLEADING SAVIOUR			
1830@	American folk tune		
IN BABILONE			
1710@	Traditional Dutch melody		

Hark! the Herald Angels Sing *(78)*
1739	Charles Wesley	1707-1788	English
MENDELSSOHN			
1840	Felix Mendelssohn	1809-1847	German
	ad. William Hayman Cummings	1831-1915	English

He Leadeth Me, O Blessed Thought *(196)*
1862	Joseph Henry Gilmore	1834-1918	American
AUGHTON			
1864@	William Batchelder Bradbury	1816-1868	American

Hiding in Thee *(158)*
1876	William Orcutt Cushing	1823-1902	American
CUSHING			
1877@	Ira David Sankey	1840-1908	American

Holy, Holy, Holy! Lord God, Almighty *(10)*
1826	Reginald Heber	1783-1826	English
NICAEA			
1861	John Bacchus Dykes	1823-1876	English

How Firm a Foundation *(199)*
1787	Rippon's *Selection of Hymns*		
FOUNDATION			
1832@	Southern folktune		
ADESTE FIDELES			
1743	John Francis Wade	1710*-1786	English

I Heard the Voice of Jesus Say *(160)*
1846	Horatius Bonar	1808-1889	Scottish
VOX DILECTI			
1868	John B. Dykes	1823-1876	English

Date	Author or Composer	Birth/Death	Nationality

THIRD MODE MELODY
| 1567 | Thomas Tallis | 1505*-1585 | English |

I Love Thy Kingdom, Lord   *(294)*

| 1801 | Timothy Dwight | 1752-1817 | American |

ST. THOMAS
| 1770@ | Anonymous | | |

I Must Tell Jesus   *(163)*

| 1894 | Elisha Albright Hoffman | 1839-1929 | American |

I Need Thee Every Hour   *(165)*

| 1872 | Annie (Sherwood) Hawks | 1835-1918 | American |

NEED
| 1872 | Robert Lowry | 1826-1899 | American |

I Think When I Read That Sweet Story of Old   *(202)*

| 1841 | Jemima (Thompson) Luke | 1813-1906 | English |

LUKE (from "Salamis")
| 1859 | arr. William Batchelder Bradbury | 1816-1868 | American |

It Is Well with My Soul   *(167)*

| 1873 | Horatio Gates Spafford | 1828-1888 | American |

VILLE DU HAVRE
| 1876 | Philip P. Bliss | 1838-1876 | American |

Jesus, and Shall It Ever Be   *(233)*

| 1765 | Joseph Grigg | 1720*-1768 | English |

FEDERAL STREET
| 1832 | Henry Kemble Oliver | 1800-1885 | American |

Jesus Calls Us   *(236)*

| 1852 | Cecil Frances Alexander | 1818-1895 | English |

GALILEE
| 1887* | William Herbert Jude | 1851-1922 | English |

Jesus, Lover of My Soul   *(204)*

| 1738 | Charles Wesley | 1707-1788 | English |

MARTYN
| 1834 | Simeon Butler Marsh | 1798-1875 | American |

ABERYSTWYTH
| 1879 | Joseph Parry | 1841-1903 | Welsh |

Date	Author or Composer	Birth/Death	Nationality

Jesus Paid It All *(111)*

1865	Elvina Mable Hall	1820-1889	American
ALL TO CHRIST			
1865	John Thomas Grape	1835-1915	American

Jesus Shall Reign Where'er the Sun *(298)*

1719	Isaac Watts	1674-1748	English
DUKE STREET			
1790*	John Hatton	1710*-1793*	English

Jesus, Thy Blood and Righteousness *(113)*

1739*	Nicolaus Ludwig von Zinzendorf	1700-1760	German
1740	tr. John Wesley	1703-1791	English
GERMANY			
1815@	att. William Gardiner	1770-1853	English
MALVERN			
1845	arr. Lowell Mason	1792-1872	American

Joy to the World! the Lord Is Come *(81)*

1719	Isaac Watts	1674-1748	English
ANTIOCH			
1836	Lowell Mason	1792-1872	American

Just As I Am, Without One Plea *(143)*

1834	Charlotte Elliott	1789-1871	English
WOODWORTH			
1849	William Batchelder Bradbury	1816-1868	American
SAFFRON WALDEN			
1890	Arthur Henry Brown	1830-1926	English
ST. CRISPIN			
1863	George Job Elvey	1816-1893	English

Lead On, O King Eternal *(263)*

1887	Ernest Warburton Shurtleff	1862-1917	American
LANCASHIRE			
1835	Henry Smart	1813-1879	English

More Love to Thee, O Christ *(239)*

1856	Elizabeth Payson Prentiss	1818-1878	American
MORE LOVE TO THEE			
1870	William Howard Doane	1832-1915	American

Date	Author or Composer	Birth/Death	Nationality

PROPIOR DEO
| 1872 | Arthur Seymour Sullivan | 1842-1900 | English |

My Country, 'Tis of Thee *(311)*
| 1831 | Samuel Francis Smith | 1808-1895 | American |

AMERICA
| 1744@ | Anonymous | | |

My Faith Looks Up to Thee *(208)*
| 1830 | Ray Palmer | 1808-1887 | American |

OLIVET
| 1833 | Lowell Mason | 1792-1872 | American |

My Hope Is Built on Nothing Less *(211)*
| 1834 | Edward Mote | 1797-1874 | English |

SOLID ROCK
| 1863 | William Batchelder Bradbury | 1816-1868 | American |

My Jesus, I Love Thee *(13)*
| 1858* | William Ralph Featherston | 1842*-1873 | Canadian |

GORDON
| 1876@ | Adoniram Judson Gordon | 1836-1895 | American |

Now Thank We All Our God *(70)*
| 1636 | Martin Rinkart | 1586-1649 | German |
| 1858@ | tr. Catherine Winkworth | 1827-1878 | English |

NUN DANKET
| 1647@ | Johann Crüger | 1598-1662 | German |

O Come, All Ye Faithful *(83)*
| 1743 | John Francis Wade | 1710*-1786 | English |
| 1841 | tr. Frederick Oakeley | 1802-1880 | English |

ADESTE FIDELES
| 1743 | John Francis Wade | 1710*-1786 | English |

O for a Thousand Tongues to Sing *(41)*
| 1739 | Charles Wesley | 1707-1788 | English |

AZMON
| 1839@ | att. Carl Gotthelf Gläser | 1784-1829 | German |

RICHMOND
| 1792@ | Thomas Haweis | 1734-1820 | English |

Date	Author or Composer	Birth/Death	Nationality

LYNGHAM
1803@ Thomas Jarman   1776-1861   English

O God, Our Help in Ages Past *(214)*
1719   Isaac Watts   1674-1748   English
ST. ANNE
1708   William Croft   1678-1727   English

O Jesus, I Have Promised *(242)*
1866* John Ernest Bode   1816-1874   English
ANGEL'S STORY
1881   Arthur Henry Mann   1850-1929   English
LLANFYLLIN
1865@ Traditional Welsh melody
DAY OF REST
1874@ James William Elliott 1833-1915   English

O Jesus, Thou Art Standing *(146)*
1867   William Walsham How   1823-1897   English
KNECHT
1793   Justin Heinrich Knecht 1752-1817   German
ST. HILDA
1871   ad. Edward Husband   1843-1908   English

O Little Town of Bethlehem *(87)*
1868   Phillips Brooks   1835-1893   American
ST. LOUIS
1868   Lewis Henry Redner   1831-1908   American
FOREST GREEN
1906   Ralph Vaughan Williams 1872-1958   English

O Love That Wilt Not Let Me Go *(217)*
1882   George Matheson   1842-1906   Scottish
ST. MARGARET
1884   Albert Lister Peace   1844-1912   English

Onward, Christian Soldiers *(266)*
1864   Sabine Baring-Gould   1834-1924   English
ST. GERTRUDE
1871   Arthur Seymour Sullivan 1842-1900   English

O Perfect Love, All Human Thought Transcending *(220)*
1883   Dorothy Frances   1858-1932   English
         (Blomfield) Gurney

Date	Author or Composer	Birth/Death	Nationality

O PERFECT LOVE
| 1889 | Joseph Barnby | 1838-1896 | English |

STRENGTH AND STAY
| 1875 | John Bacchus Dykes | 1823-1876 | English |

O Sacred Head, Now Wounded *(116)*

XII c.	Bernard of Clairvaux	1091-1153	French
1656	tr. Paul Gerhardt	1607-1676	German
1830	tr. James Waddell Alexander	1804-1859	American

HERZLICH TUT MICH VERLANGEN
| 1601 | Hans Leo Hassler | 1564-1612 | German |
| 1729 | harm. Johann Sebastian Bach | 1685-1750 | German |

O Word of God Incarnate *(140)*

| 1867 | William Walsham How | 1823-1897 | English |

MUNICH
| 1693@ | German melody | | |
| 1847 | ad. Felix Mendelssohn | 1809-1847 | German |

O Worship the King *(16)*

| 1833 | Robert Grant | 1779-1838 | Scottish |

HANOVER
| 1708 | William Croft | 1678-1727 | English |

LYONS
| 1815@ | att. Johann Michael Haydn | 1737-1806 | Austrian |

Pass Me Not, O Gentle Saviour *(148)*

| 1868 | Fanny Jane Crosby | 1820-1915 | American |

PASS ME NOT
| 1868 | William Howard Doane | 1832-1915 | American |

Peace, Perfect Peace *(171)*

| 1875 | Edward Henry Bickersteth | 1825-1906 | English |

PAX TECUM
| 1877 | George Thomas Caldbeck | 1852-1912* | English |

Praise, My Soul, the King of Heaven *(45)*

| 1834 | Henry Francis Lyte | 1793-1847 | Scottish |

LAUDA ANIMA (Benedic Anima Mea)
| 1869 | John Goss | 1800-1880 | English |

Date	Author or Composer	Birth/Death	Nationality
LAUDA ANIMA (Andrews)			
1931	Mark Andrews	1875-1939	English/ American
REGENT SQUARE			
1867	Henry Thomas Smart	1813-1879	English

Praise Ye Jehovah *(48)*

1976	Bob Jones	1911-	American
ANNIVERSARY HYMN			
1976	Dwight Leonard Gustafson	1930-	American

Praise Ye the Lord, the Almighty *(50)*

1680	Joachim Neander	1650-1680	German
1863	tr. Catherine Winkworth	1827-1878	English
LOBE DEN HERREN			
1665*	*Stralsund Gesangbuch*		

Rejoice, the Lord Is King *(52)*

1744	Charles Wesley	1707-1788	English
DARWALL			
1770	John Darwall	1731-1789	English
GOPSAL			
1746	George Frederick Handel	1685-1759	German

Rejoice, Ye Pure in Heart *(55)*

1865	Edward Hayes Plumptre	1821-1891	English
MARION			
1883	Arthur Henry Messiter	1834-1916	English
VINEYARD HAVEN			
1974	Richard Dirksen		

Rock of Ages, Cleft for Me *(223)*

1776	Augustus Montague Toplady	1740-1778	English
REDHEAD NO. 76			
1853	Richard Redhead	1820-1901	English
RELIANCE			
1895	John Henry Gower	1855-1922	English
TOPLADY			
1831	Thomas Hastings	1784-1872	American

Silent Night, Holy Night *(90)*

1818	Joseph Mohr	1792-1848	Austrian
1863@	tr. John Freeman Young	1820-1885	American

Date	Author or Composer	Birth/Death	Nationality
STILLE NACHT			
1818	Franz Gruber	1787-1863	Austrian

Softly and Tenderly   *(150)*

1882	Will Lamartine Thompson	1847-1909	American
THOMPSON			
1882	Will Lamartine Thompson	1847-1909	American

Soldiers of Christ, Arise   *(271)*

1749	Charles Wesley	1707-1788	English
DIADEMATA			
1868*	George Job Elvey	1816-1893	English

Spirit of God, Descend upon My Heart   *(245)*

1867@	George Croly	1780-1860	Irish
EMILIE			
	John Wesley Baume	1862-	English/American
MORECAMBE			
1870	Frederick Cook Atkinson	1841-1897	English

Stand Up, Stand Up for Jesus   *(272)*

1858	George Duffield, Jr.	1818-1888	American
WEBB			
1830	George James Webb	1803-1887	English/American
GEIBEL			
1901	Adam Geibel	1885-1933	German/American

Take My Life, and Let It Be   *(248)*

1874	Frances Ridley Havergal	1836-1879	English
PATMOS			
	William Henry Havergal	1793-1870	English
HENDON			
1823	Henri Abraham César Malan	1787-1864	Swiss
YARBROUGH			
1879@	Anonymous		

Take the Name of Jesus with You   *(252)*

1870	Lydia Baxter	1809-1874	American
PRECIOUS NAME			
1871@	William Howard Doane	1832-1915	American

Date	Author or Composer	Birth/Death	Nationality

Tell Me the Old, Old Story *(120)*

1866	Arabella Katherine Hankey	1834-1911	English

EVANGEL

1867	William Howard Doane	1832-1915	American

The Church's One Foundation *(300)*

1866	Samuel John Stone	1839-1900	English

AURELIA

1864	Samuel Sebastian Wesley	1810-1876	English

The King of Love My Shepherd Is *(226)*

1868	Henry Williams Baker	1821-1877	English

DOMINUS REGIT ME

1868	John Bacchus Dykes	1823-1876	English

The Ninety and Nine *(124)*

1868	Elizabeth Cecilia Clephane	1830-1869	Scottish
1874	Ira David Sankey	1840-1908	American

There Is a Fountain Filled with Blood *(126)*

1771*	William Cowper	1731-1800	English

CLEANSING FOUNTAIN
Early American Melody

There Is a Name I Love to Hear *(229)*

1855	Frederick Whitfield	1829-1904	English

BELMONT

1812@	William Gardiner	1770-1853	English

OH HOW I LOVE JESUS
XIX c. Camp meeting song

The Sands of Time Are Sinking *(174)*

1857	Anne Ross (Cundell) Cousin	1824-1906	English

RUTHERFORD

1834	Chrétien Urhan	1790-1845	French
1867	arr. Edward Francis Rimbault	1816-1876	French

The Son of God Goes Forth to War *(275)*

1812	Reginald Heber	1783-1826	English

ALL SAINTS, NEW

1872	Henry Stephen Cutler	1824-1902	American

Date	Author or Composer	Birth/Death	Nationality

The Spacious Firmament on High *(19)*

Date	Author or Composer	Birth/Death	Nationality
1712	Joseph Addison	1672-1719	English

CREATION

| 1798 | Franz Joseph Haydn | 1732-1809 | Austrian |

This Is My Father's World *(21)*

| 1901 | Maltbie Davenport Babcock | 1858-1901 | American |

TERRA BEATA

| 1915 | Franklin Lawrence Sheppard | 1852-1930 | American |

TERRA PATRIS

| 1926 | arr. Edward Shippen Barnes | 1887-1958 | American |

Trust and Obey *(254)*

| 1887@ | John H. Sammis | 1846-1919 | American |

TRUST AND OBEY

| 1887 | Daniel Brink Towner | 1850-1919 | American |

What a Friend We Have in Jesus *(179)*

| 1855* | Joseph M. Scriven | 1819*-1886 | Irish |

ERIE

| 1868 | Charles Crozat Converse | 1832-1918 | American |

When I Survey the Wondrous Cross *(129)*

| 1707 | Isaac Watts | 1674-1748 | English |

HAMBURG

| 1824 | arr. Lowell Mason from Gregorian Chant I | 1792-1872 | American |

Ye Servants of God, Your Master Proclaim *(58)*

| 1744 | Charles Wesley | 1707-1788 | English |

HANOVER

| 1708 | William Croft | 1678-1727 | English |

LYONS

| 1815@ | att. Johann Michael Haydn | 1737-1806 | Austrian |

Chronological List of Hymns

Some of the following dates are approximate. If the date of writing was not available, the date of publication was listed.

XII c. O Sacred Head, Now Wounded (Bernard of Clairvaux)
1529 A Mighty Fortress Is Our God (Martin Luther)
1561 All People That on Earth Do Dwell (William Kethe)
1636 Now Thank We All Our God (Martin Rinkart)
1677 Fairest Lord Jesus (anonymous)
1680 Praise Ye the Lord, the Almighty (Joachim Neander)
1695 Doxology (Thomas Ken)
1707 Alas! and Did My Saviour Bleed? (Isaac Watts)
1707 When I Survey the Wondrous Cross (Isaac Watts)
1712 The Spacious Firmament on High (Joseph Addison)
1719 Jesus Shall Reign Where'er the Sun (Isaac Watts)
1719 Joy to the World! the Lord Is Come (Isaac Watts)
1719 O God, Our Help in Ages Past (Isaac Watts)
1724 Am I a Soldier of the Cross (Isaac Watts)
1738 And Can It Be That I Should Gain? (Charles Wesley)
1738 Jesus, Lover of My Soul (Charles Wesley)
1739 Christ, the Lord, Is Risen Today (Charles Wesley)
1739 Hark! the Herald Angels Sing (Charles Wesley)
1739 Jesus, Thy Blood and Righteousness (Nicolaus Ludwig
        von Zinzendorf)
1739 O for a Thousand Tongues to Sing (Charles Wesley)
1743 O Come, All Ye Faithful (John Francis Wade)
1744 Rejoice, the Lord Is King (Charles Wesley)
1744 Ye Servants of God, Your Master Proclaim (Charles
        Wesley)
1745 Guide Me, O Thou Great Jehovah (William Williams)

333

1749 Soldiers of Christ, Arise (Charles Wesley)
1752 Be Still, My Soul (Katharina von Schlegel)
1757 Come, Thou Almighty King (anonymous)
1757 Hail, Thou Once-Despised Jesus! (John Bakewell)
1758 Come, Thou Fount of Every Blessing (Robert Robinson)
1765 Jesus, and Shall It Ever Be? (Joseph Grigg)
1769 Great God of Wonders! (Samuel Davies)
1771 There Is a Fountain Filled with Blood (William Cowper)
1772 Blest Be the Tie That Binds (John Fawcett)
1776 Rock of Ages, Cleft for Me (Augustus Montague Toplady)
1779 All Hail the Power of Jesus' Name (Edward Perronet)
1779 Amazing Grace (John Newton)
1779 Glorious Things of Thee Are Spoken (John Newton)
1787 How Firm a Foundation (anonymous)
1801 I Love Thy Kingdom, Lord (Timothy Dwight)
1812 The Son of God Goes Forth to War (Reginald Heber)
1816 Angels, from the Realms of Glory (James Montgomery)
1818 Silent Night, Holy Night (Joseph Mohr)
1826 Holy, Holy, Holy! Lord God Almighty (Reginald Heber)
1830 My Faith Looks Up to Thee (Ray Palmer)
1831 My Country, 'Tis of Thee (Samuel Francis Smith)
1833 O Worship the King (Robert Grant)
1834 Just As I Am, Without One Plea (Charlotte Elliott)
1834 My Hope Is Built on Nothing Less (Edward Mote)
1834 Praise, My Soul, the King of Heaven (Henry Francis Lyte)
1841 I Think When I Read That Sweet Story of Old (Jemima
        Thompson Luke)
1844 Come, Ye Thankful People, Come (Henry Alford)
1846 I Heard the Voice of Jesus Say (Horatius Bonar)
1847 Abide with Me: Fast Falls the Eventide (Henry Francis
        Lyte)
1849 Faith of Our Fathers! (Frederick William Faber)
1851 Crown Him with Many Crowns (Matthew Bridges and
        Godfrey Thring)
1852 Jesus Calls Us (Cecil Frances Alexander)
1855 There Is a Name I Love to Hear (Frederick Whitfield)
1855 What a Friend We Have in Jesus (Joseph M. Scriven)
1856 More Love to Thee, O Christ (Elizabeth Payson Prentiss)
1857 The Sands of Time Are Sinking (Anne Ross Cundell
        Cousin)
1858 My Jesus, I Love Thee (William Ralph Featherston)
1858 Stand Up, Stand Up for Jesus (George Duffield, Jr.)
1861 Battle Hymn of the Republic (Julia Ward Howe)
1862 He Leadeth Me, O Blessed Thought (Joseph Henry
        Gilmore)
1864 For All the Saints (William Walsham How)

1864 Onward, Christian Soldiers (Sabine Baring-Gould)
1865 Jesus Paid It All (Elvina Mable Hall)
1865 Rejoice, Ye Pure in Heart (Edward Hayes Plumptre)
1866 O Jesus, I Have Promised (John Ernest Bode)
1866 Tell Me the Old, Old Story (Arabella Katherine Hankey)
1866 The Church's One Foundation (Samuel John Stone)
1867 O Jesus, Thou Art Standing (William Walsham How)
1867 O Word of God Incarnate (William Walsham How)
1867 Spirit of God, Descend Upon My Heart (George Croly)
1868 O Little Town of Bethlehem (Phillips Brooks)
1868 Pass Me Not, O Gentle Saviour (Fanny J. Crosby)
1868 The King of Love My Shepherd Is (Henry Williams Baker)
1868 The Ninety and Nine (Elizabeth Cecilia Clephane)
1870 Take the Name of Jesus with You (Lydia Baxter)
1872 I Need Thee Every Hour (Annie Sherwood Hawks)
1873 Blessed Assurance, Jesus Is Mine (Fanny J. Crosby)
1873 It Is Well with My Soul (Horatio G. Spafford)
1874 All the Way My Saviour Leads Me (Fanny J. Crosby)
1874 Take My Life, and Let It Be (Frances Ridley Havergal)
1875 Peace, Perfect Peace (Edward Henry Bickersteth)
1876 God of Our Fathers, Whose Almighty Hand (Daniel Crane Roberts)
1876 Hiding in Thee (William Orcutt Cushing)
1877 Break Thou the Bread of Life (Mary A. Lathbury and Alexander Groves)
1882 O Love That Wilt Not Let Me Go (George Matheson)
1882 Softly and Tenderly (Will Lamartine Thompson)
1883 O Perfect Love, All Human Thought Transcending (Dorothy Frances Gurney)
1885 Away in a Manger (anonymous)
1887 Lead on, O King Eternal (Ernest Warburton Shurtleff)
1887 Trust and Obey (John H. Sammis)
1894 I Must Tell Jesus (Elisha Albright Hoffman)
1897 Count Your Blessings (Johnson Oatman, Jr.)
1901 This Is My Father's World (Maltbie Davenport Babcock)
1923 Great Is Thy Faithfulness, O God My Father (Thomas Obadiah Chisholm)
1945 Bob Jones University Hymn (Bob Jones)
1976 Praise Ye Jehovah (Bob Jones)

Bibliography

The following list includes the main sources used in compiling and verifying the stories and facts in this book. Since the files of the late Dr. Grace Haight were also used, as mentioned in the Foreword, where in many cases the sources were not clearly specified, it has not been possible to acknowledge every author.

Bailey, Albert Edward. *The Gospel in Hymns: Backgrounds and Interpretations*. New York: Charles Scribner's Sons, 1950.

Beattie, David Johnstone. *The Romance of Sacred Song*. London: Marshall, Morgan, and Scott, [n.d.].

Benson, Louis F. *Studies of Familiar Hymns*. Philadelphia: Westminster Press, 1903.

Bonner, Clint. *A Hymn Is Born*. Chicago: Wilcox and Follet Company, 1952.

Bonar, Andrew, ed. *Letters of Samuel Rutherford*. 1891; reprint, Carlisle, Pennsylvania: Banner of Truth Trust, 1984.

Breed, David R. *The History and Use of Hymns and Hymn-Tunes*. New York: Fleming H. Revell Company, 1903.

Bucke, Emory Stevens, ed. *A Handbook to the 1964 Methodist Hymnal*. Nashville: Abingdon Press, 1970.

Cecil, Richard, ed. *The Life of John Newton*. 1808; reprint, Grand Rapids: Baker Book House, 1978.

Clark, Willie Thorburn. *Stories of Fadeless Hymns*. Nashville: Broadman Press, 1949.

Covert, William Chalmers, and Laufer, Calvin Weiss, eds. *Handbook to the Hymnal*. Philadelphia: Presbyterian Board of Christian Education, 1935.

Douglas, Charles Winfred; Ellinwood, Leonard; et al. *The Hymnal: 1940 Companion*. New York: The Church Pension Fund, 1949.

Duffield, Samuel Willoughby. *English Hymns: Their Authors and History.* New York: Funk and Wagnalls Company, 1886.

Emurian, Ernest K. *Famous Stories of Inspiring Hymns.* Grand Rapids: Baker Book House, 1956.

Eskew, Henry, and McElrath, Hugh T. *Sing with Understanding: An Introduction to Christian Hymnology.* Nashville: Broadman Press, 1980.

Fountain, David G. *Isaac Watts Remembered.* Roundwood Gardens, England: Gospel Standard Baptist Trust, 1978.

Frost, Maurice, ed. *Historical Companion to "Hymns Ancient and Modern."* London: Clowes, 1962.

Haeussler, Armin. *The Story of Our Hymns: The Handbook to the Hymnal of the Evangelical and Reformed Church.* New York: Harper and Brothers, 1931.

Hart, William J. *Hymns in Human Experience.* New York: Harper and Brothers, 1931.

Hart, William J. *Unfamiliar Stories of Familiar Hymns.* Boston: W. A. Wilde Company, 1940.

Harvey, Robert. *Best-Loved Hymn Stories.* Grand Rapids: Zondervan Publishing House, 1963.

Hill, Richard S. "Not So Far Away in a Manger, Forty-one Settings of an American Carol," *Notes* (December 1945), pp. 12-36.

Hughes, Charles W. *American Hymns Old and New: Notes on the Hymns and Biographies of the Authors and Composers.* New York: Columbia University Press, 1980.

Hustad, Donald P. *Jubilate: Church Music in the Evangelical Tradition.* Carol Stream, Illinois: Hope Publishing Company, 1981.

Johnson, A., ed. *Dictionary of American Biography.* 20 vols. American Council of Learned Societies, 1928-1936.

Jones, Francis Arthur. *Famous Hymns and Their Authors.* London: Hodder and Stoughton, 1903.

Julian, John. *A Dictionary of Hymnology Setting Forth the "Origin and History of Christian Hymns of All Ages" and Nations.* London: John Murray, 1892.

Kerr, Phil. *Music in Evangelism and Stories of Famous Christian Songs.* Glendale, California: Gospel Music Publishers, 1939.

Knapp, Christopher. *Who Wrote Our Hymns.* Oak Park, Illinois: Bible Truth Publications, 1925.

Knight, George Litch. "Maltbie Davenport Babcock, D.D.: A Centenary Appreciation," *The Hymn* (April 1958), 37-44.

Lorenz, Edmund S. *The Singing Church: The Hymns It Wrote and Sang.* Nashville: Cokesbury Press, 1938.

McCutchan, Robert Guy. *Our Hymnody: A Manual of the Methodist Hymnal.* New York: The Methodist Book Concern, 1937.

Metcalf, Frank J. *Stories of Hymn Tunes.* New York: Abingdon Press, 1928.

Miller, Josiah. *Our Hymns: Their Authors and Origin . . . A Companion to the New Congregational Hymn Book.* London: Jackson, Walford, and Hodder, 1866.

Ninde, Edward S. *The Story of the American Hymn.* New York: Abingdon Press, 1921.

Nutter, Charles S., and Tillett, Wilbur Fisk. *The Hymns and Hymn Writers of the Church: An Annotated Edition of the Methodist Hymnal.* New York: The Methodist Book Concern, 1911.

Osbeck, Kenneth W. *Singing with Understanding: Including 101 Favorite Hymn Backgrounds.* Grand Rapids: Kregel Publications, 1979.

Price, Carl Fowler. *More Hymn Stories.* New York: Abingdon Press, 1929.

Price, Carl F. *One Hundred and One Hymn Stories.* New York: Abingdon Press, 1923.

Reynolds, William Jensen. *Companion to Baptist Hymnal.* Nashville: Broadman Press, 1976.

Reynolds, William Jensen, and Price, Milburn. *A Joyful Sound: Christian Hymnody.* 2nd edition. New York: Holt, Rinehart, and Winston, 1978.

Richards, Laura E., and Elliott, Maud Howe. *Julia Ward Howe.* New York: Houghton-Mifflin Company, 1915.

Robinson, Charles Seymour. *Annotations Upon Popular Hymns.* New York: Hunt and Eaton, 1903.

Routley, Erik. *A Panorama of Christian Hymnody.* Collegeville, Minnesota: Liturgical Press, 1979.

Routley, Erik. *Hymns and the Faith.* Greenwich, Connecticut: Seabury Press, 1954.

Rudin, Cecilia Margaret. *Stories of Hymns We Love.* Chicago: John Rudin and Company, 1944.

Ryden, Ernest Edwin. *The Story of Our Hymns.* Rock Island, Illinois: Augustana Book Concern, 1930.

Sankey, Ira D. *My Life and the Story of the Gospel Hymns and of Sacred Songs and Solos.* New York: Harper and Brothers, 1928.

Smith, Henry Augustine. *Lyric Religion: The Romance of Immortal Hymns.* London: Fleming H. Revell Company, 1931.

Stephens, Leslie, and Lee, S. *Dictionary of National Biography.* 63 vols. 1885-1900.

Tyler, John Crew. *The Blind Seer: George Matheson.* New York: Philosophical Library, 1959.

Scripture Index

Exodus
10:11   *274*
13:22   *292*
17:6   *224*
33:22   *224*

Numbers
34:4-5   *44*

Deuteronomy
32:4   *224*
32:12   *183*
33:25   *200*

I Samuel
7:12   *33*

Job
38-40   *2*
38:7   *74*

Psalms
9:9   *200*
19   *20, 21*
20:5   *56*
27:5   *207*
31:2   *159*
42   *110*
46   *261*
46:4   *292*
46:10   *157*
55:8   *207*
55:22   *180*

67   *60*
69:2   *207*
72   *299*
87:3   *292*
90   *215*
93:1-4   *59*
98:6-9   *81*
100   *1, 65*
103:1-2, 4   *71*
103:1-6   *51*
103:2-4   *46*
104   *17*
104:1, 33, 35   *17*
107:30   *207*
116:15   *227*
119:105   *141*
126:6   *63*
134   *2, 4, 65*
137:5-6   *295*
143:9   *207*
147:1   *57*
148   *54*
150   *51*

Proverbs
6:23   *141*
18:24   *180*
22:6   *98*

Isaiah
7:14   *74*
25:4   *207*
26:3   *172*

33:20-21 *292*
43:2 *200*

Lamentations
3:22-23 *189*

Haggai
2:7 *74*

Zechariah
13:1 *127*

Malachi
3:1 *74*

Matthew
1:23 *74*
2:2 *74*
3:16-17 *246*
4:18-20 *236*
5:6 *138*
7:24-25 *224*
11:28 *162*
13:36-43 *62*
14:19 *138*
16:18 *224*
16:26 *130*
20:28 *227*
22:37 *246*
23:24 *277*

Mark
4:26-29 *62*

Luke
15:4-7 *227*
24:29 *154*

John
1:14 *74*
4:14 *162*
6:32, 33, 35 *227*
6:35 *138*
8:12 *162*
8:32 *138*
10:11 *227*
13:1 *207*
14:19 *105*
15:4-5 *166*
15:7 *227*

Acts
7:54-60 *277*
7:59 *207*

Romans
3:25 *127*
6:1-4 *131*
8:1 *103*
8:28 *71*
8:37 *272*

I Corinthians
1:30 *177*
3:11 *211*
10:4 *224*
11:27 *130*
14:15 *168*
15:55-57 *105*
16:13 *258*

II Corinthians
5:8 *227*
12:9 *200*

Galatians
5:25 *246*
6:14 *130, 131*

Ephesians
2:13 *225*
3:12 *103*
3:20 *166*
5:19 *168*
5:20 *72*
6:14 *274*

Philippians
2:6-8 *102*
4:4 *53, 57*
4:6-7 *180*
4:19 *227*

Colossians
2:20 *131*
3:2 *246*

I Thessalonians
4:16 *74*
4:17 *157*

II Timothy
1:7 *266*
2:1-3 *264*
4:7-8 *49*
4:18 *293*

Hebrews
12:1 *288*
13:5 *200*

James
1:17 *190*

I Peter
5:7 *180*

I John
1:7 *251*

Revelation
3:20 *147*
4:8-11 *11*
5:11-14 *37*
7:9-12 *59*
7:9-17 *277*
19:12 *36, 272*
22:1 *37, 292*
22:2 *293*

Tune Index

ABERYSTWYTH 207
ADESTE FIDELES 201
AIR OF READING 86
AJALON 225
ALL SAINTS 95, 278
ALL SAINTS' NEW 278
ALL THE WAY 183
ALMA 207
AMAZING GRACE 101
AMERICA 31, 314
ANGEL'S STORY 245
ANTIOCH 82
ARLINGTON 258
ASCALON 7
ASSURANCE 186
AUGHTON 199
AURELIA 305
AUSTRIA 293
AUSTRIAN HYMN 293
AUTUMN 109
AVON 95-96
AZMON 44

BACCALAUREATE 136
BATTLE HYMN 309
BEETHOVEN 116
BELLEVUE 201
BELMONT 231
BERLIN 80
BETHLEHEM 80
BLESSINGS 188
BREAD OF LIFE 140
BROMSWICK 60

CANNONS 55
CHEADLE 293
CHORAL 133
CLEANSING FOUNTAIN 129
COMFORT 82
CONVENTION 201
CONVERSE 181
CORONATION 28
COWPER 129
CRADLE SONG 77
CRUSADER'S HYMN 7
CWM RHONDDA 195

DARWALL 54
DARWALL'S 148TH 54
DAY OF REST 245
DENFIELD 45
DENNIS 283
DIADEM 28
DIADEMATA 40, 272
DOMINUS REGIT ME 228
DRUMCLOG 95
DUKE STREET 299

EASTER HYMN 107
EIN' FESTE BURG 262
EMILIE 248
EMPEROR'S HYMN 293-294
ERIE 181
EUCHARIST 133
EVENTIDE 155

FAIRFORD 32

FAITHFULNESS *191*
FEDERAL STREET *235*
FENWICK *95*
FILLMORE *103-104*
FINLANDIA *158*
FITZWILLIAM *55*
FLORENCE *32*
FOR ALL THE SAINTS *289*
FOREST GREEN *90*
FOUNDATION *201*
FULDA *116*

GALILEE *239*
GASTON *45*
GEARD *201*
GEIBEL *275*
GERMANY *116*
GETHSEMANE *225*
GIARDINI *32*
GOOD SHEPHERD *35*
GOPSAL *54, 55*
GORDON *15*

HALLELUJAH *35*
HAMBURG *133*
HANOVER *19, 60*
HAYDN *293*
HE LEADETH ME *199*
HELLESPONT *248*
HENDON *251*
HERMON *32*
HERZLICH TUT MICH
  VERLANGEN *120*
HOLBORN *297*
HOLLINGSIDE *207*
HOLY TRIUMPH *82*
HOTHAN *207*

IN BABILONE *110*
INVERNESS *95*
ITALIAN HYMN *32*

JERUSALEM *82*
JESU REDEMPTOR *80*
JUDE *239*

KNECHT *148*
KÖNIGSBERG *142*

LANCASHIRE *265*

LAUDA ANIMA (Andrews) *47*
LAUDA ANIMA (Benedic Anima
  Mea) *47*
LLANFYLLIN *245*
LOBE DEN HERREN *52*
LUKE *204*
LYNGHAM *45*
LYONS *19, 60-61*

MALVERN *116*
MARION *57*
MARTYN *207*
MARTYRDOM *95-96*
MEDIA *82*
MELCHIZEDEC *116*
MENDELSSOHN *80*
MESSIAH *82*
MILES LANE *28*
MORE LOVE TO THEE *240*
MORECAMBE *248*
MORNING HYMN *110*
MOSCOW *32*
MUELLER *76-77*
MUNICH *142*

NATIONAL HYMN *311*
NATIVITY *80*
NETTLETON *35*
NEWRY *300*
NICAEA *12*
NUN DANKET *72*

O PERFECT LOVE *222*
OH HOW I LOVE JESUS *232*
OLD 104TH *60*
OLD HUNDREDTH *3-4, 65*
OLIVET *133, 210*
OPORTO *86*

PASS ME NOT *149*
PATMOS *251*
PAX TECUM *172-174*
PETRA *225*
PLEADING SAVIOUR *110*
PORTUGUESE HYMN *86, 201*
PRECIOUS NAME *254*
PROPIOR DEO *241*
PROTECTION *201*

REDHEAD NO. 76 *225*

REFUGE *207*
REGENT SQUARE *48, 75*
RELIANCE *225*
RHONDDA *195*
RICHMOND *45*
RUSSIAN HYMN *311*
RUTHERFORD *178*

SAFFRON WALDEN *145*
SAGINA *104*
SAINT MARGARET *220*
SALISBURY TUNE *107*
SANDRINGHAM *221-222*
SARUM *289-290*
SCHÖNSTER HERR JESU *6*
SINE NOMINE *289-290*
SOLID ROCK *213*
ST. ANNE *217*
ST. CATHERINE *286*
ST. CRISPIN *145*
ST. EDITH *148*
ST. ELIZABETH *7*
ST. GEORGE'S *60*
ST. GEORGE'S WINDSOR *64*
ST. GERTRUDE *270*
ST. HELEN'S *300*
ST. HILDA *148*
ST. KILDA *76*

ST. LOUIS *90*
ST. PHILIP *289*
ST. THOMAS *297*
ST. VINCENT *80*
SWEET STORY *204*

TALLY'S *60*
TERRA PATRIS *24*
THIRD MODE MELODY *162*
TOPLADY *226*
TRINITY *32*
TRUST AND OBEY *256*
TYNEMOUTH *286*

UXBRIDGE *116*

VIENNA *293*
VINEYARD HAVEN *58*
VOX DILECTI *162*

WALTON *116*
WARRENTON *35*
WEBB *275*
WINDLE *300*
WOODWORTH *145*

YARBROUGH *251*

General Index

Abney, Sir Thomas and Lady, 81, 216
Addison, Joseph, 19-20, 300
Adeste Fideles, 84
"Aldersgate experience," 42
Alexander, Cecil Frances, 236-239
Alexander, James Waddell, 117, 119, 120
Alexander, William, 237
Alford, Henry, 62-64
American hymnology, 10, 295
American melody, early, 101, 110, 129
American Revolution, 31-32, 296
Andrews, Mark, 47
Anne (queen of England), 68, 215
Anonymous hymns, 29, 76, 97, 200
Apocrypha, 70, 206
Apostles' Creed, 238, 303
Appomattox, 65
Arminianism, 195
Arne, Thomas A., 258-259
Arnold, John, 107
Arnold, Matthew, 132-133
Artaxerxes (Thomas Arne), 258
Asaph, 106
Atkinson, Frederick Cook, 248

Babcock, Maltbie Davenport, 22-24
Bach, Johann Sebastian, 44, 120, 262, 305

Baker, Henry Williams, 227-228
Bakewell, John, 108-109
Baptists, 15, 34, 140, 198, 253-254, 281
Baring-Gould, Sabine, 268-270
Barlow, Joel, 296
Barnby, Joseph, 80, 221-222, 289
Barry, C. A., 5
Barthélémon, François Hippolyte, 110
Barthold, Anna, 119
Baume, John Wesley, 248
Baxter, Lydia, 252-254
Bay Psalm Book, The, 295
Beethoven, Ludwig van, 61, 116
Bennett, William Sterndale, 52
Bernard of Clairvaux, 117-119
Bible societies, 36, 75, 173
Bickersteth, Edward, 17, 173
Bickersteth, Edward Henry, 171-173, 211
Blair, Samuel, 9
Blenheim, battle of, 20
Bliss, Philip P., 112, 159, 170
Bode, John E., 243-244
Bohemian Brethren, 114-115
Böhler, Peter, 42
Bonar, Andrew, 176
Bonar, Horatius, 125, 160-162, 180
Bonaventura, Saint, 84
"Bonnie Prince Charlie." *See* Charles Edward
Book of Common Prayer, 79

Borthwick, Jane Laurie, 157-158
Boston, Thomas, 109
*Boston Handel and Haydn
    Society Collection of Church
    Music* (Mason), 61, 133
Bourgeois, Louis, 3-4, 65
Boyd, Henry, 300
Bradbury, William Batchelder,
    145, 198-199, 204, 213, 251
Brady, Nicholas, 60
Brevint, Daniel, 224
Bridges, Matthew, 36-37, 40
Brooke, Stopford, 238-239
Brooks, Phillips, 88-90
"Brothers, and a Sermon"
    (Ingelow), 147
Brown, Arthur Henry, 15, 145
Browning, Elizabeth Barrett, 129
Buchanan, Claudius, 100
Buck, Zechariah, 245

Caldbeck, George T., 173-174
Calvin, John, 3-4, 118
Calvinism, 109, 194-195, 284
Calvinistic Methodists, 34,
    194-195
Campbell, Thomas, 104
Cantata 80 (J. S. Bach), 262
Carey, William, 299
Carlyle, Thomas, 261
Caswall, Edward, 85
Catlett, Mary, 98-99
Chalmers, Thomas, 161-162
Charles Edward, the "Young
    Pretender," 17, 59
Charles II (king of England), 67,
    178
Charlotte, Countess of Warwick,
    20
Chautauqua Literary and
    Scientific Circle, 138-140
Chicago fire of 1871, 168
Children's hymns, 76, 125, 202,
    216
Chisholm, Thomas O., 189-191
Christian Psalmody
    (Bickersteth), 17, 173
Christmas hymns, 73, 92
Church Missionary Society, 173
Church of England, 26, 40, 57,

85, 100, 173, 195, 231, 244,
    269, 276, 284
Church of Ireland, 247
Church of Scotland, 160,
    177-178
Civil War, 65, 77, 126, 197-198,
    210, 235, 310
Clapham Sect, 122
Clark, J. E., 76
Clarke, James Freeman, 307
Clephane, Elizabeth Cecilia,
    124-125
Colenso, John William, 302-303
College of New Jersey, 9
Commencement hymns, 48-50,
    263-266
Communion hymns, 129-133,
    137-140
Converse, Charles Crozat, 181
Conversion experiences, 14,
    42-43, 67, 94, 98-99, 102-103,
    106, 144, 185, 206, 209, 225,
    253
Conyers, Richard, 42
Coolidge, Calvin, 30
Cousin, Anne Ross (Cundell),
    175, 178
Covenanters, 177
Cowper, William, 100, 127-129,
    286
Creation, The (Haydn), 21
Croatian folksong, 293
Croft, William, 19, 60, 217
Croly, George, 246-248
Crosby, Fanny J., 94, 149-150,
    182-186, 216, 254
Crucifixion, 131
Crüger, Johann, 72
Crusaders, 5-7
Cummings, William Hayman, 80
Cushing, William O., 158-159
Cutler, Henry S., 278-279

Darwall, John, 54
Davies, Samuel, 8-10
Declaration of Indulgence, 68
Dirksen, Richard, 58
Disruption, The, 161
Dissenters, 215-216
Doane, William Howard, 122-123,

150, 167, 183, 240, 252, 254
Donne, John, 128
Duffield, George, Jr., 273-274
Duffield, S. W., 149
Dutch melody, traditional, 110
Dwight, Sereno E., 209
Dwight, Timothy, 295-297
Dykes, John Bacchus, 12-13, 162, 207, 222, 229

Easter hymns, 104-107, 186
Ecce Homo (painting), 114
Edwards, Jonathan, 9, 296
Egan, James, 109
Eilenburg, Saxony, 71-72
Elijah (Mendelssohn), 80, 142
Elizabeth (Hungarian saint), 5, 7
Elizabeth I (queen of England), 4
Elizabeth II (queen of England), 3, 46
Elliott, Charlotte, 143-145
Elliott, James William, 245
Ellor, James, 28
Elvey, George Job, 40-41, 64, 145, 272
English folk melody, 24, 90, 162, 270
English hymnody, development of, 60, 100, 215-216, 277
English psalmsinging, 2-3, 60, 215-216
Episcopalians, 57-58, 88-90, 92, 273, 277, 310
Evangelical Association, 164
Evangelical Lutheran Church in North America, 76
Evangelical party, 18, 122, 173
Ewing, Mrs. Juliana Horatia, 276
Excell, Edwin Othello, 100, 188-189

Faber, Frederick W., 284-286
Fallersleben, A. H. Hoffman von, 6-7
Fawcett, John, 280-283
Featherston, William Ralph, 13-15
Festegesang (Mendelssohn), 80
Fest Ouverture (Nicolai), 262
Fillmore, Millard, 103

Fischer, William G., 104
Foundry Collection (Wesley), 107
Foundry Meeting House, 105
Francis, Benjamin, 233-234
Franz II (emperor), 293
Frederick William I (king of Prussia), 120
Frederick William IV (king of Prussia), 92
Free Church of Scotland, 157, 160-162, 178

Gabriel, Charles H., 77
Gardiner, William, 19, 61, 116, 294
Geibel, Adam, 275
Geneva Bible, 2
George I (king of England), 20, 60
George II (king of England), 9, 59, 128
George III (king of England), 60, 283
Gerhardt, Paul, 117, 119
German Reformed, 51
Giardini, Felice de, 32
Gibbons, Thomas, 10
Gilchrist, Anne, 95
Gill, John, 281
Gilmore, Joseph Henry, 197-199
Gladstone, William, 121
Gläser, Carl Gotthelf, 44
Glenelg, Baron, 17-18
Gloria Patri, 71
"God Save the King," 31-32, 314
Goldschmidt, Otto, 52
Gordon, Adoniram Judson, 14-15
Goss, John, 47
Gottschalg, Alexander Wilhelm, 5, 7
Grant, Robert, 16-18, 278
Grape, John T., 112
Gray, Robert, 303
Great Awakening, 9
Greek melody, 203-204
Gregorian chant, 133
Gregory the Great (pope), 133
Grigg, Joseph, 233-235
Groves, Alexander, 138-139
Gruber, Franz, 91-92
Guildhall School of Music

(London), 80, 289
Gurney, Dorothy Frances
  (Blomfield), 220-222
Gustafson, Dwight, 49
Gwynne, Nell, 67
Gwynne, Sarah, 106

Hall, Elvina M., 111-112
Hall, Robert, 34
Handel, George Frederick, 54-55,
  60, 61, 82, 114, 133, 245
Hankey, Arabella Katherine,
  121-123
Hanover, Elector of, 60. *See also*
  George I
Harris, Eliza Anne, 204
Harris, Howell, 194
Harrison, Ralph, 259
Hassler, Hans Leo, 120
Hastings, Selina, Countess of
  Huntingdon, 27, 195
Hastings, Thomas, 45, 210, 226
Hatton, John, 300
Hauschka, Lorenz, 293
Havergal, Frances Ridley,
  249-251
Haweis, Thomas, 45
Hawks, Annie Sherwood,
  165-167
Haydn, Franz Joseph, 21, 61,
  116, 270, 293-294
Haydn, Johann Michael, 19, 61
Heber, Reginald, 11-13, 265,
  276-278
Hedge, Frederick Henry, 261-262
Hemy, Henri Frederick, 286
Herrnhut, 115
High Church party, 12, 40
Higher criticism, 219, 302
Hilda of Whitby, Saint, 148
Hoffman, Elisha Albright, 163-
  164
Holbrook, J. P., 207
Holden, Oliver, 28
How, William Walsham, 141-142,
  146-148, 288-289
Howe, Julia Ward, 306-309
Howe, Samuel Gridley, 307
Hughes, John, 195-196
Huguenots, 4, 26, 284

Huguenots, Les (Meyerbeer), 262
Hunt, William Holman, 146
Huntingdon, Lady. *See* Hastings,
  Selina
Husband, Edward, 148
Hussites, 6, 114
Hymns Ancient and Modern, 40,
  52, 221, 228, 305
Hymns and Spiritual Songs
  (Watts), 132
Hymns based on scriptural
  passages. *See* Scripture Index
Hymns, circumstances behind:
  anniversary of university, 49;
  anniversary of writer's
  conversion, 102; blindness,
  183, 218-219; breakfast
  conversation, 14, 42, 230;
  broken organ, 91-92; Civil War,
  197-198, 306-309; college
  devotions, 65; commencement
  exercises, 136, 264;
  confirmation, 243; deathbed of
  a relative, 172; deathbed of
  Rutherford, 176-177; death of
  a preacher, 272-275; dove
  fleeing from a hawk, 206;
  drowning of writer's fiancée,
  180; five-dollar bill, 183; Fourth
  of July celebration, 310;
  fundraising bazaar, 144;
  handicaps, 297; hiding from a
  mob, 206; Hussite refugees, 6;
  illness, 106, 122-123, 178, 180,
  200, 250; insane asylum, 127-
  128; invalid, 14, 144-145, 250;
  Lake Chautauqua, 138;
  mother's sorrow, 180;
  newspaper item, 125; opening
  of a meeting house, 105;
  painting (*The Light of the
  World*), 146-147; pastor leaving
  congregation, 154-155, 280-
  283; pastor's prayer, 111-112;
  penitent's prayer at a mission,
  149; persecution, 59; poem
  ("Brothers, and a Sermon"),
  147; Reformation, 261; rejected
  marriage proposal, 95;
  shipwreck, 168-170;

stagecoach ride, 203; ten-year-
old poet, 233; testimony at a
revival, 255; theological
controversy, 194, 302-303;
Thirty Years' War, 71;
thunderstorm, 224; train
wreck, 170; visit to some
friends, 249; wedding hymn,
221
Hymns from the Land of Luther,
157

Independent (churches), 34
India, 12, 17-18, 203, 314
Ingalls, Jeremiah, 103-104
Ingelow, Jean, 147
Invitational hymns, 30, 94, 151,
162, 236, 240

Jackson, Andrew, 200
James II (king of England), 68-69
Jarman, Thomas, 45
Jennens, Charles, 54
Jesuits, 5, 204
"John Brown's Body," 307, 309
Johnson, Samuel, 82
Jones, Bob, 48-49, 135-137
Jones, Sam, 188
Jude, William Herbert, 239
Julian, John, 6-7, 26, 57, 84, 109,
132, 206-207, 234, 262, 304

Kaisermarsch (Wagner), 262
Keith (Kethe), George, 201
Ken, Thomas, 64-69, 79, 110
Kethe, William, 1-3, 17, 65
Kirkpatrick, William James, 77
Knapp, Christopher, 65
Knapp, Mrs. Joseph Fairchild,
185
Knapp, Phoebe, 186
Knecht, Justin Heinrich, 148

Lathbury, Mary Artemisia,
138-139
Lee, Robert E., 200
Legend of St. Elizabeth, The
(Liszt), 5, 7
LeHunte, W. A., 154
Leland, John, 110

Liberalism, 79, 219, 247, 289,
302
Light of the World, The (Hunt),
146
Lincoln, Abraham, 308
Lindsay, Maggie, 253
Liszt, Franz, 5, 7, 181
Longfellow, Henry Wadsworth, 3
"Look-Up Legion," 139
Low Church party, 12
Lowry, Robert, 167, 183
Luke, Jemima Thompson,
202-204
Lundie, Jane, 161
Luther, Martin, 76, 118-119,
260-263
Lvov, Alexis, 311
Lyra Davidica, 107
Lyte, Henry Francis, 46-48,
154-155, 248

Macaulay, Thomas Babington,
18, 20
McCabe, Charles C., 104, 308
Madan, Martin, 31-33, 105,
108-109, 207
Malan, Henri Abraham César,
144, 251
Mann, Arthur Henry, 245
Marsh, Simeon B., 207
Mary Tudor, 2
Mason, Lowell, 44, 61, 82, 116,
129, 133, 140, 210, 226, 235,
275, 283, 313
Massie, E., 8
Matheson, George, 217-220
Mauracher, Karl, 92
Mendelssohn, Felix, 7, 80, 142,
262
Mentzer, Johann, 42
Messiah (Handel), 54, 82
Messiter, Arthur Henry, 57-58
Methodist Episcopal Church,
188
Methodists, 27, 34, 59, 106, 108,
138-139, 186, 190-191, 194,
254, 258, 300
Miller, Josiah, 68, 281
Miller, Lewis M., 138
Mohr, Joseph, 90-92

Monk, William Henry, 155

Montgomery, James, 73-75, 128, 203

Moody, Dwight Lyman, 15, 125-126, 145, 149, 151-152, 159, 166, 169, 253, 255-256

Moravians, 42, 74, 115, 206

Morning and Evening Hymns (Ken), 65, 79, 110

Morrell, Thomas B., 141, 146

Morris, James, 225

Morrison, Henry C., 190

Mote, Edward, 211-213

Mozart, Wolfgang Amadeus, 61, 116

Münster Gesangbuch (1677), 5-6

Murray, F. H., 85

Murray, James Ramsey, 76-77

Nägeli, Johann (Hans) Georg, 283

Nazi hymn, 293

Neale, John Mason, 85

Neander, Joachim, 50-52

Nettleton, Asahel, 35

Newman, John Henry, 40, 284-285

Newton, John, 97-101, 129, 207, 232, 286, 291-294

Nicaean Creed, 12

Noble, T. Tertius, 110

Novello, Vincent, 86

Oakeley, Frederick, 85

Oatman, Johnson, 187-188

Oliver, Henry Kemble, 235

Oliver, Thomas, 109,

Olney Hymns (Newton and Cowper), 100, 292

Oratorio, 5, 7, 21, 50, 80, 142

Oratory of St. Philip Neri, 284

Oxford University, 11, 20, 40, 57, 60, 64, 67, 85, 244-245, 259, 270, 284, 289, 294, 304-305

Paisley, Ian, 49

Palmer, Ray, 208-211

Palmer, Walter C., 186

Parker, Harriette Stollenwerck, 136

Parry, Joseph, 60, 207

Peace, Albert L., 220

Perronet, Edward, 26-28

Persecution, 2, 13, 26, 59, 114, 176, 178, 271

Pickett, George E., 193

Pietism, 115

Pigou, Francis, 141

Pilgrim's Progress (Bunyan), 281

Plumptre, Edward Hayes, 56-57

Prentiss, Elizabeth Payson, 240-242

Prentiss, George L., 241

Presbyterians, 9, 22-24, 75, 119, 132-133, 164, 178, 219, 234, 241, 255, 273-274

Priestley, Joseph, 34

Princeton University, 9, 109, 117, 120

Protestants. *See* Reformation

Psalm singing, 2-4, 100, 215-216, 295-296

Quietism, 115

Reading, John, 86

Reden, Karl, 181

Redhead, Richard, 225

Redner, Lewis H., 89-90

Reformation, 118, 132, 260, 263, 265

Reformation Symphony (Mendelssohn), 262

Revised Version (1885), 57

Rhythmica Oratio, 117

Richter, E. F., 7

Rimbault, Edward Francis, 178

Rinkart, Martin, 70-72

Rippon, John, 26, 28, 200-201

Roberts, Daniel Crane, 309-311

Robinson, Charles S., 172, 288

Robinson, Robert, 33-35

Robinson, William, 9

Rodeheaver Hall-Mack Company, 275

Rodeheaver, Homer, 190

Roman Catholic Church, 2, 40, 71, 84-85, 173, 261, 269-270, 284-286

Röntgen, Julius, 110

Roosevelt, Theodore, 200, 268

Royal Chapel, 305
Runyan, William M., 191
Rutherford, Samuel, 175-178

St. Matthew Passion (J. S. Bach), 120
St. Stephen's Day, 56, 277
Salvation Army, 66
Sammis, John H., 255-256
Sankey, Ira David, 14, 112, 125-126, 152, 159, 169-170
Schlegel, Katharina von, 156-157
Schlesische Volkslieder (1842), 5-6
Scott, Thomas, 100
Scriven, Joseph M., 179-181
Seiss, Joseph Augustus, 6, 8
Selection of Hymns from the Best Authors (Rippon), 201
Shakespeare, William, 3
Shaw, Oliver, 61
Sheppard, Franklin L., 24
Sherwin, William Fiske, 140
Shipley, Amelia, 12
Shrubsole, William, 28
Shurtleff, Ernest Warburton, 264-265
Sibelius, Jean, 158
Slavery, 307
Smart, Henry Thomas, 75, 133, 265-266
Smith, Gipsy, 187-189
Smith, H. Augustine, 4, 30, 270
Smith, Isaac Gregory, 74, 297
Smith, R. A., 95
Smith, Samuel Francis, 210-211, 312-314
Socinianism, 132
South Africa, 302-303
Spafford, Horatio G., 168-171
Spener, Philip Jakob, 51
Spurgeon, Charles, 34, 258
Stéphan, John, 84, 86
Stone, Samuel John, 302-305
Strasser family, 92
String Quartet in C (Haydn), 293
Sullivan, Arthur Seymour, 241, 245, 270
Sunday, Billy, 190
Sunday school, 166, 183

Symphony in D (Haydn), 270

Tallis, Thomas, 60, 162
Tate, Nahum, 60
Te Deum, 70
Tennent, Gilbert, 9
"There Is a Green Hill Far Away," 238-239
Thirty Years' War, 71, 114, 119
Thomas à Kempis, 99
Thompson, Will Lamartine, 150-152
Thring, Godfrey, 36-38, 40
Toplady, Augustus Montague, 27, 79, 108-109, 223-226
Towner, Daniel Brink, 255-256
Tractarian movement, 173
Transcendentalists, 307
Translators, 6-7, 52, 72, 85, 92, 117-120, 157-158, 194-195, 261-262
Tyler, Moses Coit, 297
Tyng, Dudley A., 273-274
Tyrolean Alps, 92

Unitarians, 34, 132, 262, 307
Unwin, Mary, 129
Urhan, Chrétien, 178

Van Alstyne, Alexander, 183
Van Dyke, Henry, 23, 313
Victoria (queen of England), 162, 219
Ville du Havre (ship), 168-169
Vincent, Charles John, 174
Vincent, John H., 138

Wade, John Francis, 84-85
Walton, Izaak, 67
Walton, James G., 286
Warren, George William, 310-311
Washington, George, 10, 296
Watts, Isaac, 44, 81-83, 93-96, 98, 130-133, 215-217, 232, 239, 257-259, 295-296, 298-300
Webb, George J., 256, 275
Webbe, Samuel, Jr., 45, 86
Wedding hymn, 40, 46, 221-222
Wells, G. C., 133
Welsh Calvinistic Methodists, 194

Wesley, Charles, 26, 29-31, 41-45, 53-55, 58-59, 61, 66, 78-80, 102-109, 115, 194, 205-207, 224, 271-272, 286, 305

Wesley, John, 20, 27, 100, 113, 216-217

Wesley, Samuel Sebastian, 305

Westminster Abbey, 20, 46, 60, 82

Whitby (monastery), 148

Whitefield, George, 26, 31, 34, 79, 100, 131, 194-195, 281, 296

White Mountain, battle of, 6, 123

Whitfield, Frederick, 230-231

Wilberforce, William, 18

William (of Orange), 67

Williams, John, 194

Williams, Peter, 194

Williams, Ralph Vaughan, 90, 110, 289-290

Williams, William, 192, 194-196

Willis, Richard Storrs, 6-7

Wilson, Hugh, 95-96

Wilson, Woodrow, 200

Winchester Cathedral, 67, 86

Winkworth, Catherine, 51-52, 72

Woodbury, I. B., 133

Wordsworth, William, 284

World War II, 293

YMCA, 255

Young, John Freeman, 92

Zinzendorf, Nicolaus Ludwig von, 113-115

Alphabetical List of Hymns

This list includes the title of each hymn given in the book. Also included are alternate titles and first lines if they differ from the normal title.

Abide with Me: Fast Falls the Eventide, *153*
Alas! and Did My Saviour Bleed, *93*
All Hail the Power of Jesus' Name, *25*
All People That on Earth Do Dwell, *1*
All the Way My Saviour Leads Me, *182*
Amazing Grace, *96*
Am I a Soldier of the Cross, *257*
A Mighty Fortress Is Our God, *259*
And Can It Be That I Should Gain, *101*
Angels, from the Realms of Glory, *73*
Ashamed of Jesus (*See* Jesus, and Shall It Ever Be)
Away in a Manger, *75*

Battle Hymn of the Republic, *306*
Be Still My Soul, *156*
Blessed Assurance, Jesus Is Mine, *184*
Blest Be the Tie That Binds, *280*
Bob Jones University Hymn, *134*
Break Thou the Bread of Life, *137*

Christ the Lord Is Risen Today, *104*
Come, Thou Almighty King, *29*
Come, Thou Fount of Every Blessing, *32*
Come, Ye Thankful People, Come, *62*
Count Your Blessings, *186*
Crown Him with Many Crowns, *35*

Doxology, *64*

Fairest Lord Jesus,   *4*
Faith of Our Fathers!,   *283*
For All the Saints,   *287*

Glorious Things of Thee Are Spoken,   *290*
Glory, glory, hallelujah (*See* Battle Hymn of the Republic)
God of Our Fathers, Whose Almighty Hand,   *309*
Great God of Wonders!,   *8*
Great Is Thy Faithfulness, O God My Father,   *189*
Guide Me, O Thou Great Jehovah,   *192*

Hail, Thou Once-Despised Jesus!,   *107*
Hark! the Herald Angels Sing,   *78*
He Leadeth Me, O Blessed Thought,   *196*
Hiding in Thee,   *158*
Holy, Holy, Holy! Lord God Almighty,   *10*
How Firm a Foundation,   *199*

I Heard the Voice of Jesus Say,   *160*
I hear the Saviour say (*See* Jesus Paid It All)
I Love Thy Kingdom, Lord,   *294*
Immanuel's Land (*See* The Sands of Time Are Sinking)
I Must Tell Jesus,   *163*
I Need Thee Every Hour,   *165*
I Think When I Read That Sweet Story of Old,   *202*
It Is Well with My Soul,   *167*

Jesus, and Shall It Ever Be,   *233*
Jesus Calls Us,   *236*
Jesus, Lover of My Soul,   *204*
Jesus Paid It All,   *111*
Jesus Shall Reign Where'er the Sun,   *298*
Jesus, Thy Blood and Righteousness,   *113*
Joy to the World! the Lord Is Come,   *81*
Just As I Am, Without One Plea,   *143*

Lead On, O King Eternal,   *263*

Mine eyes have seen the glory of the coming of the Lord (*See* Battle
    Hymn of the Republic)
More Love to Thee, O Christ,   *239*
My Country, 'Tis of Thee,   *311*
My Faith Looks Up to Thee,   *208*
My Hope Is Built on Nothing Less,   *211*
My Jesus, I Love Thee,   *13*

Now Thank We All Our God,   *70*

O Come, All Ye Faithful,   *83*
O for a Thousand Tongues to Sing,   *41*

O God, Our Help in Ages Past,   *214*
O Jesus, I Have Promised,   *242*
O Jesus, Thou Art Standing,   *146*
O Little Town of Bethlehem,   *87*
O Love That Wilt Not Let Me Go,   *217*
Onward, Christian Soldiers,   *266*
O Perfect Love, All Human Thought Transcending,   *220*
O Sacred Head, Now Wounded,   *116*
O safe to the Rock that is higher than I (*See* Hiding in Thee)
O Word of God Incarnate,   *140*
O Worship the King,   *16*

Pass Me Not, O Gentle Saviour,   *148*
Peace, Perfect Peace,   *171*
Praise God from whom all blessings flow (*See* Doxology)
Praise, My Soul, the King of Heaven,   *45*
Praise Ye Jehovah,   *48*
Praise Ye the Lord, the Almighty,   *50*

Rejoice, the Lord Is King,   *52*
Rejoice, Ye Pure in Heart,   *55*
Rock of Ages, Cleft for Me,   *223*

Silent Night, Holy Night,   *90*
Softly and Tenderly,   *150*
Soldiers of Christ, Arise,   *271*
Spirit of God, Descend upon My Heart,   *245*
Stand Up, Stand Up for Jesus,   *272*

Take My Life, and Let It Be,   *248*
Take the Name of Jesus with You,   *252*
Tell Me the Old, Old Story,   *120*
The Church's One Foundation,   *300*
The King of Love My Shepherd Is,   *226*
The Ninety and Nine,   *124*
There Is a Fountain Filled with Blood,   *126*
There Is a Name I Love to Hear,   *229*
There were ninety and nine that safely lay (*See* The Ninety and Nine)
The Sands of Time Are Sinking,   *174*
The Solid Rock (*See* My Hope Is Built)
The Son of God Goes Forth to War,   *275*
The Spacious Firmament on High,   *19*
This Is My Father's World,   *21*
Trust and Obey,   *254*

What a Friend We Have in Jesus,   *179*
When I Survey the Wondrous Cross,   *129*
When peace, like a river, attendeth my way (*See* It Is Well)
When upon life's billows you are tempest-tossed (*See* Count Your
    Blessings)

When we walk with the Lord (*See* Trust and Obey)
Wisdom of God, we would by Thee be taught (*See* Bob Jones
   University Hymn)

Ye Servants of God, Your Master Proclaim,   *58*